THE
HOME
PROBLEM
SOLVER

DON VANDERVORT

THE
HOME
PROBLEM
SOLVER

The Essential
Homeowner's Repair
and Maintenance Manual

PERSEUS PUBLISHING
Cambridge, Massachusetts

To Bobbi, Gabe, and Kit

Special thanks:

Michael Morris, Mike ("Captain Toolhead") Staats, Joe Truini, Tom ("Mr. Fixit") Brown, John Mills, and Stephen O'Hara, for their editorial assistance; Bill Oetinger for illustrations; my editor, Marnie Cochran, Senior Editor, Perseus Publishing; Marco Pavia, Senior Project Editor, Perseus Publishing; Marsha Russell for art file conversions; and my agents, Nancy Yost and Barbara Lowenstein at Lowenstein Associates, Inc.

A CIP catalog record for this book is available from the Library of Congress.
ISBN 0–7382-0122-7

Perseus Publishing is a member of the Perseus Books Group.

Find us on the World Wide Web at http://www.perseuspublishing.com

Perseus Publishing books are available at special discounts for bulk purchases in the U.S. by corporations, institutions, and other organizations. For more information, please contact the Special Markets Department at HarperCollins Publishers, 10 East 53rd Street, New York, NY 10022, or call 1–212–207–7528.

Text design by Jeff Williams
Set in 11-point Goudy by Perseus Publishing Services

First printing, August 2000
1 2 3 4 5 6 7 8 9 10—03 02 01 00

CONTENTS

5 Electrical Problems 99

6 Heating and Comfort Problems 123

7 Interior Surface Problems 145

8 Door and Window Problems 179

9 Exterior Problems 197

INTRODUCTION

Welcome to *The Home Problem Solver*, a quick-reference guide that will help you find the easiest and most direct route to diagnosing and curing common home problems.

• • •

Consider this: Today's houses are like complex machines. They have electrical, plumbing, and comfort-control systems; scores of different surfaces and materials; and hundreds of moving parts. Unfortunately, with any machine, parts break down, foul up, or fall short on occasion. With a house, this means a faucet drips, the roof springs a leak, or a window sticks. Then you have to figure out what's wrong and deal with it.

Fortunately, you don't have to be a good mechanic to take care of a house, though a few mechanical skills certainly help at times. You do need to be a good caretaker—someone capable of recognizing a problem, identifying the cause, and handling the solutions that are within your abilities. And you have to know when it's time to get help and who to call when that time comes.

When you do call a repairperson, you need to know enough about the problem to avoid being treated unfairly.

If you have the qualities of a good caretaker and know enough about your house to avoid being taken advantage of, then you can jump to the rescue quickly and effectively in a pinch, keep your house running smoothly, and make sure little problems don't grow into big ones. *The Home Problem Solver* will help you accomplish these goals.

HOW TO USE THIS BOOK

Don't worry, you are not expected to read *The Home Problem Solver* from cover to cover—it isn't meant to be that kind of book. Instead, it is designed to help you troubleshoot a problem based on the symptoms, then jump to the best and quickest solution. To use it, first ask:

1. IS THIS AN EMERGENCY?

Fires, gas leaks, burst pipes, and any other problems that can endanger people or ruin property demand prompt action. If you know the situation is an emergency—or if you are in doubt about what constitutes an emergency—turn to page 1.

It will pay to read about emergencies in the first chapter ahead of time, so you can act quickly if such a situation occurs.

Go directly to these pages for information about emergencies:

If it isn't an emergency, ask yourself . . .

2. WHERE ARE THE SIGNS OF THE PROBLEM?

Pinpointing the origin of a problem is the best first step toward solving it. This book is organized to help you do that.

Some problems are not specific to a particular location in a house, or the location may be difficult to determine without exploration. For that reason, whole house systems, including electricity, plumbing, and heating/cooling each have an independent section.

If you're not sure about the problem's location or if the symptoms are unclear, turn to page 10 for help in clarifying what to do next.

3. WHAT ARE THE FIRST STEPS TO TAKE?

Once you've determined the location and its corresponding chapter, turn to the specific symptom. Follow the step-by-step instructions or the decision chart at that point.

If the problem concerns a major appliance, turn to the chapter on appliances, beginning on page 23, then to the beginning of the section on the specific appliance. Read the brief introduction there and any special notes, then flip to the symptom. For example, if your dishwasher doesn't fill, turn to "Dishwasher" on page 30, read the introduction, then scan your way to the symptom "Doesn't fill" and follow the instructions in sequence. As a rule, these instructions will take you through the simplest, most likely remedies first.

4. TURN TO ADDITIONAL INFORMATION ON TOOLS AND MATERIALS FOR MORE HELP.

Some specialized tools and techniques are discussed at the beginning of certain chapters. The chapter on plumbing problems, for example, begins with a section on the tools and techniques of the trade, and so does the chapter on electrical problems.

1

EMERGENCY!

Emergencies that may cause danger or property loss call for immediate action. This quick-reference section offers "house triage"; it is designed to help you act quickly, decisively, and effectively in an emergency that endangers your family or home. Read through this section now so you will be prepared when or if such an event occurs.

MAJOR HOUSE FIRE

Fire is one of the most immediately critical and devastating home disasters.

In the event of a house fire, quickly get everyone outside and assembled at a pre-arranged meeting place; designate one person to call 911 or the fire department from a neighbor's home or cellular phone. Once outside, never go back into a burning building—even for the pets.

Evacuate the house quickly and calmly.

(continued)

Feel interior doors before opening them—if a door is hot, do not open it. Leave doors and windows closed unless you must open them to get out.

Stay low to the floor, on your hands and knees, where the cleanest, most breathable air is. (Smoke inhalation is the most common cause of fire fatalities.)

SMALL HOUSE FIRE

Call 911 or the fire department first.

You can control a small fire with an A-B-C fire extinguisher. To use one:

1. Pull out the pin located at the top of the extinguisher.
2. Standing about six feet back from the fire, point the extinguisher at the base of the fire and squeeze the lever. Make sure to direct the discharge at the base of the flames.

If the fire gets out of control, stop and evacuate the house immediately.

KITCHEN GREASE FIRE

NEVER pour water on a kitchen grease fire.

Instead, smother the flames by cutting off the source of oxygen. Place a lid over the pan and turn off the range.

If necessary, use an A-B-C fire extinguisher to put out the fire, but be prepared for a mess in the kitchen.

To put out an oven fire, shut the door and turn off the heat.

If the fire begins to get out of control, call 911 or the fire department. Evacuate the house immediately.

CHIMNEY FIRE

If your fireplace has glass doors, close them.

Call 911 or the fire department immediately and be ready to evacuate the house if necessary.

When a chimney fire occurs, creosote buildup on the interior walls of the chimney catches fire and flames shoot out the chimney. Where mortar between bricks is missing, flames can shoot through the chimney walls and ignite combustibles in the attic.

During a chimney fire, flames may be rolling over your head in the attic, so call the fire department even if you think the fire has been snuffed out.

It's a good idea to keep a chimney fire extinguisher on hand. Available at fireplace dealers and some hardware stores, these devices, which look a bit like a road flare, are designed to help put out a chimney fire. Follow the label instructions.

Be prepared for emergencies!

Yes, this motto can be as important to you as it is to a good Boy Scout. Know what your family should do in the event of a fire or other emergency before one occurs.

1. Develop an escape plan and practice it with a family drill. Everyone should know how to get out of the house and where to assemble safely outdoors. Establish who will be responsible for small children or the elderly or handicapped.
2. Be sure each room has at least two exits that can serve as safe escapes. If one of these is an upper-story window, provide a hook-on fire escape ladder (available at home improvement centers). Be sure that even children know how to attach and climb down these ladders, and keep the ladder in an easily accessed place.
3. Check smoke detectors periodically to be sure they're working properly. Fire departments recommend changing batteries twice a year—when you change your clocks to and from daylight savings time.
4. Make a map of where your home's water supply, gas, and electrical shutoffs are located and keep this where you can find it quickly in an emergency. Alert your family members, baby-sitters, and house-sitters to its location. And be sure your house numbers can be easily seen at night.

ELECTRICAL SPARKS OR SMOKING

Faulty electrical systems can quickly become house fires. At the first sign of a hot, smoking, crackling, or buzzing electrical outlet, switch, or fixture, quickly shut off the circuit breaker that governs that circuit. If you don't know which breaker or fuse to turn off, shut off the main circuit breaker (see page 103).

If the electrical outlet, switch, or light fixture was burning or smoking, call 911 and report the problem.

Safe electrical practices

- Avoid outlet extenders or plug-in power bars; these can overload an electrical circuit.
- Beware of worn, frayed, or broken electrical cords.

(continued)

- Use only extension cords that match (or have a larger capacity than) the wattage of the appliances that you plug into them.
- Make sure receptacles and appliances are properly grounded.
- Check the maximum size of bulb allowable for lighting fixtures and don't exceed the maximum wattage. Be especially careful not to use improperly sized bulbs in recessed light fixtures because of heat buildup.
- Never replace a blown fuse with an improperly sized substitute.

Fire Extinguisher A-B-Cs

- Keep two fire extinguishers in your home, one in the kitchen area or service porch and one in the garage, located in clear view, near the exit. Fire extinguishers are coded according to the types of fires they can extinguish.

- A green A symbol means it can put out paper, wood, cloth, trash, rubber, and many plastics fires.

- The red B symbol indicates it will extinguish flammable liquid fires, including kitchen grease, oil, gasoline, paints, and solvents.

- The blue C symbol specifies an extinguisher that will put out dry-chemical fires, including electrical fires.

- An A-B-C multipurpose extinguisher puts out all of these types of fires.

- Be sure your extinguishers are large enough to handle home fires. The minimum size to have on hand is classified "2A10BC" on the label.

- Periodically check your extinguishers to be sure they are fully charged; this is usually just a matter of looking at a small gauge mounted on the top of the unit. At least once every five years have your extinguishers serviced by a qualified service person, listed in the telephone book's classifieds under "Fire Extinguisher Repair."

GAS LEAK

A gas leak can be extremely dangerous because the smallest spark or flame can ignite gas fumes, causing an explosion. Natural gas has a garlic-like odor; if you smell this or suspect a gas leak, don't light matches (or a lighter) and don't operate electrical switches (they could ignite an explosion).

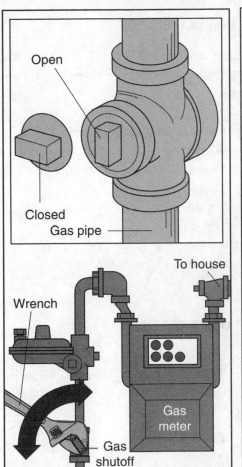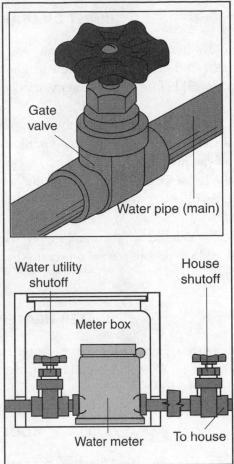

FIGURE 1.1   Gas and Water Shutoffs

Immediately:

1. Ventilate the house by opening doors and windows. If the smell of gas is strong, move everyone outdoors at once; leave the doors open.
2. Turn off the gas supply valve—located by the gas meter on the gas inlet pipe—by rotating the valve one quarter turn with an adjustable wrench (page 73). The valve's oblong stem should be perpendicular (at a right angle) to the inlet pipe to stop the flow of gas.
3. Call your gas supplier or the fire department from a neighbor's phone or a cellular phone outside the house.

(continued)

Emergency!

BURST OR LEAKING WATER PIPE

To avoid water damage to your home, you must shut off the water flow quickly if a pipe ruptures. To do this, it's important to know the location of your home's water shutoffs (see page 93) before such an emergency occurs.

1. Close the valve nearest to the leak, turning it clockwise until it stops.
2. If the flow continues or you don't know where the nearest valve is located, turn off the main water valve, usually located where the main water supply pipe enters the house (it may be either outside or inside).
3. If that doesn't work, shut off the main gate valve, located at the water meter.

Once you've shut off the water supply, fix the ruptured plumbing or call a plumber. You may be able to restore your water service by temporarily plugging the leak, as discussed on page 94.

WATER HEATER OVERHEATING

If your faucets emit steam or your water heater has boiling sounds inside, overheating may be causing a dangerous buildup of steam. Immediately turn down the water heater's temperature setting; then turn to page 67 for information on what to do.

ROOF LEAK

During a rainstorm, it's difficult to permanently fix a roof leak, but you can temporarily stop—or catch—the flow of water into your home. Because it's difficult to tell where the leak is originating, often the best and quickest solution is to completely tarp the leaking section of roof. That way, water can't find the entry point either. When the weather clears, see page 200 for information on how to find and fix a roof leak.

How to tarp a section of roof

Here is how to make an emergency cover for your roof from plastic sheeting and two-by-fours.

1. Partially unroll or unfold enough heavy (six-mil) polyethylene sheeting to cover the leaking section of roof, from eaves to peak; add about four feet extra and cut it off with a utility knife. Wrap one end around a two-by-four that is as long as the

plastic's width; staple the plastic along the two-by-four. Sandwich the assembly with a second two-by-four and nail the boards together with three or four 3-inch or 3 1/4-inch common nails.

2. Place the sandwiched end of the plastic along the eaves line and stretch the sheeting from eaves to ridge, running it over the top of the ridge and down the other side a few feet.

3. Sandwich the top end of the sheeting with another pair of two-by-fours to anchor it so wind can't carry it away. Do not nail any part of this assembly to the roof.

FOR SAFETY: Don't go onto a roof that is steeply pitched; don't step on the plastic sheeting—particularly when it's wet; and never go onto the roof during a thunderstorm.

FROZEN PIPES

When pipes filled with water are exposed to freezing outdoor temperatures, the water can freeze, blocking or eventually bursting the pipes. During very cold weather, if you turn on a faucet and the water is blocked, act quickly to protect your plumbing.

1. Open the faucet.
2. To locate the blockage, follow the faucet's supply pipe to where it passes through exterior walls or unheated areas.
3. Melt the ice. To this, you may use a heat gun, hair dryer, heating pad, heat lamp, or—in a pinch—a propane torch (be very careful to shield flammable materials from the flame). As you heat the pipe, water should drain out of the open faucet.

Prevent re-freezing by wrapping those pipes with foam insulation sleeves. Eventually, wrap all pipes that run through unheated spaces; outdoors, be sure insulation extends about twelve inches below the frost line (the average depth of ground freeze each year).

POWER OUTAGE

If your home's electrical power goes out, see page 107.

DRAIN CLOGS

For information on how to clear clogged drains, see page 75.

Home safety issues

Fundamentally, a house should offer safety and protection even during the worst of times, including earthquakes, tornadoes, floods, and blizzards. To expect safety and protection during some disasters is to ask too much of a house, but you can do a few important things to ensure that your home will be as safe as possible.

Here are a few important steps toward disaster preparedness:

1. Be sure your house is properly insured for full replacement value. Talk with your insurance agent to evaluate your coverage and understand its limitations. For example, most policies do not protect you in the event of flood or earthquakes. Determine the extent of protection—whether temporary housing is covered if major repairs are required, and so forth.

2. Document your valuables so you have proof of any losses if a disaster occurs. Photographs or video of your possessions are helpful.

3. Install smoke detectors. Every home should have a detector on each level and outside the sleeping areas (one hallway detector can serve all bedrooms within ten feet). In addition, you can install detectors in areas where fire may be a danger, but avoid placing ionization-type detectors within twenty feet of furnaces, water heaters, or kitchens, or within ten feet of bathrooms, because otherwise they may emit frequent false alarms.

4. Keep a wrench next to the gas meter for quick emergency shutoff.

5. Where high winds are a threat, rafters should be fastened to wall framing with strong, steel hurricane ties. Also, windows should be fitted with shutters that can offer protection from flying debris (once windows break, a house is much more vulnerable to wind destruction).

6. Prune back large tree limbs and dead branches from the house to minimize fire and wind hazards.

7. Where fires are a threat, be sure roofing has a Class A fire rating. In areas more threatened by high winds, wind resistant roofing is important.

8. Where earthquakes are a threat, be sure the water heater is strapped to prevent it from falling over. Be sure the wall's sill plates are securely bolted to a steel-reinforced concrete foundation.

9. Where floods are a threat, keep sandbags, sand, and a good sump pump on hand. Consider a concrete block wall to divert rising water. Be sure your home has an easy access to the roof if high floodwaters are a danger.

2

HOUSE SENSE

If you discover a new water spot on the ceiling, can you tell what caused it? Before you can repair a leak, you must discover its source through clues that may or may not be obvious. For instance, water streaming down the wall and pooling on the floor under a window may come from a roof leak; an ice dam; penetrations in the siding, flashing, or window frame . . . or even a broken pipe. Then again, maybe it's the dog.

To handle home repairs, you have to know how to read the clues. In the leak scenario, the biggest clue is whether or not it's raining or storming outside. In most cases, a storm narrows the possibilities down to rain-caused leaks in the roofing, siding, flashing, or window. Of course, if the weather is dry, you're better off to consider the plumbing first, particularly if water is spilling or spraying under pressure.

Finding the fastest and easiest route to repairing problems often boils down to understanding the rhyme and reason behind the workings of your house and then pinpointing and repairing or replacing the faulty component or mechanism. In this chapter, we'll take a closer look at how you can quickly and effectively diagnose and handle problems.

We'll also look at how to make basic decisions about whether to do the work yourself and who to hire if you don't.

TROUBLESHOOTING TIPS

The key to the art of troubleshooting problems is to combine your skills of perception and logic. As one roofer said, when trying to trace a roof leak, "Think like water." More to the point of this book, when trying to figure out what's wrong when some component of your house isn't working right or when you see or hear signs of trouble, "Think like a house."

For example, if water drips under a kitchen sink only when the basin is filled with water, you can be pretty sure that it isn't a problem with the water supply pipes or the faucet. You should suspect the basket strainer that's mounted in the sink's drain hole because this is the one part of the sink where there are seals that could leak. In fact, the chances are good that the putty seal under the strainer's flange has dried out or the strainer nut has become loose or split.

Many house-related problems occur because materials age and deteriorate. But also consider whether a person was involved when the problem occurred. People interact with houses through a variety of controls, from light switches to thermostats to faucets. If somebody was using something when it stopped working or malfunctioned, you have an important clue about the cause of the trouble. For example, if the kitchen lights flicker when the garbage disposer is turned on, you can suspect some type of wiring problem, most likely either the disposal's switch or its electrical circuit.

First isolate the problem and determine its source; then go after the appropriate solution. If you can pin down the problem to a particular system—plumbing, electrical, heating, and so forth—you're ahead of the game because you can turn to the appropriate chapter in this book and scan your way to the particular symptom. Of course, systems don't always play by the rules. Sometimes houses offer up a few surprises that require a bit more detective work.

There is no better way to get information about a specific problem than to bend the ear of a professional. Ask questions. By talking to a pro, you can get free, personalized help. Whether you discuss a leaky water heater over the phone with a plumber or talk with a hardware clerk about the right tool, plenty of free advice is available if you're willing to ask for it. One caveat: Just try to be sure the person you're asking knows what they're talking about.

BUYING A HOUSE? ELEVEN THINGS TO INSPECT

The best time to discover a house's foibles is before you buy it. This is when you'll want to uncover as many mysteries as possible in order to minimize the time and money needed

---

to fix it up later. A thorough checkup is a job for a qualified house inspector (see below), but before you pay for an inspector, do a preliminary check yourself. By checking these eleven things, you can get a pretty good idea of a house's condition.

The structure.   Look at the house from a distance. Be sure the exterior walls look perfectly vertical and flat and that the roof doesn't sag. Lightly jump in the middle of the living room floor to see if it flexes or feels solid. Be sure the interior walls are flat and the corners are straight. If there is a basement or crawl space, check to be sure the foundation walls are straight and not bowed or badly cracked. Are there standing puddles or water stains on the basement/crawl space floor? Inspect the bottom ends of all support posts or columns for rust and rot and look for any signs of insect and rodent infestation.

The roofing.   This is your first line of protection against the elements. Is the roofing in good shape, and does it look neat and properly applied? Do you see any signs of roof leaks? Check the ceilings in each room for water stains. You can inspect the roof from the ground with binoculars. Look for missing or curled shingles and rusty flashing. Check inside the attic for water stains on the rafters and underside of the sheathing. Ask how many layers of roofing are installed and when the house was last re-roofed.

Drainage control.   Look for evidence of water damage and check to be sure groundwater runoff has been handled properly. If you're looking at the house on a dry day, imagine where water will come from during a heavy rain. Be sure the ground slopes away from the base of the house and that gutters, downspouts, and drainage pipes are designed to carry excess water away from the house. Look at the ground directly below the gutters for telltale signs of erosion, which will indicate that water drips behind the gutters or that they leak or easily overflow.

Details.   Look for signs of quality workmanship. Check the moldings, quality of hardware, and tile work. Are the grout joints between the tiles in good condition? Open and close all interior and exterior doors to make sure they stay open without swinging shut and latch closed securely. Do the windows operate smoothly and close squarely?

Kitchen and bath fixtures.   Be sure sinks, toilets, showers, and tubs are all high-quality fixtures that work well. And check the water pressure while you're at it: Be sure there is plenty of flow when you turn on the faucets and the shower and flush the toilet at the same time. How old are the kitchen appliances? Check to make sure the cabinet doors open and close properly and that the drawers slide smoothly.

Electrical system.   Look around the rooms to be sure there are plenty of electrical receptacles conveniently located. Check the size of the main circuit breaker panel (see page 101 for more about this). A 100-amp panel is considered to be barely adequate in today's homes; a 150- or 200-amp panel is much better. Are the kitchen and bathroom outlets protected by GFCI outlets? Ask if there is any aluminum wiring in the house—if there is, it should be replaced.

Water heater and plumbing.   Are the pipes that run from the water heater to plumbing fixtures made of copper? If they are steel instead of copper, they'll probably require replacement at some point because of mineral deposit buildup inside them. Is the water heater gas or electric? An electric water heater is cheaper to install but can be very expensive to operate unless the house is located in a region where electric power is unusually affordable. How old is the water heater? The average life of a gas-fired water heater is twelve years; an electric model typically lasts fourteen years.

Heating.   How is the house heated? Is it air conditioned? Where are furnace registers located? Are any rooms not heated? How old is the furnace? The average life of a gas- or oil-fired furnace is about eighteen years.

Insulation.   Is the house well insulated? The first place to check is the attic. Minimum amounts are: R-19 (six inches of fiberglass, for example) in moderate climates; up to R-38 (twelve inches of fiberglass) in cold climates. If you want to check for wall insulation, remove a receptacle cover on a perimeter wall and look next to the electrical box (do not touch any electrical wires or contacts).

Fireplaces.   Are fireplaces fitted with screens or recirculating fans and glass doors, so that they heat more efficiently? Are the chimneys equipped with dampers and spark arrestors? Take a close look at the chimney foundation; it should be structurally sound and not cracked, sinking, or deteriorated. Also inspect the condition of the exterior concrete block or brick work. The mortar joints should be solid and free of large cracks or voids.

Environmental hazards.   Does the house contain any of the following potentially dangerous materials: asbestos, radon, lead paint, underground oil tank, or contaminated water?

House inspectors

Before buying a house, be sure to hire a house inspector to uncover hidden problems. Most professional inspectors have a construction background—many were formerly contractors, engineers, or city building officials. It's a house inspector's job to comb your home for shortcomings and give you a complete report. With this report, you can determine what problems you might anticipate if you buy the house, whether you want to deduct an amount from your offer to handle some of those problems, or whether you want to look for another house. The fee for this service generally runs $300 or more.

It isn't generally a good idea to hire an inspector that has been recommended by the real estate agent because the inspector's first priority may be to receive future referrals from the agent (their report may not divulge important information to avoid "killing" the deal).

Before you do hire an inspector, ask if his or her company has recently done an inspection on that particular house; if it has, you can usually buy the inspection report for about half the original cost. Finally, show up at the house on inspection day and follow the inspector around to discuss his or her findings. (Don't hire any inspector that won't allow you on site during the inspection.)

You can find house inspectors through the Yellow Pages or by contacting the American Society of Home Inspectors (http://www.ashi.com) at 85 West Algonquin Road, Arlington Heights, Illinois, 60005.

SHOULD YOU DO THE WORK?

What repairs should you—or should you *not*—try to do yourself? Whether or not you should take on a particular home repair task will depend upon a number of factors, including your abilities, your collection of tools and safety gear, your time, and your inclination to roll up your sleeves.

Unless you are a highly skilled do-it-yourselfer, avoid taking on jobs that may be dangerous, particularly difficult, or where a mistake can be quite costly. Some jobs simply are not worth the risk. For example, think twice before doing:

- Extensive electrical work
- Plumbing that involves crawling under the house
- Roofing work on a steeply pitched or high roof
- Difficult or laborious work, such as chopping out and pouring a new concrete floor
- Siding work that requires scaffolding higher than two stories
- Work where there may be hidden mysteries

Skills. Also be realistic about your skills. Don't try to take on work that you won't be able to finish or that may end up looking unprofessional. Avoid intricate work or work that requires a high degree of craftsmanship unless you're competent at the job. For example, don't plan on building raised-panel cabinets unless you possess the necessary cabinetmaking skills and machinery.

Tools.   Be aware that you'll need special tools for some jobs. You can rent tools, and you can often buy tools with what you'll save on labor, but if you don't already own the tools, you probably don't have very much experience at using them. Once again, think twice before jumping in with both feet unless you have experience.

Time.   Don't forget to take your time into consideration. Even spare time has a value—and the value of yours is worth factoring into the equation. One final thought about time: Although a professional repairperson can probably do the job considerably faster than you can, you actually may save time doing some jobs yourself because you won't be required to wait for professionals to show up.

Work + hire.   Another option is to do some of the work yourself and save the more complicated tasks for the pros. Demolition work usually can be tackled by homeowners who aren't afraid of getting a little dirty. Painting is another good way to be involved in the project and save money. But be aware that if you set up this type of arrangement, you must stay ahead of your contractor—he or she won't want to be slowed down by the need to wait for you.

HIRING HOME REPAIR HELP

Finding the right people to help with your home repairs is key to getting a quality job and good price. Many different types of tradespeople specialize in working on various house components, systems, and machines. The chart below will help you determine the right discipline to call for a particular problem. Begin with the first type of service listed; in most cases, the first one is the more affordable service, the one that can handle the problem most efficiently and effectively, or the one that can best get you started with the information you need.

If you're not sure where to look, start under the heading "Contractor." There you will find a wide variety of tradespeople, such as "Contractor, Concrete" or "Contractor, Ventilation."

Problem	Phone book listings
Air conditioning	Air Conditioning Services, Electrical Contractors, Heating and Ventilating Contractors, Air Conditioning Contractors
Appliances	Appliance Repair Services, Appliance Refinishing
Cabinets	Cabinetmaking, Woodworking, Carpenters, Kitchen Cabinets Refacing/Refinishing
Carpets	Carpet Installers, Carpet Dealers, Carpet Repair
Chimney	Chimney Service, Brick Masons
Countertops	Installer (by type of material), Countertops, Kitchen Cabinets
Doors and windows	Window Companies, Carpenters, Handyman, Fix-It Service
Drains	Plumbing Contractors, Drains Cleaned, Septic Tanks and Systems, Sewer Contractors
Electrical systems	Electric Utilities, Electrical Contractors
Foundation	Concrete Contractors, Waterproofing Contractors
Garage door	Garage Doors; Doors, Overhead
Gutters	Gutters and Downspouts, Handyman, Fix-It Service
Heating/cooling systems	Heating Service, Heating and Ventilating Contractors, Air Conditioning Contractors
Locks	Locksmiths
Lighting	Lighting Dealers, Electrical Contractors
Natural gas	Gas Utility, Appliance Repair Service
Paint	Painting Contractors, Spray Painting and Finishing

Problem	Phone book listings
Pests	Exterminating and Fumigating, Pest Control, Insect Control
Plumbing systems	Plumbing Contractors, Handyman, Fix-It Service
Plumbing fixtures	Fixture Dealer, Plumbing Contractors, Plumbing Fixture Parts
Remodeling	General Contractors, Remodeling Contractors
Roof	Roofing Contractors
Security systems	Burglar Alarm Systems
Sewer	Sewer or Septic Contractors, Excavating, Septic Tanks and Systems, Sewer Contractors
Siding	Siding, Painting Contractors; Building Cleaning, Exterior
Skylight	Roofing Contractors
Smoke damage/odor	House Cleaning
Telephone system	Your telephone company, Telephone Installer, Telephone Equipment
Tile	Tile Ceramic Contractors and Dealers
Ventilation	Heating Service, HVAC Contractors, Ventilating Contractors
Vinyl floors	Flooring Installers
Wallboard	Handyman, Fix-It Service, Carpenters, Painting Contractors
Wallpaper	Painting Contractors, Wallcovering Contractors, Decorating Companies
Water heater	Water Heater Repair, Plumbing Contractors
Wood floors	Floors, Laying; Floors, Refinishing and Resurfacing
Woodwork	Carpenters, Handyman, Fix-It Service, Floor Waxing and Cleaning

For problems with products or some materials—such as appliances, flooring, or carpeting—always check the conditions of your warranty before hiring a repairperson. By using factory-authorized service people, you may save on the cost of the repair, if the material is under warranty. And if you don't use authorized service people, you may void your warranty.

THE VERSATILE HANDYMAN (OR HANDYWOMAN)

A handyman is often an excellent choice for handling a variety of home repairs—especially small jobs that many contractors won't touch. Most people who give themselves this title have a range of skills—from wiring to plumbing to carpentry—and charge considerably less per hour than licensed tradespeople such as electrical contractors or plumbers. And handymen and women work across trades—during a single house call, a good handyman can fix your dripping faucets, replace a light switch, and repair the gate latch. But it is imperative that you find a handyman who is competent at a variety of trades and is fair in his or her dealings with you. Be aware that when you hire a handyman, you don't know what you're getting unless the person comes with high recommendations. Unlike licensed contractors and subcontractors or factory-authorized repair people, no particular accreditation is required for a handyman in many states.

CONTRACTORS

For major improvements, a remodel, or a similar job that involves several trades, you'll want a general contractor—a construction professional who knows several trades and hires tradespeople called subcontractors or "subs" to handle various aspects of the work, such as the plumbing, electrical, concrete and, drywall. Some contractors work with their subs; some just supervise. The contractor is responsible for coordinating and paying the subs and purchasing materials, and generally works on the basis of a firm bid. Contractors must be licensed or certified in most states; be sure yours is, and that he or she carries worker's compensation and liability insurance.

CHOOSING GOOD HELP

The best way to find reliable, capable tradespeople is through referrals from friends or neighbors who have had similar work done and were happy with the service. If you can't get recommendations, talk to local building supply dealers or turn to the Yellow Pages— your most likely source of names if you're dealing with a home-repair emergency. So that you're not left to this device in a pinch, it pays to have the names and numbers of good repair services on hand. It's also smart to check with the local chapter of the Better Business Bureau to make sure there isn't a history of consumer complaints against the pro you plan to hire.

Making a selection.   Select two or three potential tradespeople or companies (three to five for major construction work), call them, describe your problem, and ask:

1. Their hourly rate or method of charging and whether they charge for time spent coming to the job or picking up materials. Also ask whether a basic fee for checking the problem can be applied toward the final bill for fixing it.
2. Whether they are licensed or factory-certified for a particular product. Will the person with the license or certification be doing the actual work?
3. How much experience they have with your repair problem.
4. Whether they can handle the problem as quickly as you need to have it taken care of. Pinpoint the time of their visit to avoid wasting the day waiting.

When a repairperson arrives.   Review the work to be done and request a written description and price on their letterhead. This formal estimate should include:

1. Details about his or her fees and rates
2. A "not-to-exceed" amount to limit the maximum price you will pay
3. Written confirmation of any guarantees made
4. His or her signature as well as yours—but do not sign a partial or incomplete contract
5. An exact description of the work to be done and materials to be used

A formal estimate.   For all but the simplest repairs, you should secure a formal estimate. But be aware that many problems may be concealed behind walls or above ceilings and the repairperson can't be expected to anticipate every ugly surprise. If he or she can't give you a tight estimate, set a fixed rate for the investigative work that can become part of the overall price if he or she does the repairs.

Before making a final payment or signing off on the finished work, be sure to inspect it carefully. Ask for a written receipt that states "Paid in full" to avoid liens or other legal claims later.

HIRING A GENERAL CONTRACTOR

For major improvements or remodeling, you'll probably want a general contractor who is responsible for organizing and coordinating all of the trades involved in completing the work. Find a general contractor the same way you would find a repairperson, as discussed above—ideally, through personal recommendations. Call and pre-qualify several contractors, checking to be sure that they can handle the work and your schedule. Then meet with three or four of them individually, and request the names and numbers of a few of their satisfied customers. Call those references to check whether they were happy with the contractors and note any problem areas. Be sure each candidate is licensed and insured for worker's compensation, property damage, and personal liability insurance. And whenever possible, always visit past clients' homes to see the contractor's work first hand.

Request a formal bid from each candidate that you're considering seriously, based on exactly the same plans or specifications. Don't jump for the lowest bid—this may indicate inexperience or desperation on the contractor's part.

Chemistry with your family is an important contractor qualification. Remember, they will be in your midst doing major construction, and there will be times when you may need to deal with difficult issues. Also, probe their level of experience and their level of commitment to your project—ask how long they've been in business and whether they will have other ongoing jobs while they're working on yours. If they have other work coinciding with yours, ask how much personal supervision they will give to your job.

When you've settled on one contractor, you can follow up by asking the name of their insurance carrier and agency and then calling to check on their coverage. Also ask to see their contractor's license.

When the job is finished, if you feel you've been cheated or wronged, you may lodge a formal complaint with the contractor's licensing board (this is one of the reasons it's important to work with licensed professionals). Through that board, you may request arbitration or a hearing. You can also contact the Better Business Bureau or bring suit against the contractor and/or his or her company or bring the matter before small claims court.

If the contractor doesn't pay for the materials or the subcontractors, the people owed money may be able to place a lien against your property. You can protect yourself from this on a large project by adding a release-of-lien clause to your contract and issuing your payments to an escrow account to be held until the work is completed.

A GOOD CONTRACT

The best way to avoid legal hassles or misunderstandings between you and your contractor is to have a clear, binding contract that outlines everyone's expectations and responsibilities. This contract, signed by both you and your contractor, should specify in detail all of the work to be done and the materials to be used, the completion schedule, and how payments will be made.

Here's a closer look at what the contract should include:

- The names and addresses of the project and the builder.
- Details of all work to be performed as well as the start and completion dates. You may want to consider a penalty clause if the job isn't completed on time (excluding delays for strikes, material shortages, or natural disasters). But if you do, also insert a bonus clause to pay the builder more money if the job is finished ahead of schedule.
- Details about the materials to be used, including brand names, model numbers, and quality markings. The more detail, the better. Avoid the phrase "or equal," unless you make it clear that substitutions can't be made without your approval. If you set up a separate budget for particular items, such as plumbing fixtures, be sure that the budget figure is high enough to purchase the items you want.
- Details about when and how payments will be made. Do not pay more than one-third up front. Making an initial payment and then paying in installments as the work progresses is a common practice, but don't let the finished work fall behind the payments (after the initial payment).
- Details of responsibilities, such as demolition and trash collection. Will there be a dumpster on the job? If so, where will it be dropped. Even a small dumpster will ruin a lawn and sink into an asphalt driveway on a hot day. Leaving it at the curb is a good idea, but not all towns allow it. Where will the contractor stage materials—lumber piles, cabinets, roofing, plywood—when they arrive? If anything is stolen, who will be responsible? (For safety, consider asking the contractor to have the crew clean up the site at the end of every day.)
- Don't sign a completion statement or pay the final payment until the completed job has passed final inspection.

BUILDING PERMITS

For many different types of home repair and improvement jobs, permits are required. Though simple repairs usually don't call for permits, additions or major changes—particularly those that involve electrical, heating, plumbing, and structural work—usually demand that you get the appropriate permits from the local building department. If you're working with a contractor or subcontractor, this professional usually handles the permit process.

If you are undertaking major changes and your tradesperson suggests that you don't need a permit, be wary and check with the building department yourself. In most cases, getting a permit means the work will be inspected by the necessary officials. As a homeowner, this is good for you. Your contractor's work will be scrutinized by another set of knowledgeable eyes, and the results must adhere to building codes, which set minimum safety standards for both materials and construction techniques.

Building codes insure that your home will be safe for your family and any future families who live there. If work is done without a permit and discovered later, building officials may require that you bring the work up to permit standard—or even dismantle and redo the work—before they will give it a completion or occupancy approval.

For most permits, you must pay fees, typically based on the value of the project. Don't overestimate the value of your work—it may cost you more in permit fees.

DO-IT-YOURSELF REPAIR TIPS

Here are a few helpful tips to keep in mind when you're doing your own repairs to appliances, fixtures, and systems in your home:

1. Use an instant camera or make a sketch of how things fit together before you take them apart—so you know how to reassemble them. As you begin to disassemble the unit, line up all the parts in the exact order in which they were removed. That will keep everything in order and make it easy to reassemble the unit.
2. Take the worn or defective parts with you when you go to the hardware store or home improvement center so you can find a perfect replacement.
3. Rubber washers, gaskets, small fittings, and other inexpensive parts that have a limited life should be replaced along with the defective part. Otherwise, you may find yourself disassembling everything for another repair in the near future. When you are replacing something that has several inexpensive parts—like a sink trap (page 80)—it sometimes pays to replace all of the components.

3

APPLIANCE PROBLEMS

When they work, major appliances add to the many conveniences of daily life, but when they rattle, flood, and stop with a thud, they remind us of how reliant we have become upon mechanical and electronic devices.

Fortunately, most major home appliances will run reliably for a long time. And when appliances do break down, an appliance repairperson can usually hustle over on a house call to handle the problem on short notice. But appliance repairs can be pricey—easily $100 or more per hour, plus parts, for even simple repairs. And many repairs are done on a flat-rate basis; you may pay $75 for a repair that takes fifteen minutes. If you can fix something yourself with little effort, you can spend your hard-earned cash on something more fun than a stalled garbage disposal or drippy dishwasher. This chapter covers major appliances in alphabetical order and will show you how to handle simple appliance repairs and how to decide when it's smarter to defer problems to professional repair people.

As a rule, it's wise to buy appliances that have proven reliability, a trait that you can usually determine by checking up on current ratings in *Consumer Reports* (back issues are available in libraries). You can also ask friends or relatives whether they've bought appliances that they're particularly happy with. Opt for appliances that have strong warranties. There's nothing more satisfying than calling a factory-authorized repairperson, having them solve the problem, then seeing them leave at no charge with nothing more than a "thank you."

If your appliance is under warranty, be sure the service person you call is factory authorized. The display of the brand name in an advertisement in the Yellow Pages does not signify that the person you have called has warranty authorization. If you use an unauthorized repairperson, the manufacturer probably won't cover the fee and, worse, the warranty may be voided.

A caveat: Appliances differ from one manufacturer to the next, so they are covered generically here. Though the locations of components may be different in your particular appliance, the basics are the same in most cases.

APPLIANCE BASICS

Tools and parts

The tools you'll need for repairs will depend on the situation; they are discussed along with the repair steps and on pages 73 and 104. Appliance parts are available through stores or outlets that specialize in appliance parts or from an appliance service company that has a location with a parts counter. Look in the Yellow Pages under the heading "Appliances, Major, Parts."

Check the owner's manual

An owner's manual is a critically important tool for the care of any appliance. When you buy a new appliance, be sure to file all owner's manuals and warranties where you'll be able to find them later. If you don't have your owner's manual to an appliance, call the manufacturer and request a copy for your make and model (see the resources on page 229 for manufacturers' phone numbers). Owner's manuals are also available through appliance parts dealers.

Check the power

Nearly all appliances rely upon electricity for some part of their operation—to run motors, create heat, provide light, or power the controls. If the power goes out, most appliances don't work. With that in mind, check the power first when an appliance doesn't work at all. Here's how:

1. Be sure the appliance is plugged in and turned on. If necessary, check the receptacle that the appliance is plugged into. To do this, simply plug in a working lamp, small power tool, or a voltage tester (page 105-106). If the device works, you know the receptacle is active.
2. If none of the test devices work, the receptacle is dead for some reason. Go to the electrical panel and check the circuit breaker or fuse that serves the appliance's circuit (see page 104). If necessary, reset the circuit breaker or replace the fuse.
3. If the receptacle works, but the appliance doesn't, unplug the appliance and check its power cord. If necessary, repair the cord (page 111).
4. If you have an owner's manual, check it to see whether the device has an overload fuse or reset switch. If you don't have the owner's manual, look for a reset switch or fuse. You may have to remove a cover panel to do this—unplug the appliance first. Don't remove the cover from an appliance if there are warnings posted to the contrary. Don't hesitate to call the manufacturer's customer information number for repair advice. You may be surprised at the helpful information they will provide.
5. Always turn the power off when working on an electrical appliance, and don't forget to turn it back on when you've made your repairs.

Refrigeration principles

Air conditioners, heat pumps, refrigerators, freezers, and other appliances that produce "cold" share basic refrigeration technology. In fact, appliances such as heat pumps and dehumidifiers that draw heat or humidity out of the air also utilize refrigeration principles. Here's how they work:

Cooling appliances don't really create "cold," they remove heat from the air. To do this, a compressor pushes a refrigerant through copper tubing between two sets of coils, one a condenser and the other an evaporator. With a whole-house air conditioner, the condenser is located outside and the evaporator is mounted on top of the indoor air-handling unit. With a portable air conditioner, dehumidifier, refrigerator, or freezer, both the condenser and evaporator coils are part of the appliance.

As the refrigerant moves from condenser to evaporator, it changes from liquid to gas and back to liquid, absorbing or releasing heat and changing pressure. Cold, high-pressure refrigerant moves through the condenser coil, which, because it is cold, pulls the heat out of the air. As warm air cools on the condenser coils, the air releases moisture as condensation (dehumidifying the air). As the refrigerant absorbs heat at the evaporator, it becomes a vapor and travels on to the compressor, which boosts its pressure, converting it back into a liquid. This liquid must release its heat, which it does through the condenser coils. As it loses its heat, it becomes a high-pressure liquid and moves full circle back toward the evaporator coil.

This complete refrigeration system is called a "sealed" or "hermetic" system and should be repaired only by certified professionals.

Air conditioners carry the indoor heat out; heat pumps will carry heat out or bring it in to warm your home's interior spaces (they're reversible). All of these appliances rely upon electricity to run the compressor and power fans that blow air across the coils.

AIR CONDITIONER

See Heating and Comfort problems on page 126.

DEHUMIDIFIER

If your home doesn't have air conditioning, it may rely upon a dehumidifier to reduce uncomfortable, muggy humidity in room air. A dehumidifier uses refrigeration principles (see above) the way an air conditioner does, but it doesn't cool the air—in fact, it warms it slightly. It is a box that contains cold evaporator coils, warm condenser coils, a fan, and a reservoir or drain to catch water (Figure 3.1). The fan blows moisture-laden room air over the cold coils, where water condenses and drips into the pan or drain. The drier air then blows across the warm coils and back into the room.

For a dehumidifier to operate, its fan must have electric power, the evaporator coils must contain a proper charge of refrigerant, and the controls must work properly. In the same way that a thermostat controls a heater or air conditioner, a dehumidifier is cycled off and on by a humidistat that measures a room's humidity.

Many dehumidifiers have an overflow cutoff ("float") switch that prevents the unit from spilling over with the water that has been drawn out of the room air. Sometimes this switch goes bad and must be replaced. Nine times out of ten, a problem with a dehumidifier can be traced to electrical parts—not to the compressor. If you (or a repairperson) discover that the problem is being caused by the compressor and the unit is out of warranty (most have a one-year limited warranty), strongly consider replacing the unit rather than trying to have the compressor repaired. If you're thinking about having the unit repaired, be sure to ask for an estimate.

FOR SAFETY: Always unplug a dehumidifier before working on it.

THE HOME PROBLEM SOLVER

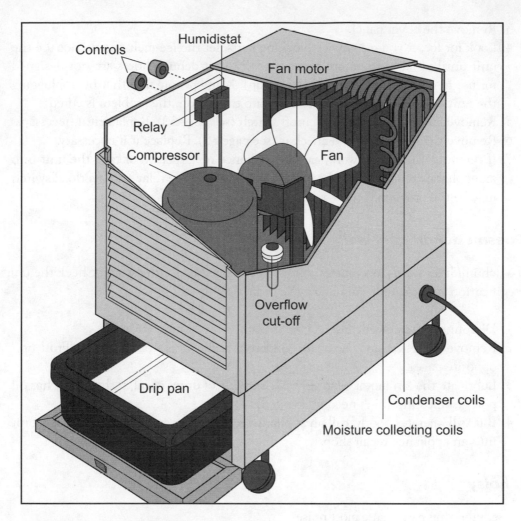

FIGURE 3.1   Dehumidifier

Doesn't run

If your dehumidifier shows no signs of life:

1. Check the power (page 24). Be sure it is plugged in to a working outlet and turned on.
2. Unplug the dehumidifier unit and check the power cord. If necessary, replace the cord (page 111).

3. Remove the cover panel.
4. Look for ice. If you see any ice blocking parts, let the ice melt and do not use the unit until room temperature exceeds 65°F (most dehumidifiers are not designed for use in colder spaces and may freeze up). Many people find that by unplugging the unit and waiting about thirty days into the season, the problem is cured.
5. Remove and test the overflow cutoff switch (see page 30). Replace it if necessary.
6. Remove the humidistat and check it (see page 30). Replace it if necessary.
7. If the unit still doesn't work, call an appliance repairperson or take the unit into an appliance repair shop—the compressor motor or the relay and overload switch may be the problem.

Doesn't dehumidify well

If a dehumidifier seems incompetent, it may be undersized for the space. Check the unit's specifications to be sure it can handle the room size.

1. Disconnect the power cord.
2. Remove the cover and clean the condenser and evaporator coils (see "Frost up," opposite page).
3. Lubricate the fan motor bearings with a couple of drops of oil, if the motor has oil ports (some units don't need to be oiled).
4. If it still operates poorly, call an appliance repairperson for advice or take the unit into an appliance repair shop.

Is noisy

Loose, vibrating parts cause most noises.

1. Disconnect the power.
2. Remove the cover and look for loose screws or vibrating parts and check to see if the rubber compressor mounts have hardened so that they no longer absorb the unit's movement. If they have, replace them.
3. Wiggle the fan to see if it is loose on its shaft. If it is, tighten the mounting fasteners. Lubricate the motor's bearings if suggested by your owner's manual.
4. If it still makes noise, call an appliance repairperson or take the unit into an appliance repair shop.

Frosts up

A dehumidifier will often frost up if room temperatures are colder than about 65°F. If your room temperature isn't this cold, airflow to the unit may be restricted or blocked entirely.

1. Be sure the unit is set far enough from the wall so that airflow isn't restricted.
2. Clean the evaporator coils. To do this, unplug the dehumidifier and take off the outer cover. Allow excess moisture to evaporate from the coils. Then, using a brush attachment on a vacuum cleaner, remove all dust buildup. If necessary, cover the motor and electrical parts with plastic sheeting and spray with water.

Leaks water

If water drips or pools at the base of your dehumidifier:

1. Disconnect the power.
2. Check the pan or reservoir and empty it if necessary, or make sure the drain isn't clogged.
3. Straighten any kinks or bends in the unit's hose.
4. If it still leaks, check and/or replace the overflow cutoff switch (see page 30). Then, if necessary, call an appliance repairperson or take the unit into an appliance repair shop.

Gives off an odor

Odors are generally caused by stagnant water or chronically dirty condenser coils.

1. Unplug the unit.
2. Empty the reservoir; mop up any damp areas; and clean the coils with a brush and a garden hose.

Note: You can have a dehumidifier's coils steam cleaned at an appliance repair or auto repair shop, but if you do this, have the unit checked after the cleaning to be sure the electrical components haven't been disturbed. Allow to dry in a warm place for at least twenty-four hours.

Humidistat test (advanced):

You can test the humidistat fairly easily, using a volt-ohm meter (pages 105-106). Just set the meter to RX1 scale and attach its leads to the humidistat's terminals. Rotate the humidistat's knob as far as it will turn in both directions. If the volt-ohm meter registers zero ohms through only part of the humidistat dial's range, the humidistat is working. If it registers zero through the entire range, it's broken and must be replaced.

Overflow cutoff switch test (advanced):

Using a volt-ohm meter (pages 105-106), you can tell if the overflow cutoff switch works or not. Clip the leads to the terminals on the switch. Depress the bar or trip lever on the switch. If the meter's needle doesn't fluctuate between continuity and no continuity as the switch is clicked back and forth, the switch is probably faulty and will need replacement.

DISHWASHER

A dishwasher is essentially a watertight cabinet that sprays dishes with hot water and soap, drains out the dirty water, then dries the dishes. A hot water supply hose or tube hooks up to a valve that distributes the water to one or more spinning spray arms; a motor pump beneath the lower spray arm recirculates wash water and pumps out the dirty water; and an electric heating element or a hot-air fan dries the dishes. Controls, including a timer and switches, sequence and activate the various cycles.

Many dishwashers have an air gap attached to their drain line. Typically mounted behind the sink, the air gap prevents wastewater from being sucked back into the dishwasher. With a dishwasher that doesn't utilize an air gap, the drain hose usually makes a high, arching loop up under the countertop; this also prevents wastewater from siphoning back into the dishwasher.

FOR SAFETY:
1. Before working on it, always unplug the dishwasher from its electrical receptacle or shut off the circuit that powers it (see page 103).
2. Turn off the hot water supply valve beneath the sink before disconnecting or working on the dishwasher's supply valve or hose.
3. Don't work inside the dishwasher immediately following a wash cycle; various parts, especially the electric dryer element at the bottom, may still be hot.

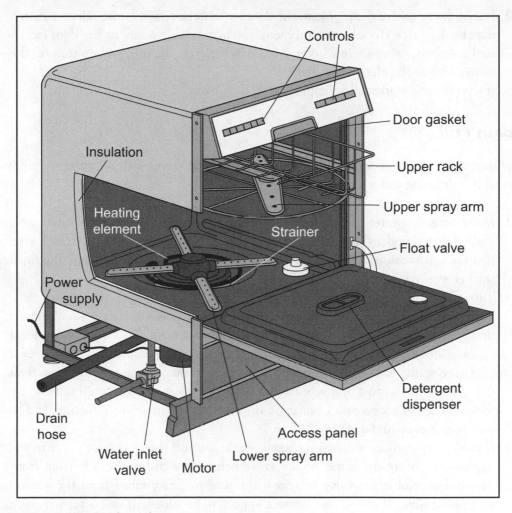

Controls

Door gasket

Insulation

Upper rack

Upper spray arm

Heating element

Strainer

Float valve

Power supply

Detergent dispenser

Drain hose

Access panel

Water inlet valve

Motor

Lower spray arm

FIGURE 3.2   Dishwasher

Doesn't run

If you turn on the dishwasher and nothing happens:

1. Be sure the power is on (page 24), the door is latched, and the control is turned on. Also make sure the appliance cord is plugged into the electrical receptacle under the sink (some are hardwired and don't come unplugged).

2. If that doesn't solve the problem, the door switch, the timer, or the selector switch may be defective. To solve the problem, you may be able to adjust the door latch's strike slightly, using a screwdriver (before working on the dishwasher, turn off the power to it at the electrical panel).

3. If that doesn't work, call an appliance repairperson.

Doesn't fill

If a dishwasher runs but doesn't fill, either something is wrong with its water supply system or it is draining water too soon.

1. Make sure the water is turned on. Check the hot water supply stop valve, normally located under the sink. Open it all the way by turning it counterclockwise. If there is no reason this would have been turned off since the last time the dishwasher worked, go on to the next step.

2. Turn off the power to the dishwasher.

3. When the dishwasher is cool, look for the float inside—usually a small plastic dome or cylinder mounted at the tub's base, near the front. When you move most types of floats up and down, you can hear them click because they trip a lever (they are spring loaded). Lift out the float mechanism and clean around the float tube; many floats must be disconnected from below—to do this you'll have to remove the lower access panel. Rinse off the float; then replace it in the tube and be sure it moves up and down freely.

4. If you're experienced with minor repair work, shut off the hot water valve to the appliance. Locate the water intake valve behind the dishwasher's bottom front panel; disassemble the valve to reveal the screen; clean debris from the screen; and reassemble. If the screen doesn't appear to be blocked, call a repairperson (they will probably need to replace the water intake valve).

5. If none of this helps, call a repairperson. Any of several parts, including the water inlet valve, the pressure switch, and the timer or selector switch, may be faulty.

Doesn't stop filling

If the dishwasher's water flow doesn't automatically shut off, the float switch is faulty or the timer is stuck on "Fill" or the water inlet valve is stuck open.

To test the float switch, you'll need an inexpensive volt-ohm meter (or multi-meter), as discussed on pages 105-106.

1. Unplug the dishwasher.
2. Reach into the cabinet and lift the dome-shaped plastic float switch. If it doesn't lift, remove the plastic top from the stem, scrub the stem clean, and then replace the dome. If it moves up and down freely, go on to step 3.
3. Note which wires are attached to the float switch's terminals and, using small pieces of tape, label them for later reference.
4. Set the volt-ohm meter's dial to Rx100 or, if the meter is digital, to a kΩ or just Ω and touch the two probes to the terminals. When you lift the float, the tester's needle should show an infinity reading, and when you let the float drop, the needle should show 0. If it doesn't, the switch is broken and will need replacement. Unscrew it from the tub and replace it.

Doesn't drain

Following a cycle, a small pool of clean water inside the tub is typical. Excessive water means the pump isn't pumping water out properly, the drain hose isn't carrying it to the drain pipe, or the house's drain lines are backed up (see page 75). If dirty water spews from the air gap, the drain line is kinked or clogged. Note: If you've recently installed a garbage disposer, be sure the knockout plug for the dishwasher was removed when the connection was made (see your disposer instructions).

1. Remove the cover from the air gap at the top of the sink (usually a short, chrome, domed cylinder that sits at the back of the sink) and, using a wire, clean it. Also check the entire length of the drain hose for kinks and blockages, especially at the drain connection to the disposer or drain line.
2. Once the dishwasher is cool, shut off the power to it, and—if your dishwasher is made to allow this—remove the strainer, located under the bottom spray arm at the base of the cabinet (see Figure 3.3, following page). Unscrew the hubcap, lift the spray arm off, and remove any clips that hold the strainer to get it out. Scrub it clean with a brush; then replace it.
3. Determine whether the sink trap or house drain line is clogged (see page 76).
4. If it still doesn't drain properly, the drain hose may be clogged or the drain valve may need replacement. At this point, it's usually best to call a repairperson. You can check the drain hose for obstructions, but this sometimes involves pulling the dishwasher out from under your counter to access the hose, disconnecting the hose at both ends, and flushing it out with a faucet or garden hose.

FIGURE 3.3   Dishwasher Strainer

Doesn't wash well

A common cause of poor washing is improper loading—dishes block or impede the spray arms or prevent the soap dispenser from opening. On the other hand, if your dishwasher has chronic problems with washing, the problem may not be your dishwasher. Your home's water pressure may be too low; the water may be too hard; you may not be using the right amount of detergent; or the water temperature may not be hot enough.

Water pressure.   In order to fill to appropriate levels, water pressure should be from 20 to 120 pounds per square inch. If you suspect that your water pressure may be low, turn off all water; then put a half-gallon jug under the kitchen water faucet. Turn on the hot water full blast. If the jug doesn't fill within fourteen seconds, your water pressure may be too low for proper dishwasher operation. Call your city water utility to discuss options or avoid drawing water elsewhere in the house or yard during dishwasher cycles.

Too little or too much detergent.   The right amount of detergent to use depends upon how dirty your dishes are and how hard the water is. To find out how hard your water is, call your local water utility and ask. Hardness is measured in grains—the more grains of hardness, the more detergent you'll need. If your water has twelve grains or more of hardness, fill both dishwasher soap cups completely with detergent. If that doesn't work, consider installing a water softener.

Here are detergent recommendations:

Water hardness	Tablespoon of detergent
0 to 3 grains	1
4 to 6 grains	2
7 to 9 grains	3
10 to 12 grains	4

Water temperature. To check water temperature, hold a meat thermometer under the hot water faucet for two minutes; if it doesn't register a minimum of 140°F, turn up the temperature dial on your hot water heater (page 63). Note: Some newer dishwashers heat the water automatically—it isn't necessary to turn up your hot water heater if you have one of these.

FOR SAFETY: If you have small children in the house, it's safer to leave your water heater set below 120°F; scalding is a major cause of serious children's accidents.

If your dishwasher has worked fine in the past, but suddenly your dishes aren't clean after the dishwasher completes all cycles:

1. Check your water heater's temperature dial to be sure it hasn't been changed recently.
2. Be sure dishes haven't prevented the detergent dispenser from opening properly during the wash cycles or kept the spray arms from turning, the lower arm from rising, or the spray from reaching the upper rack's dishes.
3. During the wash cycle, listen to the spray arm spinning inside. If it seems to be spinning poorly, clean out the spray holes in the spray arm(s) with a stiff piece of wire—wait for the machine to cool, then remove the spray arm(s) by unscrewing the hub cap and lifting the arm(s) off.

Washing leaves spots or film

If your dishes or glassware appear filmy or spotted following a complete wash cycle, the first thing you need to do is determine whether the film is removable or permanently etched. To do this, soak a glass in undiluted white vinegar for about fifteen minutes. Or you can wash the glass with warm water and concentrated dishwasher detergent or a high-phosphate detergent (such as Glass Magic), according to label directions.

If film comes off, it is probably caused by hard water minerals, improper amounts of detergent, or unsuitable water temperature. An adjustment of the amount or type of de-

---

tergent you're using and of your hot water heater's water temperature may solve the problem. (See "Doesn't wash well" on page 34.) But before you do either of these things, put a rinse additive (such as Jet-Dry) in the rinse dispenser to improve the sheeting action of the water.

Permanent etching is often caused by a combination of soft water and excessive heat or detergent. If glassware is permanently etched, there isn't anything you can do to make it clear again. But you can avoid future etching by taking these steps:

1. Be sure hot water entering the dishwasher is no hotter than 140°F; don't use extra hot settings such as "Power Scrub"; and use the "Energy Saver" dry cycle.
2. Adjust detergent amount (see chart on page 35).
3. Don't pre-rinse your dishes before loading them in the dishwasher. Food particles on the dishes actually help the detergent and drying agents clean better.

Leaks

If you have nuisance water leaks around the base of your dishwasher, you may be using a detergent that is sudsing too much. Cut back on the amount of detergent you use and see if that makes a difference.

Water that spills through the door vent is usually caused by improperly loading dishes. Leaks from the door itself may be caused by a faulty door gasket or door tightness adjustment. Also make sure the dishwasher is sitting level (you can adjust the front feet up or down, and many units have some type of levelers at the rear).

Water under the dishwasher may be originating from a leaky hose or loose hose connection. Remove the lower front panel and check the hoses. The pump seal may be defective, too; replacing this is a job for an appliance repairperson.

An older dishwasher may corrode at the bottom, but this is fairly uncommon. If this is the case with your dishwasher, it's time for a new one.

Makes noise

Noise may be coming from faulty parts, but it also may be caused by improperly loaded dishes; check your owner's manual for proper loading methods. Next, when the dishwasher is completely cool, look in the openings around the pump at the bottom of the dishwasher's interior; be sure no implements or hard debris such as bones, fruit pits, or silverware are stuck in them.

Be sure your dishwasher is sitting level. Adjust the feet beneath the unit by screwing them up or down. If there are lock nuts on the feet, make sure they are tight.

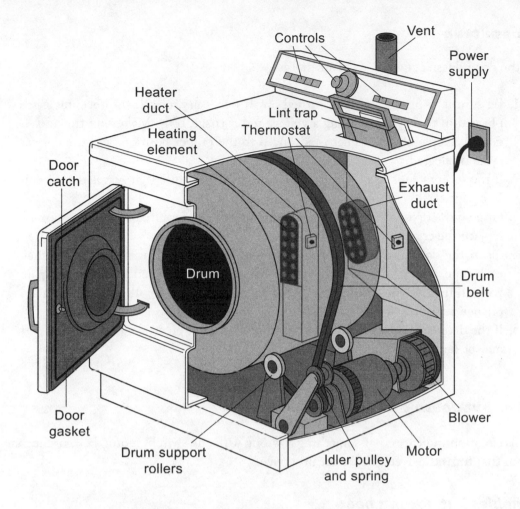

FIGURE 3.4   Clothes Dryer

A thumping or chattering sound during the filling cycle usually indicates that the inlet valve needs to be replaced. Unless you're handy with this sort of repair, this is a job for a repairperson.

DRYER

Problems with a clothes dryer normally involve the heat source or the motor that tumbles the clothes: Clothes don't dry because it doesn't get hot enough or the drum doesn't rotate.

Doesn't run

If the dryer doesn't start or make any noise:

1. Be sure it is plugged in and turned on. If necessary, check the receptacle it's plugged in to for power, using a voltage tester (page 106). Make sure the door is closed completely, the timer is advanced to the proper position, and the correct cycle is selected.
2. If the receptacle is dead, check the circuit breaker or fuse that serves that circuit (see page 104).
3. Unplug the dryer and check the power cord and the terminal block. If necessary, replace the cord.
4. Open the door and check the door switch. Press and release it: It should click each time. If it doesn't, it's probably broken. If you're experienced at home repair, you can remove the switch, test it, and replace it if needed; otherwise, call an appliance repair service.
5. If the dryer still doesn't work, a thermal fuse or other electrical or electronic part may be faulty. Call a service person.

Runs but doesn't tumble

This situation indicates that something is wrong with the switch, motor, belt, or mechanism that turns the drum. Call a repair service.

Tumbles but doesn't heat

When this happens, something has interrupted the heat source. Run the dryer for a couple of minutes to see if it gets hot. Be sure you don't have the dial or controls on a non-heat setting such as "Fluff" or "Wrinkle Control."

Electric dryer.   No heat may mean that the circuit breaker or fuse that controls the power has blown—check and replace or reset (page 104). Be aware that a dryer may have two breakers or fuses: The motor will run when one works, but the heating element requires both.

Gas dryer.   Recheck the control's setting to be sure it's not on a heat-free setting. Check the gas valve behind the dryer to be sure the gas supply is turned on. Also make sure the house's main gas valve is turned on. On an older dryer, make sure the pilot light is burning. If it isn't, re-light as discussed on page 139 or in your owner's manual (pilot light instructions are often mounted next to the pilot light on the burner, too). Note: Most modern dryers have electronic ignition instead of a pilot light. If yours has electronic ignition and isn't heating, call a qualified repairperson.

Takes too long to dry

Dryers need to be properly vented, otherwise the moisture in the air can't be properly carried away.

Vents that go out the roof are particularly problematic—the dryer may take far too long to dry clothes, and the vent pipe may even drip water that can't be exhausted. Minimum size for a dryer's roof vent is four inches. If your dryer has chronically poor drying, then, if possible, have the vent moved so that it exits a house wall near the dryer.

The vent should be made of four-inch rigid aluminum duct and elbows or, where absolutely necessary, flexible metal (but not flexible thin foil). Do not use flexible plastic duct—it restricts air flow and is combustible.

The dryer should vent outside—never into a crawl space, wall, ceiling chimney, or other type of flue. The bottom of the exhaust hood should be located at least twelve inches above the ground.

If your dryer is properly vented but still takes too long to dry clothes, then the vent is probably blocked with lint. Here is what to do:

1. Check the lint trap and clean it.
2. Be sure the dryer isn't pushed so close to the wall that it pinches off the airflow through the vent's air duct hose.
3. Check the point where the air duct vents away from the house. Be sure plants, birds, or other things haven't blocked it. If the duct vents out the roof, it could easily be blocked with lint.
4. Disconnect the air duct hose from the back of the dryer and clean out built-up lint. Note: For safety, first turn off the gas or power to the dryer; then unplug the dryer; in the case of a gas dryer, this means you will have to re-light the pilot light later, if the dryer has one (page 139).
5. If necessary, clean out the ductwork from the dryer to the exterior wall where it vents; this may involve disconnecting sections. One trick that sometimes makes this job easier (but only if the dryer duct is fastened firmly at all connection points) is to blow lint and debris through the duct and out the exterior wall vent with an electric leaf blower.

Is noisy

Some noises are caused by objects bouncing around inside the drum or by loose, vibrating dryer parts. Scour the interior of the drum for loose objects.

If the noise is being caused by defective parts—notably a worn or defective drum belt, idler pulley, support roller, or worn motor bearings—it's best to call an appliance repair service.

Smells of natural gas

Of course, this problem applies to gas dryers only. If you smell natural gas near your gas dryer, do not light matches or a lighter and don't operate electrical switches or anything that might spark and ignite an explosion.

Immediately shut off the gas valve that serves the dryer.

A mild smell. In this case, ventilate the area, *wait until the air is clear*, and re-light your pilot light (see page 139).

A strong smell. If the smell is strong, move everyone outside, leaving the doors open to ventilate the house. Then turn off the gas supply valve to the house—located by the gas meter on the gas inlet pipe—by rotating the valve one quarter turn with an adjustable wrench (pages 73-74). The valve's oblong stem should be perpendicular (at a right angle) to the inlet pipe to stop the flow of gas.

Call your gas supplier (or the fire department) from a neighbor's phone or a cellular phone outside the house.

GARBAGE DISPOSER

A garbage disposer is a simple device; it is essentially a motor that drives rotating impellers that, in turn, grind up food waste so it can be flushed down the sink drain. Simple problems are easy to fix; with a serious problem, you're usually better off replacing the entire unit. When you buy a new disposal, installation instructions are included.

But before you scrap your old disposer, check the manufacturer's warranty. (To contact manufacturers, see the resource guide on page 229.) Some warranties cover parts and labor for five years or more.

When using a disposer, be sure to flush it with plenty of water—two gallons per minute. Avoid grinding fibrous materials such as artichokes and corn husks, shells, large whole bones, and nonfood debris such as plastic and aluminum foil.

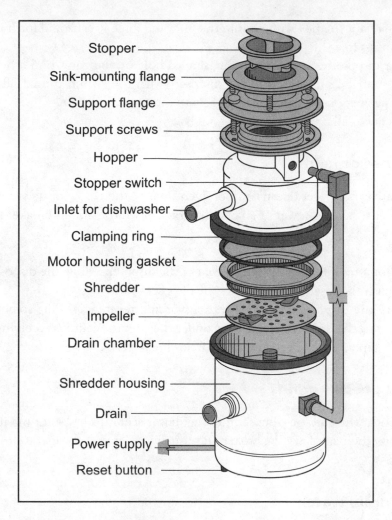

Stopper

Sink-mounting flange

Support flange

Support screws

Hopper

Stopper switch

Inlet for dishwasher

Clamping ring

Motor housing gasket

Shredder

Impeller

Drain chamber

Shredder housing

Drain

Power supply

Reset button

FIGURE 3.5   Garbage Disposal

Hums but doesn't grind

When a disposer hums but doesn't grind, the impellers are jammed. The problem is often a piece of bone, fruit pit, or the like stuck between an impeller blade and drain hole. Don't try to run the disposer when it's jammed—this can burn out the motor.

1. Under the sink, look at the bottom of the disposer for a hex-shaped hole. If you see one, look for a hex wrench that fits the hole (it's often attached to the

disposer). Fit the hex wrench into the hole and force it back and forth in both directions to free the impellers.

2. If your disposer doesn't have a hex-shaped hole or you can't find a hex wrench, put a short broom stick into the disposer (with the switch turned off!), force it down against one of the blades, and try to rotate the impeller.

3. If this fails, call a repair company for advice.

Doesn't run or hum

When a garbage disposer doesn't run or even hum at the throw of its switch, it usually means it isn't receiving power or an overload has caused the circuit breaker to shut down the unit.

1. Look for a reset button on the bottom of the disposer. Allow the disposer to cool; then push the reset button and try the disposer again.

2. Be sure the disposer is plugged into a working receptacle. Plug something that works into the disposer's receptacle under the sink to see if it's receiving power. If it isn't, replace the fuse or reset the circuit breaker.

Runs but doesn't grind

If you can hear the garbage disposer running, but it seems to be "spinning its wheels" by not grinding, the blades may be broken. It's usually easier and cheaper to just replace the entire unit.

Doesn't drain water

When water stands in the sink, it means the drain is clogged either in the disposal or further down the drain line. This isn't a disposer problem . . . it's a plumbing problem. See page 75 for information on unclogging the drain.

HUMIDIFIER

A humidifier puts water vapor into a home's air. Room-size tabletop and console humidifiers are controlled by a humidistat that turns the unit off and on when humidity levels stray from a set range. Though a humidistat allows more or less "automatic" operation, you need to dial it up and down as the temperature changes in order to maintain fairly constant indoor relative humidity levels.

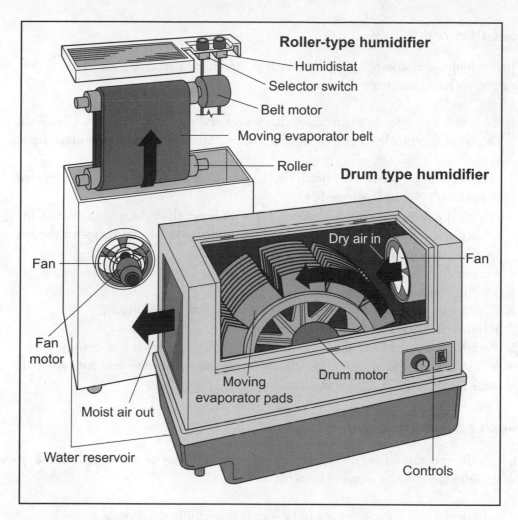

Roller-type humidifier
- Humidistat
- Selector switch
- Belt motor
- Moving evaporator belt
- Roller

Drum type humidifier
- Fan
- Dry air in
- Fan
- Fan motor
- Moving evaporator pads
- Drum motor
- Moist air out
- Water reservoir
- Controls

FIGURE 3.6   Humidifiers

Evaporative humidifiers are the most popular type. With humidifiers of this sort, a quiet fan blows an air stream through a wet medium, such as a sponge or dampened grill. Some evaporative humidifiers have fiber, honeycomb-type panels that wick water upward from a reservoir; others employ a foam or cloth drum that spins through a water-filled trough as air passes by. When the water gets too low, most evaporative humidifiers shut off automatically.

Doesn't run

When a humidifier doesn't run, it generally means it isn't receiving electrical power or the controls have automatically shut it off.

1. Be sure it's plugged in to an outlet that works and that it's turned on. Check the electrical receptacle for power, using a working lamp, appliance, or voltage tester (page 106).
2. If the receptacle seems to be dead, check the circuit breaker or fuse that serves the humidifier's circuit (see page 104).
3. Check the setting on the humidistat. If it's set lower than the room's relative humidity, the humidifier won't go on; in fact, it may take several hours for the humidistat to respond to the room's changing humidity.
4. Be sure the humidifier's reservoir is full of water.
5. Unplug the humidifier unit.
6. Check the power cord. If necessary, replace the cord (page 111).
7. Remove the humidifier's cover panel.
8. Remove the humidistat and check it (see page 30). Replace it if necessary.
9. If it still doesn't work, call an appliance repairperson, take the unit into an appliance repair shop, or replace the unit.

Doesn't humidify well

If a humidifier doesn't do a good job or runs constantly, it may be undersized for the space or humidified air may be escaping from the room.

1. Check the unit's specifications to be sure it can handle the room size.
2. Be sure your home's doors and windows are closed; also check the fireplace damper.
3. Be sure the reservoir has plenty of water.
4. Be sure air movement to and from walls or curtains are not blocking the unit.
5. Disconnect the power cord.
6. Clean the unit according to the manufacturer's recommendations.
7. Lubricate the fan motor bearings with a couple of drops of light oil, if the motor has oil holes (some units are oil-less).
8. If it still operates poorly, call an appliance repairperson or take the unit into an appliance repair shop.

Is noisy

Loose, vibrating parts cause most noises in a humidifier.

1. Disconnect the power.
2. Remove the cover and look for any vibrating parts. Tighten screws, if necessary.
3. Wiggle the fan to see if it is loose on its shaft. If it is, tighten the mounting fasteners. Lubricate the motor's bearings, if suggested in your owner's manual.
4. If it still makes noise, call an appliance repairperson or take the unit into an appliance repair shop.

Leaks water

If water drips or pools at the base of your humidifier:

1. Disconnect the power.
2. Check the pan or reservoir and empty it if necessary.
3. Be sure the wick, hose, or other water delivery system isn't kinked or fouled.

Gives off an odor

Odors are common because water stagnates in the humidifier's tank.

1. Unplug the unit.
2. Empty the reservoir, mop up any damp areas, and clean the tank and evaporator belt with a mixture of one gallon water. Add two tablespoons of chlorine bleach to the water for stubborn smells.

MICROWAVE OVEN

Because microwave leakage can be hazardous and high wattage is present, limit your microwave repairs to light bulb changes, if the light bulb is easily accessible. For other repairs, call a qualified technician to make repairs on a microwave oven. If it doesn't work and the light doesn't go on, be sure its receptacle is receiving power (see page 24).

OVEN

Both gas and electric ovens, though fundamentally different in the way they heat foods, share a few types of problems. Here's a closer look:

Bake or broil element faulty

The solution to this problem depends on whether the oven is electric or gas.

Electric oven.   If your electric oven's bake or broil element isn't working properly, either it isn't receiving electric power or the element or the oven control may need to be replaced. In many cases, the wiring to the elements can be burnt or broken.

1. Be sure the controls are set on the proper setting.
2. Be sure the stove is plugged in and/or check the circuit breaker or fuse that serves that circuit (see page 104).
3. Call an appliance repairperson or replace the element yourself as follows.
4. Unplug the oven and let any hot parts cool.
5. Unscrew the mounting screws that secure the element bracket to the oven and pull out the element far enough to access its terminals. Note which wires are attached to each of the terminals; then disconnect the wires (pull off the wire clips or unscrew the wires).
6. Take the element to a parts dealer, along with your oven's model and serial number, and buy a replacement (preferably the manufacturer's suggested replacement part).
7. Reverse the process to reinstall.

Gas oven.   When a gas oven doesn't get hot, it generally means that it isn't receiving gas, that the gas valve isn't distributing gas to the oven burner, or that the ignition system—either an electronic ignition or pilot light—isn't working properly. A common problem with ovens that have a pilot light is that the pilot light has gone out.

NOTE: Gas ovens ranges less than ten years old have a sophisticated fault code system that governs their ignition. Always call an approved warranty service provider to handle problems with these ranges.

Here's how to troubleshoot your gas oven:

1. Be sure the controls are set on the proper setting.
2. Be sure the oven or stove is plugged in and/or check the circuit breaker or fuse that serves that circuit (see page 104).

3. Check the gas valve to be sure the gas supply is turned on (also make sure the house's main gas valve is turned on).
4. On a stove with a pilot light, make sure the pilot light is burning. If it isn't, relight as discussed on page 139 or in your owner's manual.
5. Adjust the pilot flame (older stoves only), as discussed on page 139.
6. Turn off the gas and unplug the stove (or turn off its circuit at the electrical panel).
7. Clean out the oven burner ports, using a stiff wire.
8. Plug in the oven or stove (or turn on its circuit) and turn the gas back on. Relight the pilot (if it has one).
9. If the oven still doesn't work, call an appliance repairperson.

Doesn't maintain temperature

When an oven doesn't maintain the set temperature, first make sure no one is allowing the heat to escape by opening its door. If not, the oven control either needs to be recalibrated (see below) or replaced. To have the control replaced, call an appliance service person.

Calibrating oven thermostat

If your oven does not have a calibration right on the knob, call an appliance repair person. If it does, you can calibrate it as follows:

1. Remove the oven temperature knob by pulling it off its shaft.
2. Notice the current setting; then move the pointer in either direction to adjust its temperature slightly up or down. It's intentionally difficult to move the pointer; on some models, you'll have to remove a couple of screws. Figure that moving it one notch will change the setting by 10°F.
3. For more accurate calibration, call an appliance repairperson.

Bakes unevenly or burns food

When foods are burned, soggy, or baked unevenly, it generally means that heat isn't being distributed evenly throughout the oven, that it's escaping out the door, or that the controls are out of adjustment.

1. Remove any aluminum foil from racks or the bottom of the oven.
2. Check the door gasket and, if necessary, have it replaced.

3. Be sure nothing is obstructing the vent.
4. Reposition the oven racks so baking pans aren't too close to the heat sources.
5. Check your baking pans. If they're dark, they may be burning your food. Reduce temperature by 25°F when baking in dark metal or glass pans.
6. Recalibrate the controls (see page 47).

RANGE/COOKTOP (GAS)

Most problems with gas cooktops have to do with the flame—either it isn't quite right or it's nonexistent.

Burner doesn't light

Most new gas cooktops have "electronic ignition," a spark igniter that starts the flame as gas flows through the burners. If, when you turn on a burner, it fails to spark but you hear sparking at other burners, the igniter or the burner switch probably needs replacement by an appliance repairperson.

If your range has a pilot light, be sure the pilot light is lit (see page 139).

RANGE/COOKTOP (ELECTRIC)

Before doing any work on the cooktop, always unplug the range or turn off the power at the main electrical panel (page 103). Do not hesitate to call a professional appliance repair person if you have any doubt about your knowledge or abilities when repairing an electric range.

Surface element doesn't work

When an electric element doesn't work, either it isn't receiving electric power or it's likely that the element or receptacle it plugs into is faulty.

Check the other elements. If none work, the circuit breaker has probably tripped. Reset it at the electric panel (page 104). If this reoccurs, call an appliance repairperson.

If just one burner isn't working, try to pinpoint the source of the problem—likely a bad element/burner or a problem with its connection receptacle. In some cases, it's the switch or the wiring. To replace a bad switch or repair the wiring or replace the receptacle, call an appliance repairperson.

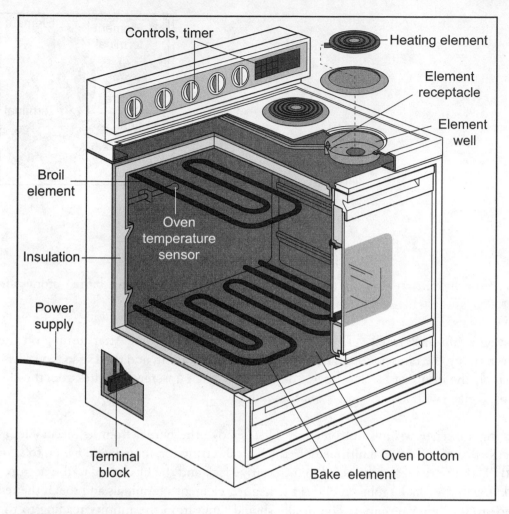

FIGURE 3.7   Range

Testing a burner that plugs into a receptacle.   This is an easy test. After turning off the cooktop's power at the main electrical panel (page 103), just unplug the nonheating burner, plug it into another working receptacle, restore the power to the cooktop and test it. If the burner works, you know its original receptacle is probably faulty. If it doesn't work in the good receptacle, the burner is bad and should be replaced. Buy a replacement and simply plug it into the receptacle.

When you remove the burner, look for burned wires or a charred receptacle. Check the receptacle or terminal block to see if it's cracked, loose, or looks burned. If you notice

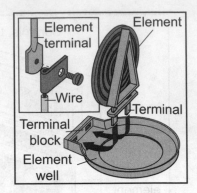

FIGURE 3.8   Plug-in Burner

any of the above signs, replace the faulty component, too. If the male burner prongs are corroded, always change the female receptacle it was plugged into.

Testing a flip-up burner.   This test requires a little more work. After turning off the power, tilt up the burner, unscrew the small screw that holds it, and then slide it out. Disassemble the insulator block by prying off the clips. Then unscrew the wires from the element, replace with a new burner, and reassemble.

Testing a burner with a multi-meter.   First remove the burner from its receptacle, as discussed above. Set the multi-meter to the Rx100 setting (or, for a digital meter, to Ω or kΩ). With the red lead connected to the positive jack and the black lead to the negative jack, touch the black probe on one of the heating element's terminals and touch the red probe to the other terminal. The needle should jump from the infinity reading to the right, indicating a properly "closed" circuit. If it doesn't, try the probes on a different part of the metal contacts. Still no reading? Touch the two leads together to make sure the meter is working (the needle should jump). If it works, there is an internal break in the element, and it will need to be replaced.

When you're finished, turn the power back on.

When a single burner doesn't heat properly:

1. Turn off the power.
2. Determine the type of burner.
     If it's a plug-in, test the faulty burner in another receptacle.

- If it works, replace the original receptacle.
- If it doesn't work, replace the burner.
- Replace other faulty components.

  If it's a flip-up burner:
- Disassemble and replace faulty burner and any other faulty parts.
3. Restore power.
4. Test.

   If it doesn't work, call a repairperson.

REFRIGERATOR AND FREEZER

As a rule, refrigerators are the most dependable of all large appliances. Even so, they do fail to do their jobs adequately on occasion, and when they do, the results can be disastrous because expensive food can spoil in a hurry. Though most problems call for a repairperson, there are a few simple repairs you can handle yourself.

How a refrigerator works

Refrigeration principles are discussed in depth on page 25. With refrigerators, it's important to know that cold air is produced in the freezer section and then blown through an air duct (usually adjustable) into the refrigerator box.

Doesn't run

To operate, a refrigerator needs electricity. If the refrigerator's light doesn't work and it's motor doesn't run:

1. Check the power, as discussed on page 24.
2. Be sure the cold control is turned on.
3. If you discover that the refrigerator is plugged into a working outlet and that the cold control is on, but the device shows no signs of life, leave the door closed to retain the cold air and call an appliance repairperson.

Runs but doesn't cool

If a refrigerator doesn't cool at all, the problem is often with basic electrical controls—almost never with a need for a boost of refrigerant. Do not assume that the problem is re-

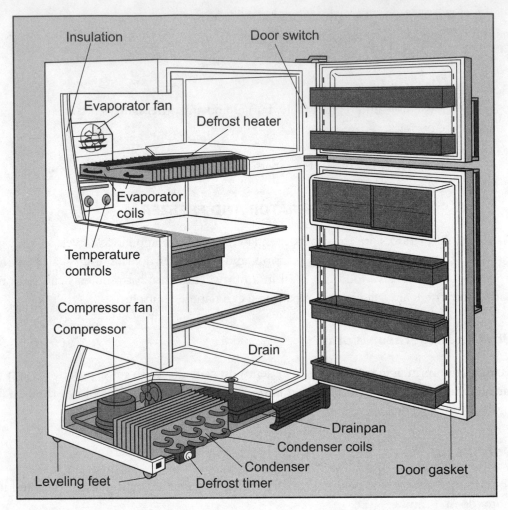

Insulation   Door switch

Evaporator fan

Defrost heater

Evaporator coils

Temperature controls

Compressor fan

Compressor

Drain

Drainpan

Condenser coils

Condenser

Leveling feet

Defrost timer

Door gasket

FIGURE 3.9   Refrigerator

lated to the compressor or the hermetic system—these types of problems happen only rarely. Usually, it is an electrical problem.

1. Check the cold control. Be sure it is set to "cold." Normally, the temperature inside the refrigerator should be about 37°F.
2. Listen for the freezer fan inside the freezer. When the freezer fan is running, it means the defrost timer and the cold control in the refrigerator are both set to cool.

3. Listen for the compressor fan where the compressor is located (typically behind or beneath the refrigerator). When the freezer fan is operating, the compressor fan should also be working (most of the time).

4. If one of the fans is not working or the compressor is off, the refrigerator will offer very little cooling or none at all. Call a repairperson.

Cools poorly or runs constantly

If the refrigerator's light works and you can hear it running but it cools poorly or runs without stopping, any of several problems may be at fault. First, make sure nothing is blocking the passageway between the freezer and refrigerator compartments—if airflow is restricted by, for example, a loaf of bread situated in front of the passageway, the refrigerator won't get cold. Be aware that a refrigerator will tend to run longer when it's full of food, when the door is opened frequently, and when the room temperature is hot.

If your refrigerator runs without stopping (unless you turn it off), it may be low on refrigerant. Without a full charge, it cannot reach the low temperature that the cold control dial summons. More likely, it is a defrost problem in which a component in the automatic defrosting system is faulty. This component could be a defrost heater, a defrost timer, or a defrost terminator.

Before you call a repairperson, do the following:

1. Determine whether the refrigerator section is being cooled. If you see frost at the top of a "frost free" refrigerator even when the cold control is set low, it means the refrigerator probably has a full charge of refrigerant. If this is the case, the thermostat may be faulty or out of calibration.

2. Try turning the cold control both up and down. If the compressor doesn't shut off, the cold control may be broken. Call a repairperson. During the repair, it is a good idea to have the defrost timer and heaters checked to ensure that they are working correctly.

3. Look at the condenser coils, located at the bottom of the refrigerator (behind the kick plate) or, in some cases, at the back. These coils disperse heat from inside the refrigerator out into the room with the aid of a fan. If the coils are dirty, the refrigerator won't operate efficiently, so clean them (see page 54).

4. To put off having the refrigerator repaired for a few days, you may be able to defrost it manually with a hair dryer—if you can access the cooling coils in the freezer section. Excessive moisture in the coils can turn into a frozen mass, reducing efficiency. Be very careful when using the hair dryer; do not stand in a puddle

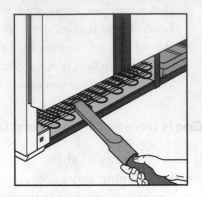

FIGURE 3.10 Cleaning Refrigerator Coils

of water—there is a serious danger of electrical shock! Also be careful not to melt the plastic parts.

How to clean refrigerator coils

It is very important to clean condenser coils on forced-air refrigerators such as side-by-side and built-in models at least twice a year (if you have a refrigerator with the black coils mounted on the back, these coils don't require semiannual cleaning).

Here's how to do it:

1. Pull the refrigerator away from the wall and unplug it or, if it's a built-in model, turn off its circuit breaker.
2. Remove the cover panel to reveal the coils. On most models, the kick plate or top trim plate simply lifts off. You may have to remove a few screws to remove a back cover.
3. With a long, narrow nozzle on your vacuum, clean out all of the dust and debris (at an appliance parts store, you can also buy a special, long-handled brush that looks somewhat like a bottle brush for this job).
4. Replace the cover and then plug the electrical cord back in or turn the circuit back on.

Refrigerator freezes foods

If your refrigerator freezes its contents, even when the cold control is set to its lowest setting, its cold control is probably defective. Call an appliance repairperson.

THE HOME PROBLEM SOLVER

As a rule, refrigerators are designed to maintain 37 to 40°F in the refrigerator box and 0 to 5°F in the freezer box. Setting either compartment to lower temperatures generally costs you extra in energy dollars.

Light stays on when door is closed

Yes, it's difficult to tell if this is happening, but you should be able to see the light go off when the door is a fraction of an inch from closing. You can also feel the bulb (be careful!) when you first open the refrigerator in the morning—it will be hot if it has stayed on.

A light bulb that stays on will warm the refrigerator's interior, cutting down on efficiency. Test the light switch button that the door closes against—when you push it in all of the way, the light should go off.

If the light stays on even when the door is closed, the light switch is defective and must be replaced. If you are adept at simple repairs, this is a job that you may be able to handle yourself—be sure to unplug the refrigerator before working on it. Otherwise, call an appliance repairperson.

Defrosts improperly

Most modern refrigerators defrost automatically. They have a defrost timer, a defrost heater, and a defrost terminator. When a frost-free refrigerator is running, it builds up frost on the tubing in the back of the freezer wall. Normally, the defrost timer automatically cycles the refrigerator to defrost for about twenty minutes every six to eight hours—it essentially heats up coils to melt the ice. If it isn't working right, ice remains on the tubing, and eventually this ice restricts airflow through the refrigerator.

On some refrigerators, you can manually advance the defrost timer, a small black box that may be located almost anywhere but is usually located on the ceiling of the fresh food section. Advance it until it clicks into the defrost mode (you should be able to hear the heaters come on). If this works, the defrost timer is defective and will need to be replaced—but this will keep it running for a little while. If it doesn't work, the problem is probably the heater or the terminator. Call the manufacturer for advice (see resources, page 229).

Rattles when it runs

Vibrating noises are generally caused by loose parts (such as loose condenser coils or compressor "tubing rattle") or rollers and feet that sit unevenly on the floor. Look for any part that is loose. Then remove the bottom trim piece by lifting it off of its supports and check the feet at the front of the unit. If necessary, turn the adjustable feet up or down so they contact the floor squarely.

Ice maker doesn't make ice

An icemaker receives water through a small, 1/4-inch water supply line that runs from the refrigerator to a water pipe, where it is connected by a tap valve. The water supply line enters a valve in the refrigerator that is controlled by an electric solenoid and that sends water through a fill tube into a mechanized icemaker assembly. There, the water freezes and is dumped into an ice bin. When the bin is full, ice lifts a bail wire that turns off the icemaker.

If the water's route is blocked or the solenoid doesn't work—or if the bail wire is lifted—the icemaker won't make ice. Also note that your home's water pressure must be strong enough to serve the needs of the icemaker (see your owner's manual). Here are a few steps you can take to get your icemaker working:

Be sure the bail wire above the ice tray is in the down position.

1. If the icemaker doesn't make ice but you can see the arm swing into motion and you hear a buzz for about ten seconds after it is finished, the water valve is asking for water that isn't arriving. This means the valve and the solenoid are probably okay, but the water supply is not. Be sure the water supply line isn't kinked behind or beneath the refrigerator (1/4-inch copper tubing is much better than plastic fill line).
2. Check to see if something has caused ice to back up around the mechanism—this can cause the fill tube to freeze, blocking the mechanism. See "How to thaw an icemaker," on the opposite page. When ice cubes are small and seem to be getting smaller, it generally indicates a frozen fill tube.
3. Check the water line that enters the back of the freezer for a blockage. Find the water shutoff valve behind the refrigerator or under the sink, turn it off, unscrew the copper line from the back of the refrigerator, put the copper line in a bucket, turn on the valve, and see if pressurized water pours out.
4. Check the tap valve, where the icemaker's supply tube connects to the water pipe; a bad tap valve may cause the problem. If necessary, replace the inlet valve and the tap valve. For the tap valve, use the type that requires you to drill a 1/4-inch hole (as opposed to the "self piercing" type). You can do this yourself, or call a repairperson or plumber and ask them to install an in-line water filter when replacing the valve to prevent future blockages.

NOTE: The water line attaches to a solenoid at the back of the refrigerator, then travels to the icemaker. The solenoid may be defective or may not be receiving power. You can try removing the sediment screen inside the solenoid and flushing it with water to clean it; be sure to respect any seals or diaphragms. Again, be sure to unplug the refrigerator first. Unless you're skilled at home repairs, this job is better left in the hands of an appliance repairperson.

Leaks

Leaking under a refrigerator may be caused by a condensation tube that doesn't drain into a pan or by a clogged freezer drain.

How to thaw an icemaker

If your icemaker has frozen up, here's how to thaw it:

1. Unplug the refrigerator.
2. Remove the ice bin and remove loose ice from the icemaker.
3. Find the fill tube—the white rubber-like hose—that delivers the water into the icemaker.
4. Pull the small metal clip off of the housing that holds the fill tube down (not all icemakers have this clip).
5. Warm the hose and surrounding mechanism. To do this, you can train a hair dryer on the icemaker to melt any ice blocking the mechanism. Sop up dripping water with a rag. Be very careful when using the hair dryer near water, and do not stand in a puddle of water—there is a serious danger of electrical shock! Also be careful not to melt the plastic parts. If you don't want to use a hair dryer, you can soak the supply tubing with hot water, using a turkey baster and catching the overflow in the empty icemaker bin. In some cases, it may be easier to remove the icemaker to thaw out the fill tube.

Icemaker doesn't shut off

If the icemaker keeps making ice, even when full:

1. Lift the bail wire to shut it off.
2. Empty the bin, remove the icemaker, clean it, and reinstall it.

3. If the problem persists, consider having an appliance repairperson remove and replace the entire icemaker and valve, a relatively affordable repair. With this type of problem, it's often better to replace the unit rather than to pay for repair.

WASHING MACHINE

A washing machine is basically a big tub that repeatedly fills and drains with water, spins to wring clothes dry, and has a device for stirring things up—either an agitator in the middle of a top-load machine or a rolling drum in the case of a front-loader. The four cycles that every washer performs are fill, wash, drain, and spin. Though there are a number of problems that you can fix quite simply, washing machines have a variety of devices and controls that—when they go wrong—are better left in the hands of an appliance repairperson.

Doesn't run

If the washer doesn't operate or make any noise when set on any cycle, or if it stops suddenly when it should continue onto the next cycle, it may not be receiving electrical power or, if the motor stopped midcycle, the machine's overload protector may have tripped. In this case, take out some of the articles to reduce the load and let the protector reset itself; then restart. Otherwise:

1. Be sure it is plugged in and turned on. If necessary, check the receptacle it's plugged in to for power, using a working lamp, appliance, or voltage tester (page 24). Be sure the washer lid is closed completely.
2. If the receptacle seems dead, check the circuit breaker or fuse that serves that circuit (see page 104).
3. Unplug the washer and check the power cord. If necessary, replace the cord (page 111).
4. Open the lid and check the lid switch and the tab on the lid that it pushes against. Press and release the switch: if it doesn't click when you do this, it's probably broken. If you're experienced at home repair, you can remove the switch, test it, and replace it if needed; otherwise, call an appliance repairperson.
5. If the washer still doesn't work, the controls may be faulty. Call a serviceperson.

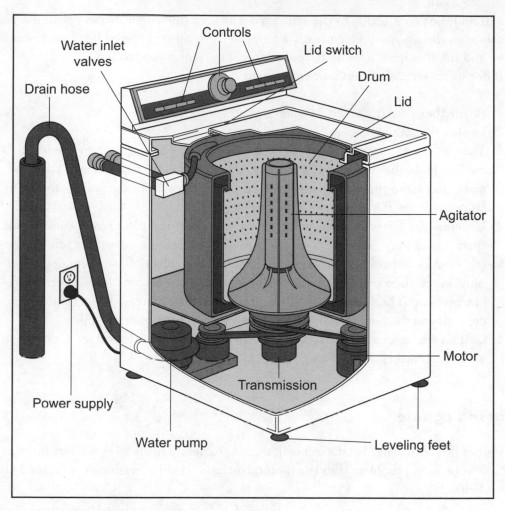

FIGURE 3.11   Washing Machine

Filling or water temperature problems

If the washer doesn't fill properly, or if only one temperature of water fills the tub, either something is probably keeping water from entering the machine or it's draining before the tub fills completely.

Set the controls to the first wash cycle and then try each water temperature setting.

If both hot and cold water seem to be entering the washer with good pressure, water may be draining out prematurely during the fill cycle, through siphoning action. Be sure the drain hose's connection to the standpipe is at least thirty-four inches above the floor (otherwise, discuss the problem with a plumber). An air gap placed between the drain hose and the standpipe in order to prevent backflow is also good to have.

If hot works but cold doesn't, or vice versa:

1. Be sure both the hot and cold water faucets are turned on.
2. Be sure the supply hoses are not kinked.
3. Turn off the faucets. Unscrew the hoses from the faucets and drain them into a bucket. Hold the bucket under the faucets and test them to make sure they both work and have plenty of pressure (see page 81 for information on replacing faucets). Screw the hoses back onto the faucets.
4. Unscrew the hoses from the inlet valves and clean the filter screens just inside them; these may be clogged. To do this, pry out the screens with a screwdriver (this can be difficult; the screens may be inside the valves), flush them under running water, then put them back into the hose. If the screens look defective, replace them. Then screw the hoses back onto the valves. Be careful not to cross-thread the hose threads when screwing them back onto the valves.
5. Call an appliance repairperson; there may be a defective inlet valve or a problem with the controls.

Doesn't agitate

If washer fills with water but doesn't agitate, the problem is likely to be a faulty lid switch, a broken belt, or a problem with the motor. Note: direct-drive washing machines do not have belts.

1. Check the spin cycle. If this works, the motor is operating and the belt is not broken. If it doesn't, the belt may be loose or broken. If you're fairly handy, tighten or replace the belt; otherwise, call an appliance repairperson.
2. Check the lid switch and the tab on the lid that strikes it. If the plastic tab is broken, the washer may halt during certain cycles. Press and release the switch: if it doesn't click each time you do this, it's probably broken. If you're experienced at home repair, you can remove the switch, test it, and replace it if needed; otherwise, call an appliance repairperson.
3. There may be a problem with the controls or the agitator solenoid may be broken; call a repairperson.

Doesn't drain

If the machine fills and agitates but does not drain, something is probably wrong with the drain hose or the pump. The fact the washer fills and agitates tells you that the motor works and that the belt is okay (though some units have a separate belt for the pump, and direct-drive washing machines don't have belts).

1. Be sure the drain hose isn't kinked.
2. Check the tab on the lid that strikes the lid switch; if it is broken, the washer may stop during the drain cycle. Press and release the lid switch: if it doesn't click each time you do this, it's probably broken. If you're experienced at home repair, you can remove the switch, test it, and replace it if needed; otherwise, call an appliance service person.
3. The water pump may be broken or clogged with a small article of clothing, or the controls may be broken; call an appliance repairperson.

Doesn't spin

If the washer seems to complete all of its cycles, but it doesn't spin:

1. Be sure the load of clothes is not lopsided. If the tub becomes unbalanced, it may spin erratically or not at all. Sometimes you can just open the lid and reposition the clothes. This automatically resets an off-balance shutoff switch. Just close the lid and retry.
2. Check the lid switch and the tab on the lid that strikes it. If the plastic tab is broken, the washer may halt during the spin cycle. If the switch doesn't click when you press and release it, it's probably broken. If you're experienced at home repair, you can remove the switch, test it, and replace it if needed; otherwise, call an appliance repairperson.
3. The belt may be loose, worn, or broken. If you're fairly handy, tighten or replace the belt; otherwise, call an appliance repairperson.
4. There may be a problem with the controls; call an appliance repairperson.

Shakes, vibrates, or walks

A washer usually shakes or vibrates when it isn't sitting firmly and level on the floor or when it has an out-of-balance wash load. First eliminate the possibility of the latter—

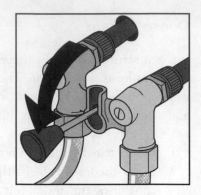

FIGURE 3.12   Washing Machine Water Shutoff

adjust the load if it has scrunched up on one side of the tub. Then check the machine for solid, level support. To work properly, the floor must be flat, level, and strong enough to support the heavy, water-filled washer without deflecting under the load.

1. Unplug the washer.
2. Look under the front of the washer and make sure all feet are resting firmly on the floor.
3. Make sure that the front legs have locking nuts to keep them tight and that the legs have rubber caps. If they don't, pick up these parts and install them.
4. Make the front feet as short as possible by screwing them up into the machine. Place a level on top of the washing machine and adjust the front feet slightly to level the washer, but do not fully extend them. Keep them as short as possible.
5. If necessary, tilt the washing machine forward. This will let the back feet self-adjust (most recent models do this automatically). Recheck with the level and adjust the front feet again.
6. Plug in the machine and run it empty through the spin cycle to see if it still vibrates.
7. If it does, call a repairperson or the manufacturer to ask about possible solutions.

Leaks

Leaking water usually comes from hoses or connections. Be sure the water appearing to be a leak isn't drain water from a backed-up standpipe (see page 75 for information on clearing clogged drains).

NOTE: To prevent serious flood damage that can occur if washing machine supply hoses burst, be sure to install "no-burst" stainless steel mesh hoses.

1. Check the fittings where hoses connect to the faucets and to the back of the washing machine. Also look for worn or leaky hoses. Tighten couplings or hose clamps if necessary, or replace hoses altogether (be sure to turn the water off before removing hoses and to drain them into a bucket after disconnecting them).
2. Determine whether the machine is oversudsing during wash loads—this can cause the entire washing machine to overflow. Reduce suds by pouring a mixture of one half cup of white vinegar and one quart of water into the washer. Then switch to less detergent or use a low-sudsing variety.
3. Call a repairperson. The machine may have a faulty basket gasket or tub seal and bearing that must be replaced.

WATER HEATER

Water heater problems normally become self-evident: a hot water faucet fails to summon hot water; you see puddles or a leak near the water heater; or the tank emits strange sounds. Though many gas utility companies will make a free house call to solve problems with a gas heater's burner or gas supply, it helps to know how to solve basic outages yourself. Most water heater problems are relatively easy to handle if you understand how a water heater works.

How a water heater works

A water heater is essentially a large water tank with a gas burner or electric heating elements that warm the water. Most hot water tanks are heated by a gas burner because gas is more affordable as a heat source in most parts of the country. A thermostat dial on the outside of the heater or on the gas valve sets the desired water temperature; a thermostat senses the water's temperature in the tank and turns the heat source off and on to maintain the set temperature.

The tank is hooked up to two pipes at the top of the unit: a cold water supply pipe that fills the tank and an outgoing hot water pipe that serves hot water (under pressure in the tank) to the faucets and fixtures throughout the house. The cold water pipe should be equipped with a valve that can shut off the flow to the tank; many plumbing systems also have a valve on the hot water side. As hot water exits the tank, cold water replaces it through a diffuser dip tube that extends down inside the tank.

Appliance Problems   63

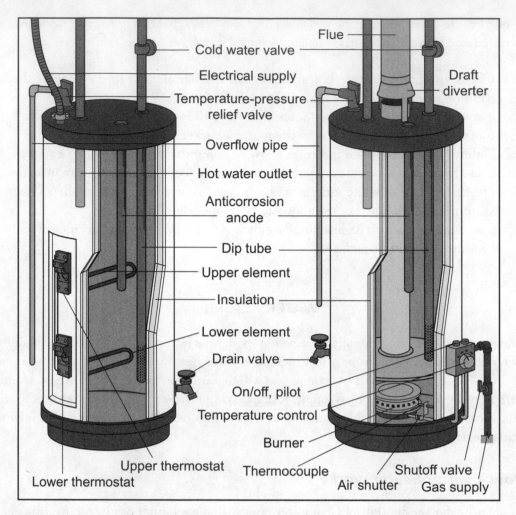

Cold water valve
Flue
Draft diverter
Electrical supply
Temperature-pressure relief valve
Overflow pipe
Hot water outlet
Anticorrosion anode
Dip tube
Upper element
Insulation
Lower element
Drain valve
On/off, pilot
Temperature control
Burner
Upper thermostat
Thermocouple
Shutoff valve
Lower thermostat
Air shutter
Gas supply

FIGURE 3.13   Hot Water Heaters: Electric (left) and Gas (right).

A gas water heater is fueled by natural gas (or, in some cases, kerosene or propane). A gas valve controlled by the thermostat delivers gas to the burner. A pilot light or electronic spark, similar to the one on a gas stove top, ignites the gas. The burner heats the bottom of the tank and the water gets hot. Gas water heaters also need a vent at the top to expel exhaust from the burner to the outside.

An electric water heater draws its energy from a heavy electric cable and doesn't have a burner; instead, one or two separate heating elements controlled by thermostats cycle on and off to heat the water. Electric water heaters don't create combustion gasses, so they don't have a vent at the top.

At the base of the water heater, a drain valve allows you to drain the tank or flush out sediment.

Last but not least, there is a magnesium or aluminum rod inside the tank, called the anode rod. Through ionization, this rod minimizes corrosive elements in the water.

To protect it from exploding under pressure, a water heater has a temperature and pressure (T&P) relief valve at or near the top of the tank; this valve opens automatically if pressure or heat exceeds a given limit—normally 150 pounds of pressure or 210°F.

If you smell gas near the water heater, shut off the pilot light, close the gas shutoff valve, and call your gas utility for assistance. For information about gas leaks, see pages 4, 40.

Always shut off the power to an electric water heater before working on it.

Do not work on an electric water heater if there is standing water pooled on the floor near the appliance. Shut off the circuit to the water heater and call an appliance repairperson.

No hot water (gas water heater)

If a gas water heater fails to heat water, it usually means there is no flame at all.

1. Be sure the thermostat dial is set high enough. If it isn't, adjust it to about 120°F. Turn on a hot water faucet and wait a few minutes to see if the water heater burner ignites.
2. Be sure the gas is turned on.
3. Turn the gas control knob to PILOT to prevent the burner from igniting if you intend to look inside.
4. Remove the metal cover at the bottom of the water heater and look to see if the burner or pilot light is lit. If the burner is on, replace the cover and turn up the thermostat slightly. If there is no pilot light burning—a small flame at the end of the pilot gas supply tube—the pilot has gone out. Note: Newer water heaters may have a glow plug or spark ignitor instead of a pilot—follow the instructions in your owner's manual if you have this type or call the manufacturer (see resources, page 229).
5. Smell for gas. If you smell a garlic-like scent, turn the gas valve control to OFF (you may have to push down as you turn it). Wait until the gas smell has dissipated before relighting the pilot light, as discussed below (instructions are normally located on the water heater near the gas valve). If the gas smell is strong and doesn't dissipate, immediately turn off the gas supply valve, ventilate the space, and call your utility company from a neighbor's phone (see information on gas leaks, page 4).

---

6. If the pilot won't light, the thermocouple may be defective; either call your gas utility to check the appliance (a free service in many areas) or call an appliance repairperson.

7. If the pilot lights but the burner doesn't ignite, check the thermostat. Turn on a hot water faucet and wait a couple of minutes. If the water heater doesn't ignite, leave the hot water running and try lowering—then raising—the temperature setting on the dial until the burner ignites. If the burner doesn't go on within a few seconds, have the water heater checked out by an appliance repairperson.

8. If the burner ignites, replace the cover and turn the thermostat back to an appropriate setting (about 120°F).

How to relight a gas water heater

Check the side of the water heater or your owner's manual for step-by-step instructions. The manufacturer will typically advise you to:

1. Turn the gas valve to OFF and wait a few minutes.
2. Turn the gas valve to PILOT, push down on it (or a red button next to it), and hold it down to begin the flow of gas through the pilot gas supply tube.
3. Holding the button or valve down, quickly use a log-lighter (or regular lighter) to ignite the gas at the end of the pilot gas supply tube. You may have to hold the flame there for a few seconds if there is air in the gas line.
4. Continue holding down the control button for a minute or two after the pilot is lit, long enough for the pilot to heat the thermocouple—a heat sensor on a wire that automatically shuts off the gas when the pilot goes out. Then release the control button.
5. If the pilot goes out or won't light, turn the valve to OFF, wait a few minutes, and repeat the process.
6. Once the pilot light stays lit after releasing the control button, turn the control to the ON position. At this point, depending upon the thermostat control setting, the burner should ignite.
7. If the pilot doesn't stay lit after a couple of attempts, call your gas utility or an appliance repairperson.

No hot water (electric water heater)

When an electric water heater fails to heat water, either the power to the water heater has been interrupted, or there is a problem with the controls or the heating elements.

1. Be sure electricity is being delivered to the appliance. Check the main switch on the water heater and the circuit breaker (or fuse) that serves the water heater (see page 104).
2. Check the high temperature cutoff in the water heater. Open the panel and push the reset button.
3. Call an appliance repairperson.

Reduced hot water supply

If your water heater suddenly seems to supply less hot water, and it isn't leaking (see above), flush the water heater tank to be sure mineral deposits are not reducing the heater's efficiency.

If that doesn't do the job, the dip tube that supplies cold water to the tank may be broken or cracked. This plastic tube is suppose to direct cold water to the bottom of the water heater tank, but if it breaks or splits, cold water pours in at the top of the tank and mixes with the hot water that's on its way out into your hot water pipes.

Either have the dip tube replaced or, if the water heater is out of warranty and showing other signs of age, consider having the entire water heater replaced.

Water not hot enough (gas water heater)

When a gas hot water heater doesn't provide enough hot water:

1. Turn the thermostat dial to a hotter setting. If the flame ignites when you do this, leave the dial set at that setting and check your water temperature in about one hour. To do this, put a meat thermometer into a cup and let hot water from the kitchen tap flow into the cup for about a minute. Then read the setting.
2. Check the pilot light to be sure it hasn't gone out.

Water heater overheats

If steam or excessively hot water shoots out of faucets or you hear boiling sounds inside the hot water heater, the appliance may not be shutting off at its set temperature. The job of the temperature and pressure (T&P) relief valve is to release excessive pressure from steam buildup, but this valve may have been improperly installed or it may be faulty. Either way, this condition can be dangerous, both because hot water and steam can scald people and because enough pressure could build up to rupture the water heater. To prevent this:

1. Immediately turn down the water heater's temperature setting.
2. Allow the water to cool.
3. Call an appliance repairperson or a plumber.

Water heater leaks

If water pools around the base of your water heater or you hear the sound of water sizzling on the hot burner, it doesn't necessarily mean that the tank or plumbing is leaking. In many cases, condensation forms when cold water fills the tank, then drips down. If the problem appears when the tank is first filled or during chilly seasons when incoming water is particularly cold—but then disappears when the water has had a chance to warm up—it usually indicates condensation. Another possibility is that the water may be coming from the temperature and pressure (T&P) relief valve, a condition that demands the immediate attention of a plumber or appliance repairperson.

1. Look for signs of a leak along pipes, at valves, and around the tank area. If you discover a leak, repair the problem yourself or call a plumber. If the tank itself has a leak, have your water heater replaced. Be sure the drain valve at the bottom of the tank isn't slightly open.
2. Look for drips at the temperature and pressure (T&P) relief valve; this valve releases water if it senses excess pressure, generally because the temperature is set too high. If this appears to be the case with your water heater, follow your owner's manual for the proper procedure.
3. If there is no water dripping from the T&P valve, minimize using hot water for a couple of hours and check the water heater again. If the leaking has stopped, the problem is probably condensation. Check for obstructions in the vent (gas water heaters only). If you find any, shut off the water heater and clean out the flue. If the problem persists, call a plumber.

Water heater makes strange noises

Noises can be caused by expanding and contracting metal parts, by drips (as discussed above), or, more likely, by minerals and hard-water scale accumulations inside the tank. When heated, dissolved hard-water minerals recrystallize and form scale that cakes onto interior surfaces of water heaters, making them less efficient and more likely to fail. Strange noises occur when steam builds up beneath the scale. If water sounds like it is

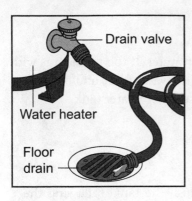

Drain valve

Water heater

Floor
drain

FIGURE 3.14   Hot Water
Heater Drain Valve

boiling inside the tank, it could indicate overheating and a dangerous pressure build up; see page 67 for information.

- To minimize corrosive minerals through ionization, water heaters have a magnesium or aluminum anode rod inserted through the top of the tank.
- To avoid scale in the first place, open the drain valve at the base of the tank and flush about a gallon of water every few months (Figure 3.14). Follow manufacturer's recommendations when you do this. Be sure to hook up a hose or allow for proper drainage of the scalding hot water before opening the valve.
- In some cases, electric water heaters may have a buildup of scale on their heating elements that causes similar sounds. Have the elements replaced.

Hot water smells bad

If your water has a strange odor, first determine whether the problem is with the source water or the hot water heater. In most cases, it's caused by a reaction between the hot water heater's anode rod and water that has a high concentration of sulfate.

Turn on a cold water faucet to see if the cold water smells. If it does, the problem is more likely with your source water.

Let the hot water run for two or three minutes. If it smells a bit like rotten eggs, the anode rod in the water heater may need replacement. This is a job that's usually best left in the hands of a plumber. If your water heater is past its warranty and showing other signs of aging, consider having the entire water heater replaced.

Hot water is discolored

Iron, copper, and other minerals can cause discoloration in water. If the problem is with both hot and cold water, consider installing a whole-house water filter and/or a water softener. If the problem is only with the hot water, flush the water heater tank:

1. Turn off the hot water heater's gas valve or electricity.
2. With the tank turned off, let the water cool.
3. Turn off the water inlet valve.
4. Open the drain valve at the base of the tank and flush the tank, following the manufacturer's recommendations. Hook up a hose or allow for proper drainage of the hot water before opening this valve.
5. Close the drain valve, turn the water back on to fill the tank, and turn the gas valve or electricity back on (relight the pilot if applicable).

4

PLUMBING PROBLEMS

Plumbing problems normally become self-evident pretty quickly: drains clog up; faucets drip; broken pipes spray; and so forth. Most minor plumbing problems are relatively easy to fix if you understand the basics of how the systems work. Considering that plumbers now cost over $80 per hour in many areas, you can save significantly by making your own repairs when possible.

Of course, some repairs are easier to do than others. Many just take time; some are a major hassle—particularly those that involve working on pipes that are hidden behind walls or under floors, or are otherwise difficult to access.

A plumber can handle nearly any problem that involves pipes, from replacing a garbage disposal to unclogging a bathtub drain, but if your problem is a stopped-up drain, you're usually better off calling a drain-clearing service because these services are usually less expensive. See more about working with plumbers and other services on page 14.

PLUMBING BASICS

Your home's plumbing actually involves several systems that work separately and, in some cases, together. Water is delivered to your home under pressure through the water

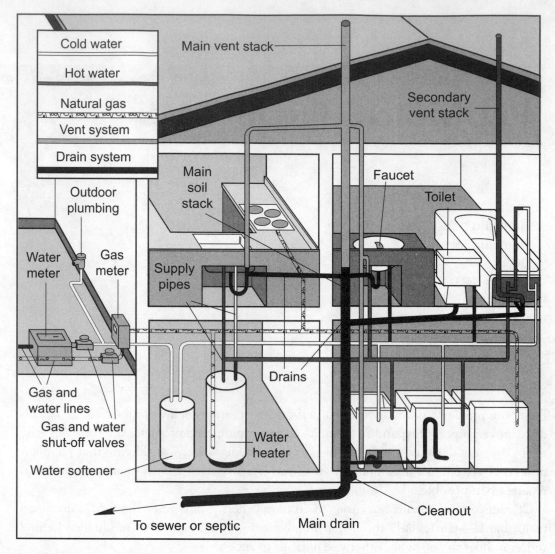

FIGURE 4.1 House Plumbing

supply system—galvanized steel or copper pipes that carry it to faucets, plumbing fixtures, outdoor hose-bibbs, sprinklers, and the like.

Drain and waste plumbing is not under pressure like the supply system—gravity is the only force that moves water and waste to the sewer or septic system. Vent piping is coupled with the drain and waste plumbing in order to exhaust sewer gasses (normally out the roof) and to allow pressure equalization so drains can drain.

Gas piping is totally separate from the water system, but utilizes pipes that look similar to water supply pipes. Gas pipes deliver natural gas from your utility to various gas-fired appliances.

PLUMBING TOOLS

Here are a few tools that can be helpful for plumbing jobs.

Pipe wrenches

Pipe wrenches have adjustable, toothed jaws designed for gripping and turning threaded pipes and pipe fittings. They're made in several sizes, from twelve to eighteen inches long; the larger the wrench, the larger the pipe it will fit. Pipe wrenches are used in pairs—one to grip the pipe, the other to turn the fitting.

Lock a pipe wrench onto a pipe or fitting so that, during turning, the force will be applied against the permanent jaw, not the adjustable one. When turning appearance-grade pipes, such as those with chrome finish, protect the material from scratches by wrapping the pipe wrenches' jaws with duct tape.

Adjustable wrenches

This type of wrench will adjust in size to fit a range of nuts, bolts, or fittings that have flat sides. These come in several sizes; a ten-inch wrench, which can open up to a 1 $1/8$-inch span, is a good, general-purpose size. When using an adjustable wrench, always position it so that the force pushes against the fixed jaw.

Rib-joint pliers

For gripping and turning pipes, nuts, and fittings, rib-joint pliers are very handy. With these pliers, a pivot slides along a slot and engages in channels at various positions to adjust the size of the jaws so they will firmly grip objects from small to large.

Locking pliers

Locking pliers offer a clamping action so they will lock onto an object such as a bolt or a pipe. A knurled screw mounted in one handle adjusts the size of their grip.

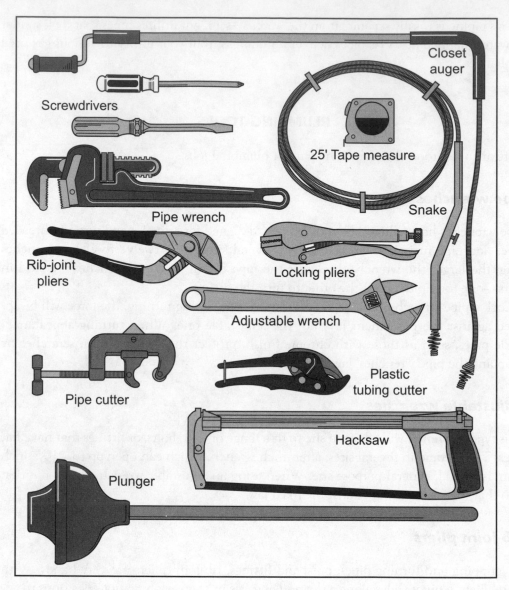

FIGURE 4.2   Plumbing Tools

Hacksaw

A hacksaw will cut nearly all types of pipe, from steel to plastic. A conventional hacksaw has a removable ten- or twelve-inch-long, fine-toothed blade that's held taught by an adjustable steel frame. For making cuts where the frame of a conventional hacksaw won't allow access, you can use a "mini" or "flush-cut" hacksaw—its blade protrudes straight out from the handle.

Screwdrivers

Screwdrivers are needed for a variety of plumbing tasks, from changing faucet washers to disassembling plumbing-related appliances. You'll want an assortment of sizes and types, including two or three sizes each of standard, flat-bladed screwdrivers and Phillips screwdrivers. A "4-in-1" driver is a handy option; it has a removable shank with interchangeable Phillips and standard tips in two sizes each. Be sure the driver fits the screw's head snugly, otherwise it will mangle the screw and the tip of the driver.

Measuring tape

A few plumbing jobs, such as measuring runs of pipe, call for a retractable steel tape measure. Get a twenty-five-footer because you'll be able to extend its blade unsupported for several feet.

Pipe cutter

Two types of pipe cutters can be helpful to you for do-it-yourself jobs. First, a plastic-tubing cutter, which looks similar to a pair of pruning shears, can make quick cuts through rigid and flexible plastic tubing, such as sprinkler pipe. Second, a pipe cutter with a sharp cutting wheel and an adjustable jaw grips onto a copper or steel pipe; you rotate it around the pipe, repeatedly tightening it until it cuts all of the way through.

Drain clearing tools

Toilet and sink plungers, "snakes" or drain augers, toilet augers, and hydraulic "blow bags" are helpful to have on hand in the event of a clogged drain. For more about these tools and how to use them, see pages 76-78.

DRAINS

Here is the sequence of events to use when trying to solve various types of drain problems. You'll find more about each of these steps in the material that follows.

1. If a drain is simply moving slowly, a clog may be starting to form or the vent system (see below) may be blocked. You can use a chemical drain cleaner to open a slow-moving drain, but beware: their caustic nature can damage certain kinds of pipes and upset the delicate chemical balance of a septic system. And if the drain becomes fully clogged, the caustic solution that fills the pipes and backs up into the bathtub or sink can burn your skin and make it dangerous to plunge or use a snake to clear the drain.
2. Plunge the drain at the fixture.
3. Try to clear out a hair blockage in a sink or tub drain with the help of a straightened coat hanger (bend a small hook at one end). To do this, first remove the pop-ups (hair and debris can collect around these assemblies). See more about removing pop-ups below.
4. Connect a hydraulic bladder to a garden hose and try to blast out the clog.
5. Try to clear the blockage with a snake, working from the fixture.
6. Try to clear the blockage with a snake, working from a branch cleanout.
7. Call a plumber.

How to locate a drain blockage

Each plumbing fixture in your home carries wastes to the sewer or septic tank via a system of drainpipes. Also connected to this system are vents, which expel sewer gasses out the roof. Each fixture has a "trap," a U-shaped pipe (or in the case of the toilet, part of the fixture) that contains water to block sewer gasses from entering your home.

To locate the blockage, check other toilets, sinks, and tubs to see if they're draining properly. If only one fixture is clogged, the stoppage is usually located in that fixture's trap or branch drain.

If other fixtures are backed up, the blockage is probably beyond where they join a branch line. Backups at lower points of the system—or throughout the entire system— usually mean the main stack or sewer line is clogged. For these blockages, it's usually best to call a plumber.

How to plunge a drain

When a drain is clogged, whether it's a sink, a toilet, or a tub, the first thing to do is try breaking up the clog by plunging with a "plumber's helper." Be sure you have one on hand that has an elongated bell shape; the bell folds up so that the plunger becomes flatter and cup shaped for sinks and tubs. A plunger always works better if you put enough water into the fixture to cover the plunger. If plunging doesn't break up the clog, either blast open the drain with a hose and hydraulic bladder or use a drain auger to snake out the drain.

Plunging a toilet.   Fill the bowl about half full. Push the bell shape of the plunger down into the drain and, maintaining a tight seal, rapidly pump ten to twenty times with short strokes. If water doesn't flush down, resort to a closet auger (see below).

Plunging a sink or tub.   First remove the strainer and pop-up. Stuff a rag or sponge into a plastic bag and use this to plug the overflow hole. If one side of a double kitchen sink is blocked, stuff this plug into the drain hole of the other side. Fill the fixture with enough water to cover the plunger's flat rubber cup (fold the bell shape up inside). Plunge steadily up and down fifteen or twenty times; intersperse a few powerful pushes. Keep the plunger tightly sealed against the fixture. A plunger doesn't usually work on floor or shower drains, but it's worth a try; be sure the water level covers the plunger.

How to water-blast a drain

There is a tool that's easier and cleaner to use than a snake for breaking loose clogs—a "blow bag" or "hydraulic ram," essentially an expanding rubber bladder that, when attached to a garden hose and pushed down into the offending pipe, fills with water, expands, then blasts clogs loose. These simple little devices cost about $10 and will work on most clogs. You have to use them judiciously, however, being careful not to break loose the connections of a plastic-pipe drain system.

1. Push the blow bag about six inches into the drainpipe, and be ready (with a bucket) for water to back up out of the pipe. If you are using one on a bathtub, push it down the overflow pipe until it passes the tee at the tub drain.
2. Turn on the water and allow the bag to fill and seal itself inside the pipe. Then it should pulse with blasts that break loose the clog.
3. Be ready to turn off the water immediately if it doesn't work.

How to snake a drain

Plumbing snakes (also called augers) are made in two varieties: drain augers and closet augers. Most people are familiar with the drain auger, a long, tightly wound flexible metal cable with a corkscrew auger at one end and a crank at the other. The closet auger is a little less familiar; it's a very short variety of the snake with a rigid end that is easier to push down into the toilet.

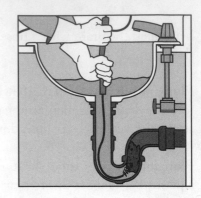

FIGURE 4.3   Snaking a Drain

Here's how to use a drain auger:

1. Wearing gloves, push the cable into the drain while turning the auger's handle clockwise. Keep repositioning the grip within a few inches of the entry point as you feed the snake into the drain.
2. When you feel the auger reach the blockage, keep turning and pull back a bit to chew away and dislodge the blockage.
3. Push forward again to grind away and, eventually, drive the auger through the blockage.
4. If possible, pull the blockage back out through the pipe. At this point, the job is a mess; have a bucket and rags ready and pull the cable back through an old towel or heavy rags.
5. If pushing the auger into the drain from the fixture doesn't work, try to find a branch cleanout (a sanitary-T fitting with a plug in one fork, located along the drainpipe that runs from the fixture to the main soil stack, often visible in a basement or crawl space). With a large bucket under the cleanout, slowly back out the plug with a wrench. Be ready: water and waste may gush out.
6. Run a drain auger in through the branch pipe as described in steps 1 through 4. If there doesn't appear to be a clog in the branch, the blockage may be in the main waste and vent stack or in the sewer line.
7. You can try to find the main cleanout and repeat this snaking effort, or you can try running an auger down the vent stack from the roof (be very careful up on the roof). Then again, maybe it's a better idea to call a plumber or drain clearing service at this point.

Floor drain clogged

When water backs up and pools at a basement floor drain, the drain trap, floor drain line, or sewer line is blocked. In most cases, you should call a plumber or drain clearing service. Some floor drains have a cleanout plug beneath the drain cover that allows an auger to bypass the trap; remove the plug and snake-out the line as described above.

Sink or tub doesn't drain

A slow-draining tub or sink usually means the drain is clogged. On a sink, first try using a plunger and, if that doesn't work, clean out the trap.

While you're at it, you may discover it's time to replace the entire trap. You may save a little by buying only one piece, but you'll pay for it later when you have to repeat the labor. When reassembling the trap, be careful not to overtighten the slip-joint nuts.

A tub is often fouled with hair. Pull out the pop-up stopper (if it has one) by wiggling the lever and lifting the stopper. Ease it out and remove hair from the linkage.

Otherwise, use a blow bag or snake-out the drain (see page 77).

If you've done both, consider the vent line—be sure it isn't blocked with a bird's nest or other debris. You can snake it from the roof (but be careful not to drop the snake into the pipe!).

If your home is served by a septic system, your tank and/or drain field may be overloaded.

Foul odors from drain

Unless there is visible sewage from a backup, foul odors occur when sewer gasses enter a room through drain and vent pipes. This happens most often in a seldom-used bathroom or basement area. Water in the trap (see "How to locate a drain blockage" page 76) evaporates, eliminating the barrier it provides. If refilling the fixture or pouring water into the drain doesn't solve the odor (after you've aired out the room), the cause may be something else, such as a dead rodent.

Sink trap leaks

If the leak is occurring at one of the joints between pipes, try tightening the slip nuts. On a metal trap, tighten them hand tight plus about a half turn (use slip-joint pliers to grip the nut). On a plastic trap, just hand tighten and, if needed, give the nut about a quarter of a turn with slip-joint pliers. If that doesn't work, loosen the nuts and remove the large rubber slip washers or cone-shaped plastic washers that provide the watertight seal at

---

each joint between the trap's pipes. Rubber washers may leak as the rubber hardens over time. If they're hard or deteriorated, replace all of them. Plastic-pipe traps are more likely to leak if the pipes or washers become misaligned—so check the alignment.

If the washers are in good condition and everything is aligned, check the pipes for rust or corrosion. If the pipe is corroded or cracked, take it with you to the hardware store to buy an appropriate replacement—replace the entire trap (PVC traps are inexpensive, durable, easy to work with, and don't corrode the way chromed brass drainpipes do).

Replacing a sink trap

Put a bucket beneath the trap and, using slip-joint pliers, disconnect the slip-joint nuts that hold the trap to the tailpiece and drainpipe. Be ready for water to pour out of the disconnected pipe momentarily.

Once you have the trap apart, clean it out with a wire coat hanger and replace any faulty parts. Then reassemble everything.

First tighten the slip joint nuts by hand while fitting everything; then tighten with the pliers—but don't overtighten. Run the water and look for leaks. If you spot leaks, tighten the nuts a little more. If everything appears to be fine, place a newspaper under the sink and check the paper for signs of drips again tomorrow.

Faulty sink pop-up stopper

If your sink pop-up won't pop up or seat properly, fixing it is quite easy—usually just a matter of adjusting a few parts. The culprit is often a buildup of hair around the base of the stopper or the pivot rod mechanism. Or the clevis (see Figure 4.4) may be out of adjustment. Here's how to fix it:

1. With a slight twist, try to lift out the stopper. If it seems to be linked to the mechanism, reach under the sink and unscrew the pivot rod retaining nut and pull out the pivot rod to disengage it.
2. Lift the stopper from the drain. Clean off all hair and debris. If the stopper is broken or the seal around its underside looks worn, replace it.
3. Face the hole at the bottom of the stopper toward the pivot rod's location, and drop the stopper back into the drain hole. Insert the pivot rod so that it engages the hole in the bottom of the stopper; then tighten on the retaining nut with the stopper in its up position.
4. Loosen the set screw on the clevis and adjust the strap up or down so that it operates the pivot rod to open and close the stopper. Retighten the set screw.

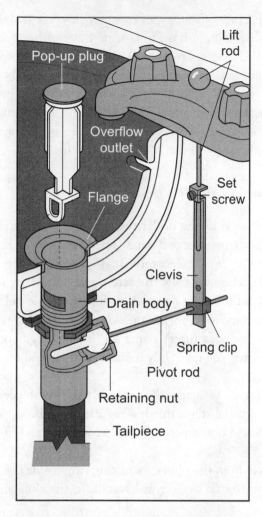

FIGURE 4.4 Sink Pop-up Assembly

FAUCETS

Unfortunately, faucets are far from standardized, so it's difficult to generalize about repairs. Most problems can be fixed by disassembling part or all of a faucet and replacing washers, seals, or other parts. It's a good idea to keep a faucet repair kit on hand—one that contains a variety of washers, O-rings, and similar seals (these are available at hardware stores and home centers).

Nearly all faucets have one of four types of water-flow control mechanisms: cartridge, compression, ball, or disc. Single-handle faucets have either a cartridge, ball, or disc mechanism. Dual-handled faucets are either cartridge, disc, or compression faucets.

Of all these types, compression faucets are more likely to drip because they have washers or seals that restrict water flow by closing against a valve seat when you turn the handle—and these washers or seals can wear out. The other mechanisms are called "washerless" because they don't use washers for the off-and-on action; even so, they do have O-rings or neoprene seals to keep them from leaking.

How to disassemble a faucet

First turn off the water supply valves under the sink and place a towel in the sink to prevent scratches and to catch any dropped parts. Then remove the handle. To do this, use a small, flat screwdriver to pry up the decorative cap, button, or plug (used to hide a screw) at the top of the handle. Then unscrew the screw and pull or pry off the handle. You are now ready to disassemble the faucet (see details for each style below). Be sure to lay out the parts in order as you remove them, so you won't have trouble reassembling the faucet. And be sure to note the manufacturer's name on the faucet (if you can find it) and take the old parts with you when you go to buy replacements.

Compression-style faucet. Unscrew the bonnet from the faucet base, using slip-joint pliers. Then remove the valve stem; this has reverse threads, so unscrew it by turning it clockwise. Once you have it out, replace all rubber washers and O-rings.

Ball-style faucet. To tighten the plastic adjusting ring inside the cap, you turn it with a special flat adjusting tool (or fit two screwdrivers into the slots and cross their blades to turn the ring.

For a spout leak, unscrew the cap, using locking-jaw pliers (wrap the jaws with duct tape to prevent scratching the faucet's finish). Lift out the ball and replace the rubber seats and springs on both sides of the valve.

If the faucet leaks around the spout, replace worn O-rings.

Cartridge faucet. To release the cartridge, use a pair of pliers to pull the retainer clip straight out. Pull out the cartridge and replace the O-rings and seals to fix leaks.

If the faucet drips, you may need to replace the entire cartridge.

Disc faucet. Most ceramic disc faucets don't drip or leak because they're made to be almost maintenance free. Two ceramic discs regulate the flow of water: a movable upper disc turns or lifts and lowers against a fixed lower ceramic disc. Though these faucets are washerless, they do have inlet and outlet seals that may leak, or sediment may build up inside the inlets and cause leaks. Be sure the faucet is in the "open" position when replacing seals.

Reduced faucet flow

If your tap water suddenly runs slow, something is probably blocking its flow. (If it runs chronically slow, see "Low water pressure" on page 93.)

1. Check the supply valves under the sink—be sure they're fully open.
2. Unscrew the aerator on the end of the spout, if there is one, and clean it out thoroughly with hot water and an old toothbrush.
3. If these measures don't work, shut off the water to the faucet and disassemble the faucet to check for debris or a dislodged faucet washer.

Faucet drips or leaks—general

At the first sign of a drip, don't torque down on a faucet in an effort to stop the drip—in most cases, this will just damage the faucet. Instead, disassemble the parts far enough to replace the washers or seals that are failing to seal off the faucet's flow. If you have an older faucet that is chronically leaky, consider replacing it with a new, high-quality model.

Refer to Figures 4.5 and 4.6 for the locations of washers, seals, and O-rings—drips and leaks nearly always mean these parts need replacement. Failed washers or seals usually cause drips—to replace them, you must disassemble the faucet. Leaks around the handle usually mean that the O-rings on the stem need to be replaced or that the packing nut or adjusting ring needs to be tightened; to do this you normally just need to remove the handle. See the illustrations and the instructions for each faucet type for more information.

Hose bibb drips

A seat washer controls water flow inside a hose bibb. When this washer wears out, the faucet drips. To fix it, turn off the water supply to the faucet, disassemble the handle, remove the valve, replace the washer, and reassemble everything.

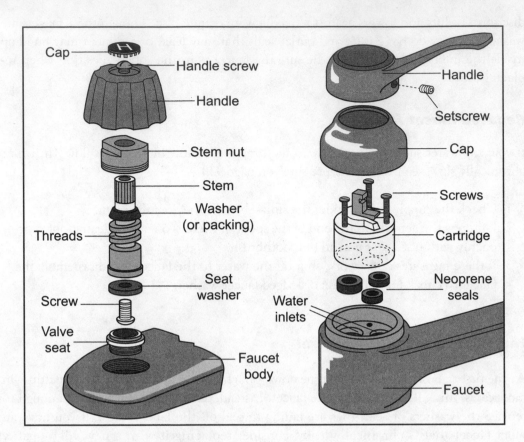

Cap

Handle screw

Handle

Stem nut

Stem

Washer
(or packing)

Threads

Seat
washer

Screw

Valve
seat

Faucet
body

Handle

Setscrew

Cap

Screws

Cartridge

Neoprene
seals

Water
inlets

Faucet

FIGURE 4.5   Faucets

FIGURE 4.6   Replacing
Faucet Packing

TOILETS

Toilets may have a variety of problems, from clogging up to running incessantly. Here is how you can handle the main hassles.

Clogged

If flushing the toilet causes sewage to back up in your bathtub or another fixture, it usually means there is a clog in the main drainpipe—the stack. Though you can attempt to snake this out, you're usually better off calling a plumber.

If your toilet is clogged but not backing up elsewhere, don't try to flush it, or it may overflow. Instead:

1. Remove the lid from the tank and raise the flapper valve to let a little water pass through so you can see whether the toilet is indeed clogged.
2. If it is, first try plunging with a bell-shaped plunger (see page 76).
3. If this doesn't do the job, snake-out the toilet with a special closet auger, as discussed on page 77.
4. If that doesn't work, call a plumber or drain clearing service.

Flushes poorly

If a toilet has been working fine but suddenly flushes or drains very slowly, the problem is usually a clogged drain. See page 77 for information on clearing the drain.

If you've plunged and snaked-out the drain but your toilet still flushes poorly, it may be the toilet's siphoning action. When a toilet is flushed, water rushes from the tank, through the valve seat, around the rim, and through a siphon jet chamber built into the porcelain at the front of the bowl. As the water encircles the rim, some washes down through the rinse holes in the underside of the rim. The rush of water causes a cleansing action and creates enough force to push waste out through the back of the bowl and down into the waste pipe.

First open the tank and check the water level. A low water level means there may not be enough force to kick off the siphoning action. Toilets are designed so that the tank, when filled to the top of the overflow tube, holds enough water for a good flush. Water-saving devices such as dams, bottles, or bending the float rod will foil the design. You're better off getting a toilet that's designed to be a water-saving fixture. Flush the toilet and make sure the flapper allows all of the tank's water to complete the flush.

If the water level looks fine, the rinse holes may be clogged with mineral deposits, particularly where hard water is a problem. You can clear the rinse holes located just under the rim or near the back of the bowl by using a short piece of coat hanger (but first turn off the toilet's shutoff valve and flush the toilet to get rid of most of the bowl's water).

Lime remover can dissolve minerals built-up in the toilet's channels, but this will take eight hours or more. The idea is to dam up the orifices so the lime remover can go to work—pack the holes with wet paper towels and hold them in place with a generous supply of plumber's putty; then pour a bottle of lime remover into the overflow tube and let it sit.

It's also possible that the toilet was made back in the late 1980s, when designs were shifting toward water-saving toilets but the technology had not been refined, in which case you may want to buy a new toilet.

Runs

A toilet runs because either the flapper (or tank ball) needs replacement or the valve is faulty. Determine the problem part by squeezing a few drops of food coloring into the tank to color the tank's water. After a few minutes, the water in the bowl will begin to turn color if the flapper is the problem. Otherwise, it's the valve.

Replacement flappers and stoppers are available for all types of toilets for under $10. Flappers are particularly simple to install. Just slide the collar down the overflow tube, center the flapper over the valve seat, and hook up the lift chain to the trip lever so that it has a little slack. Instructions are given on most flapper product labels.

Replacing the flush valve is a bit more involved—you have to disassemble most of the toilet's innards and, on a bowl-mounted tank, disassemble the tank from the bowl. Call a plumber for this unless you're comfortable handling this type of work. Complete instructions should be included on the new valve's package.

Toilet flapper closes too quickly

If the flapper has an adjustment, check it to see if it's set up properly. Check the chain's length—pull it tight; then back it off one link and attach it (Figure 4.8).

Tank sweats

In humid climates, warm room air can condense on the cooler surfaces of a toilet and drip onto the floor. The simplest solution is to empty the water from the tank and glue a foam

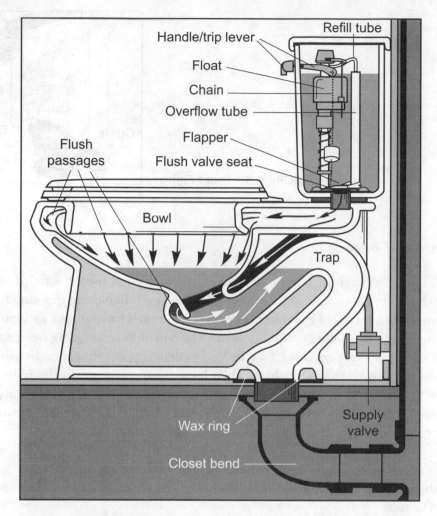

Handle/trip lever

Refill tube

Float

Chain

Overflow tube

Flapper

Flush valve seat

Flush passages

Bowl

Trap

Wax ring

Supply valve

Closet bend

FIGURE 4.7   Toilet

toilet tank liner on the tank's inner surfaces—this will reduce the amount of sweating. For a more thorough and permanent solution, talk to a plumber about installing a tempering valve on the cold water line that supplies the toilet. This draws a little hot water from a hot water pipe and mixes it with the cold water entering the toilet tank to raise the tank's temperature.

Plumbing Problems

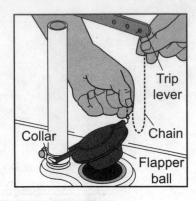

FIGURE 4.8   Toilet Flapp

Leaks around base

If you find water around the base of your toilet, the problem is usually a failed wax ring between the toilet's base and the closet bend (waste pipe). Replacing this ring involves pulling the toilet, so be sure the water is not coming from a leaking tank or supply connection (see below). Another possibility is that the tank may be sweating (see page 86).

If the tank is not sweating, check for a leaking tank or supply connection by using a rag to dry the floor around the toilet's base. Then lay a newspaper beneath the toilet's tank, wait a few minutes, and check it for drips. If there is no sign of leaking but the water reappears around the base, the wax ring is probably guilty. Before you start this repair, buy a new wax ring (the type with a rubber collar offers more secure drainage).

1. Turn off the water supply valve behind the base of the toilet.
2. Flush the toilet and drain as much water from the tank as possible. Then sponge out the rest.
3. Pop the plastic covers off of the closet flange nuts that mount the toilet to the floor on both sides (you may have to pry them off with a screwdriver).
4. Using a wrench, remove the nuts from the bolts, turning them counterclockwise.
5. Gently loosen the toilet from the floor, rocking it back and forth. It's heavy, so watch your back and don't let it topple over. Lay it down on its side.
6. Stuff a rag into the mouth of the drain opening.
7. Wearing rubber gloves, use a putty knife to scrape and peel the old wax off of the bottom of the toilet and the top of the floor flange.
8. Press the new wax ring onto the base of the toilet, with the collar pointing down.
9. Lift the toilet up and set it back onto the flange, with the bolts through the mounting holes. This is a little bit tricky—you don't want to miss when placing

the bowl onto the floor flange because this could damage the wax ring, so have someone help you line it up before you seat it on the flange. A plumber's trick is to push a couple of large drinking straws onto the mounting bolts first; slip these through the holes in the toilet's base and just slide the bowl down into place.

TUBS AND SHOWERS

Tubs and showers tend to work without mishap for years, except for clogs, which are commonly caused by hair buildup in the drain (see "Drains," page 75). Occasionally, pop-up stoppers fall out of adjustment, shower heads clog, or a few other problems occur.

Faulty tub pop-up stopper

If your bathtub pop-up doesn't open or seat properly, your tub may drain slowly or, worse, drain when you don't want it to. Adjusting it is easy.

A bathtub pop-up is a two-part mechanism: first, the stopper, which has a rocker arm that extends back toward the drain; and second, the overflow assembly, a lever that lifts or lowers a rod with a spring-like end. When you flip the overflow lever up, it pushes the rod down on the stopper's rocker arm, which raises the stopper. Flip the lever up, and it lifts the rod, allowing the stopper to drop down and plug the drain. Depending upon the type of pop-up, you adjust the way the stopper seats either by adjusting the length of the striker rod or by adjusting the rocker arm.

Adjusting the overflow assembly. Remove the screws that secure the overflow cover plate and pull the plate and lever away from the overflow hole, partially pulling out the mechanism. Adjust the nut that lengthens or shortens the rod assembly—lengthen it to raise the stopper higher or shorten it to let it drop lower. Then push the assembly back in and replace the cover plate.

Adjusting the stopper. Lift it out of the drain. Clean off hair and debris and adjust the nut on its underside to shorten or lengthen its connection to the rocker arm. Then work the arm and stopper back down into the drain hole.

Showerhead problems

Showerheads eventually wear out or become clogged with lime deposits. When this happens, they generally work poorly and look worse. This is the perfect time to replace the head with a newer, low-flow model or a hand-held shower type of head—and the job is

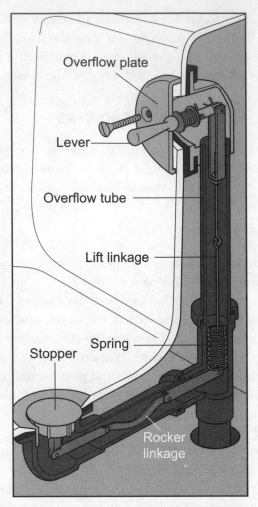

Overflow plate

Lever

Overflow tube

Lift linkage

Spring

Stopper

Rocker linkage

FIGURE 4.9   Tub Pop-up Assembly

easy. You'll need locking-jaw pliers and a pipe wrench and/or an adjustable wrench for unscrewing the old head.

1. Put duct tape on the tools' jaws to protect the finish on the shower arm and new showerhead. Use pliers or a pipe wrench to prevent the shower arm from turning while you unscrew the old shower head (counterclockwise) with the other wrench or pliers.

2. Wrap the shower arm's pipe threads with a couple layers of Teflon tape (clockwise).
3. Then simply screw the new head or shower hose attachment piece back on.

Shower runs hot and cold

If your shower sprays freezing cold water when the dishwasher or washing machine kicks on, or scalds you when someone flushes a toilet, you have two basic choices:

1. Organize shower schedules with appliance schedules or . . .
2. Have a pressure-balancing valve installed on the hot and cold water lines that supply the shower faucet. Unless you're quite familiar with doing your own plumbing work, this is a job for a plumber.

Porcelain rust

Rust on porcelain is usually the result of a dripping faucet and high iron content in the water. One household remedy is scrubbing the stain with a mixture of lemon juice and salt. If scrubbing doesn't do it, soaking might; saturate a rag with the mixture and lay it on the blemish for a few hours. Then scrub it again. If there's still a stain, ask your local hardware dealer or home center about commercially available rust and iron removers.

Shower pan leaks

Though grout can be repaired (see page 163) and you can recaulk joints (page 164), if the shower pan is leaking, you'll need to have it repaired by a tile installer or roofing contractor. Contact your homeowner's insurance company; repairing the damage may be covered. To check the shower pan for leaks:

1. Remove the shower drain screen.
2. Plug the drain with an expandable plug, purchased at a hardware store or home improvement center.
3. Fill the shower pan with water to within about one inch from the top of the step and mark the water line. Wait a few minutes. If the water level goes down and wetness shows up beneath the shower, the pan is leaking.

Bathtub spa jets don't work

If your bathtub spa jets suddenly cease to work:

1. Check the electrical panel's circuit breaker to see if it has tripped. If it has, reset it.
2. If that doesn't solve the problem, consult your owner's manual to see if the pump has a "high limit manual reset" or a separate circuit breaker on the equipment; if it has either of these, try resetting them.
3. Still doesn't work? Turn off the spa's electrical circuit and call a serviceperson. The problem could be anything from a loose wire to a faulty float switch to a bad pump. (Be sure to let the serviceperson know you've turned off the circuit.)

Fiberglass tub scratched

Fiberglass tubs have "gelcoat" surfaces that can be restored with a lot of rubbing and buffing. For this job, you need to get a three-part kit made for the removal of fiberglass oxidation and sold at marine products stores. Follow the label directions. This job normally involves buffing the scratches with a special compound, applying a seal coat, then buffing again with rubbing wax.

WATER SUPPLY SYSTEM

If your house is hooked up to a conventional municipal water system, fresh water travels through the water utility's pipes until it reaches the meter in front of your home. It passes through the meter, where usage is measured, travels through a large gate valve, and then runs through one or more water pipes to your house and property.

Inside your home, that cold-water pipe branches off to deliver cold water to all faucets and water-using fixtures and appliances, including your water heater (it may go to a water softener as well). A second run of pipes carries heated water from the water heater to all faucets, fixtures, and appliances that use hot water. Often, hot- and cold-water pipes parallel each other. See Figure 4.1 on page 72.

Supply pipes carry water under pressure—normally about fifty pounds per square inch (psi). Because of this pressure, if a pipe or fitting springs a leak, the water usually sprays out with considerable force.

Most supply pipes are copper, soldered together with elbows, tees, and other fittings. Threaded galvanized iron pipes are also common, particularly in older homes, but are being phased out because they tend to get clogged by mineral deposits over time. Plastic pipes often supply water to outdoor sprinkler systems.

Low water pressure

Water pressure may be low for a couple of reasons. If all of your neighbors have low water pressure, there may not be much you can do except to contact your water supplier and complain about the problem.

If your home is the only one with low pressure—or if only parts of your house have low pressure—then there is probably a restriction in your pipes or valves. The most common problem is older pipes that have become clogged with lime deposits.

1. Request a check by your water supplier. They may discover that a supply valve is partially closed.
2. Try to find the restriction by determining which fixtures suffer from low pressure and which don't.
3. If the problem seems to be at a single faucet or shower head, check for a flow restriction, clogged aerator, or dislodged washer. Remove the showerhead (page 91), the aerator from the faucet (if there is an aerator), or the faucet (page 81) and look for a restrictor—a rubber or brass disk—or a washer that has become dislodged.
4. If the problem persists, contact a plumber to check for obstructions or solve the problem by adjusting your home's pressure regulator, if there is one, or installing a water pressure booster pump.

How to shut off the water

When the water supply system leaks or a repair is needed, you'll have to shut off the water. It's best to do this at the valve that's closest to the problem. That way, the rest of the house will still have a functioning water supply.

For a faucet, toilet, or similar fixture, first look for a stop valve that's connected to the water supply tubes, located directly under the fixture. This is normally a chrome-plated or plastic valve; beneath sinks, one serves hot and one serves cold. Turn the handle clockwise to shut it off. If this is too difficult to turn by hand, grip it with a pair of ribjoint pliers (see page 73).

If you don't find a shutoff valve there, you can shut off the valve that controls the flow to the entire house, normally located near where the cold water pipe enters (outside in warm climates, inside in cold climates). In some cases, this valve is located on a pipe right before the water heater. In some cases, this valve has a red handle. To turn it off, rotate the handle clockwise.

To turn off the water both to your house and to the rest of your property (including sprinkler systems, hose bibbs, and so forth), look for the main valve just to the house side of your water meter, which is normally out by the street. Turn it clockwise until it stops; this valve should be completely open or completely closed—it is not used to control the amount of flow.

Burst pipe

It helps to have a pipe clamp (4.10) on hand, just in case a pipe bursts—especially if you live in a climate where pipes are likely to freeze. You can buy these quick-repair, screw-on devices at a hardware store.

1. Shut off the valve that controls water flow to the damaged pipe (see above).
2. Apply a pipe clamp. In a pinch, you can make one by wrapping the burst section with a strip of rubber (from an inner tube, for example), then clamping the wrap with an adjustable hose clamp, a pipe sleeve clamp, or a C-clamp.
3. Call a plumber or replace the damaged section of pipe.

Frozen supply pipes

Where temperatures dip below freezing, water inside supply pipes can freeze, block water flow, and burst pipes. If water flow is blocked and a pipe is bulging:

1. Open the faucet nearest to the bulge.
2. Trace along the pipe to where it extends outside of heated spaces.
3. Thaw the ice in the pipe with a heat gun, heat lamp, or hair dryer, heating the pipe to the supply side of the blockage. Or wrap the pipe with rags and pour boiling water onto the rags.
4. Once the ice has melted and the water is flowing freely, close the faucet.
5. Protect the weather-exposed pipe with a jacket of foam insulation.

Pipes make noise

Pipes may make noise because of any of several problems.

Rattles.   Sometimes pipes vibrate against your home's framing members as water travels through them. If you can gain access to them where they rattle—from the basement, for

---

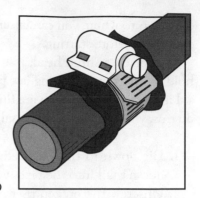

FIGURE 4.10   Pipe Clamp

example—the quickest and easiest way to solve the problem is to put foam insulation sleeves onto them and refasten them securely.

Chattering.   If pipes chatter when you turn on certain faucets, replace the faucet washers.

Water hammer.   If pipes make loud banging noises when you turn off a faucet or when water-using appliances run, recharge the water supply system with air to help cushion the water's flow when it reaches faucets. To do this, turn off the main water supply valve and drain the water from the supply system by opening all faucets halfway—remember to open the lowest faucet in the house. Then close the lowest faucets and turn on the main water supply. Work your way up through the house, turning off the faucets as water begins to flow through them. If the problem continues, call a plumber.

OUTDOOR SPRINKLERS AND PIPING

Outdoor sprinklers are vulnerable to damage and a variety of problems. Most problems are easy and inexpensive to repair—those that involve automatic timers or electronic components may require a plumber or sprinkler specialist (unless you replace the entire component).

Water gushes from riser

When water gushes freely from a sprinkler but stops when you turn off the sprinkler control or valve, the sprinkler head is loose or has fallen off, or the riser is broken. To fix this problem, replace the head, the riser, or both. For a ground-level sprinkler, you'll need to

---

Plumbing Problems   95

dig down to where you can unscrew the riser from the threaded tee or elbow. Turn off the sprinklers before starting.

To replace a shrub head, just unscrew it by turning it counterclockwise. If necessary, hold the riser with locking-jaw pliers and turn the head with an adjustable wrench.

Lawn sprinklers, which are flush to the ground, are more difficult to grip and turn. To do this, you can buy a "universal head wrench" at the hardware store.

1. Dig down to the threaded tee or elbow, clearing away all surrounding soil so it doesn't fall into the pipes when you disconnect them.
2. Unscrew the broken riser by turning it counterclockwise. Use a pair of slip-joint pliers to turn it, if needed. If a plastic riser has broken off inside the tee or elbow, tap a chisel into the broken piece, wedge the chisel against one edge, and turn it counterclockwise. Be careful not to damage the tee or elbow's threads.
3. Replace the riser with a new one of the same length.
4. Flush dirt from the line by turning on the sprinkler valve for a few seconds before replacing the head.

Sprinkler head is clogged

If dirt or debris has clogged a sprinkler head, causing it to spray unevenly or not at all, it's time to clean it. Do this with the sprinkler turned off.

1. First try a quick simple cleaning—just try to clear the head's water slit or hole with a piece of small-diameter, stiff wire or a knife blade.
2. For hard-to-clean heads and some other types, unscrew the head and check for a small filter screen. Flush the screen and/or the head with running water.
3. If the problem is with a pop-up brass head, clean any debris away from the wiper seal on the stem. If several heads in a row have this problem, the water pressure may be too low to raise all of the heads properly. Be sure the sprinkler valve is turned all the way on. You can also replace the heavy brass heads with lightweight plastic types

Sprinkler spray patterns are off

If spray patterns are directed the wrong way, you can simply turn the sprinkler head in the right direction. You can also substitute a head with a different pattern—a half- or full-circle pattern, for example. Or, you can change the adjustment of adjustable heads; turn the sprinkler on and plan to get wet when you do this.

A small screw on the top of stationary spray heads adjusts water flow; turn it counter-clockwise with a small screwdriver to open it or clockwise to decrease spray. If the screw is completely open, try increasing or decreasing the flow at the valve.

On rotary-style heads, look for the spray-limit adjustment on the head.

To find an underground leak

If you suspect that water may be leaking from a broken pipe or fitting somewhere underground, here's how to know for sure:

1. Turn off every faucet, fixture, and appliance that uses water—even the icemaker.
2. Open the water meter's cover so that you can see the gauge.
3. Mark the rim of the gauge where the needle is pointing (if there are several dials, mark the one that indicates one-cubic-foot increments).
4. Leave the water shut off for thirty minutes; then see if the needle has moved from the mark. If it has, your plumbing is leaking somewhere (unless someone used a faucet or the toilet without your knowledge).

You can look for signs of a leak, such as sink holes or mushy areas of ground, but you may have to have a professional find the leak. For a leak-detection service, look in the Yellow Pages under "Pipe and Leak Locating."

5

ELECTRICAL PROBLEMS

Of the many kinds of home repairs, electrical ones tend to intimidate homeowners the most. Not only does wiring seem confusing, but the specter of electrical shock is scary. What most people don't know, however, is that doing certain jobs on your home's electrical systems can be easy and safe if you follow basic safety precautions. The key to safety is to *always disconnect the power from an electrical system before working on it*.

Some electrical systems are safer and easier to work on than others: most low-voltage, telephone, doorbell, and cable television wires, for example, are relatively harmless and easy to handle compared to standard-voltage lights and receptacles.

ELECTRICAL BASICS

Lights, receptacles, and appliances are all connected to the primary standard-voltage system that is delivered through power lines by your electrical utility, then routed throughout your home's wiring. *Before working on any elements of the primary electrical system in your home, you must disconnect the power. Turning off a wall switch does not necessarily turn off the power to its fixture or receptacle; you must shut off the power at the circuit breaker.*

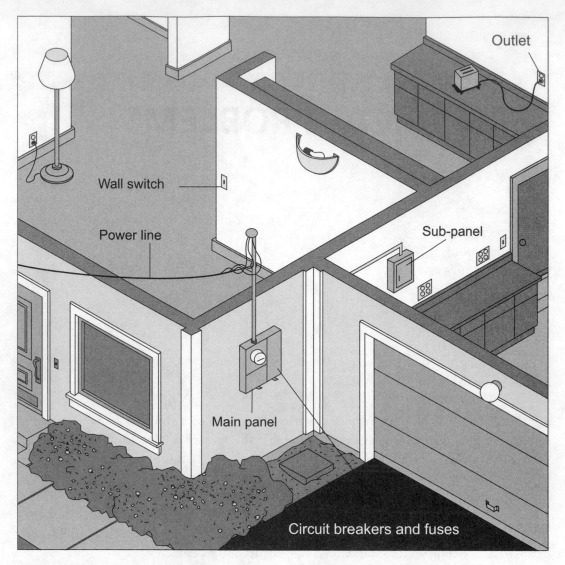

FIGURE 5.1 House Electrical System

Three wires enter most homes from the power pole: two hot (charged) wires and a third "neutral" wire. Each hot wire provides 120-volt current for conventional lights, receptacles, and appliances when paired with the neutral wire, which is normally kept at zero volts or "ground potential." When both hot wires are used together with the neutral, they power large 240-volt appliances such as air conditioners and electric ovens.

THE HOME PROBLEM SOLVER

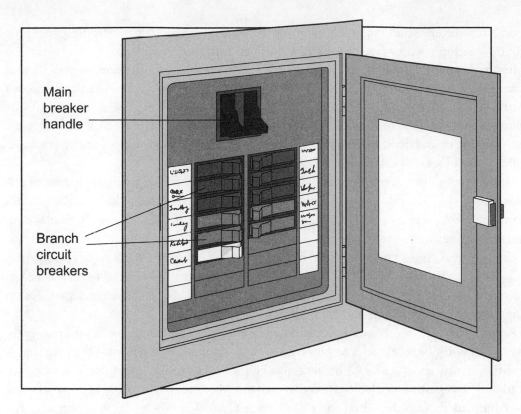

Main
breaker
handle

Branch
circuit
breakers

FIGURE 5.2   Main panel

In addition, most homes have low-voltage electrical systems, with transformers that convert standard power to a lower, safer voltage (typically from six to twelve volts) for doorbells, intercoms, security systems, low-voltage interior and exterior lighting, and the like. Low-voltage electricity is also delivered through telephone lines for ringing phones. Audio and video or cable television signals travel through cables that, under normal circumstances, have no voltage.

The main panel

Next to or near your home's electric meter is a metal box that is the main distribution center for your home's electrical power. This main panel receives the three incoming electrical service wires and routes smaller cables and wires to secondary subpanels and electrical circuits throughout your house. For safety, it should be grounded: a continuous conductor (often, solid copper) runs from the neutral connector inside the panel to a ground—either a water pipe or a metal rod driven into the ground.

Inside the main panel are circuit breakers, fuses, or levers for disconnecting all of your home's electrical circuits from the incoming power lines. Most homes built in the last thirty years utilize circuit breakers as the disconnect devices: these are essentially switches that you can turn off or that will automatically "trip" (turn off) if they detect a short circuit or overload that could cause a fire or hazard. Older homes may have fuses, pullout fuse blocks, or disconnect levers.

Many homes also have subpanels located elsewhere; these are smaller versions of the main panel. Large cables run from the main panel to a subpanel; then smaller circuit wiring carries power to specific appliances or areas of the house. Subpanels usually contain circuit breakers or fuses like those in the main panel.

Circuit breakers and fuses are rated according to the maximum amount of current they will allow or protect—typically fifteen or twenty amps for lighting and receptacle circuits. Ovens, electric water heaters, electric clothes dryers, and high-usage appliances require larger-capacity wiring and circuit breakers or fuses.

A ground-fault circuit interrupter (GFCI) circuit breaker should guard kitchen, bathroom, and outdoor receptacles to prevent shock or electrocution danger—they are highly sensitive to any short. A GFCI breaker may be located in the main panel, in a subpanel, or included as part of an electrical receptacle (this is usually identifiable because of small reset buttons mounted at the center—see page 115). When a group of receptacles has failed in the kitchen, bath, or outdoors, the GFCI circuit breaker is the first thing to check. Restoring power is often just a matter of resetting the breaker.

Circuits

Electricity travels in a circle. It moves along a "hot" wire toward a light or receptacle, supplies energy to the light or appliance, then returns along the neutral wire to the source. This complete path is a circuit. In house wiring, a circuit usually indicates a group of lights or receptacles connected along such a path.

Mapping your electrical circuits. Inside your electrical panel, you may discover that an electrician or previous homeowner has installed notations or lists that tell which circuit breakers or fuses control particular circuits. If your panel doesn't contain a reference like this, it's a good idea to map your circuits so that, when the need arises, you can quickly find the right circuit breakers or fuses to shut them off or reset them.

Though the following instructions refer to circuit breakers, the same techniques apply to panels that utilize fuses or other types of disconnect devices.

Keeping a circuit record. If each circuit breaker isn't already numbered inside the electric panel, number them. Make a list that you can post on the inside of the door. Numbers should correspond to each circuit breaker. After each number, note which devices the breaker controls. For an even more thorough mapping, you can sketch a floor plan and make notes on it that identify the breaker numbers for each light and receptacle throughout the house. Another helpful tip: mark the back of switch and receptacle covers with the circuit breaker's number.

Tracing your home's circuits. This is something you should do in daylight with a helper. Be aware that all of your home's power will be off at times and, when you're done, you'll have to reset clocks, timers, and the like. A helpful hint: receptacles are usually on circuits separate from lighting; major appliances such as furnaces, microwaves, washing machines, electric dryers, and electric ovens often have dedicated circuits.

1. At the electrical panel, turn off all the circuit breakers.
2. Identify any large, double (240-volt) circuit breakers first. Flip one on. Determine which major electrical appliance(s) it supplies by turning on each electric appliance (don't forget equipment such as the furnace and pool pump) until you find the ones that work.
3. Repeat with other large circuit breakers and major appliances.
4. Have a helper plug a small lamp (or electrical device) into a standard room receptacle. (If you're alone, use a radio that's turned on.)
5. Turn breakers on and off until you reach the one that turns on the lamp. Leave that breaker on and have your helper plug the lamp into other nearby receptacles; note all the ones controlled by that breaker.
6. Room lights will go on and off during this process. Note the circuit breaker that controls each set of lights.
7. Repeat this process with other receptacles.
8. Continue until you've located and noted all receptacle and lighting circuits.

How to turn off the power

The main circuit breaker, usually located inside the main panel (at the top), shuts off all of the electricity to the house. In a dire emergency, this is the one to turn off. Otherwise, shut off only the breaker that serves the problem circuit—that way, other parts of your house will continue to have lights and power. *The main circuit breaker does not shut off the wires that run from the main panel breakers to the electric meter—these are always "hot."*

Electrical Problems

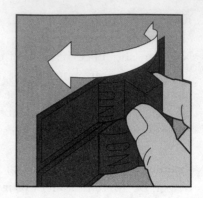

FIGURE 5.3   Circuit Breaker

When you open the main panel's cover, be sure there are no exposed electrical wires except for an exposed (noninsulated) solid copper ground wire. A protective panel should conceal all wiring—only the breakers or fuses should be exposed.

If this is not the case, call an electrician to have your electrical panel made safe—*touching the wrong wire or bare metal contact in an exposed electrical panel can electrocute you. Never touch bare metal contacts inside a disconnect panel.*

To shut off a circuit breaker.   Simply flip it to "off."

To reset a circuit breaker.   First turn it to "off"; then flip it to "on."

To shut off a circuit protected by a pullout fuse block.   Grasp the block's handle and pull it toward you. Once the block is out, you can remove the fuse from its mounting clips in the block—a special tool called a "fuse puller" makes this an easier job.

To shut off a circuit protected by a screw-in fuse.   Grasp the fuse's glass rim and unscrew it (counterclockwise). Do not put your fingers near the socket. If a fuse is blown, replace it with a good fuse that has the same amperage rating (both circuit breakers and fuses should be sized according to the wire used in the circuit they protect).

ELECTRICAL TOOLS

Most electrical wiring jobs are relatively easy to handle with a few inexpensive tools. If you want to do fairly sophisticated repairs, you'll want a multi-meter, available at consumer electronics stores or home improvement centers.

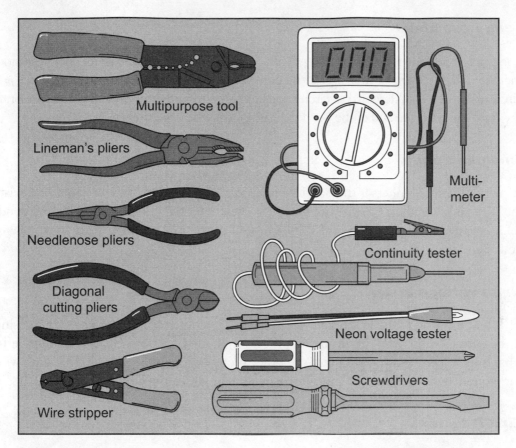

FIGURE 5.4 Electrical Tools

Wire stripper

Most electrical wires run inside a sheath of *insulation*, a plastic, rubber, or paper coating that prevents bare conductors from shorting against each other or shocking you. When splicing wires or connecting them to devices, you must remove the insulation, a relatively simple job when you have the right tool—an inexpensive wire stripper.

The stripper should be set so that it cuts the insulation but doesn't nick the wire (use the slot that matches the wire conductor's size, if it is indicated on the stripper). Hold the wire with one hand, bite into the insulation with the stripper, about $1/2$ inch to $3/4$ inch from the wire's end, rock the stripper back and forth, and pull the insulation off the end of the wire.

Long-nose pliers

Long-nose pliers are great for bending small loops at wire ends or for cutting off wires (most include a wire-cutting section). Use the pointed end of the pliers to form a smooth, $3/4$ - circle at a wire's end, designed to circle around a screw terminal (always hook the wire onto the terminal with the end of the bend sweeping clockwise from the wire).

Lineman's pliers

A pair of lineman's pliers is the best tool to use for cutting heavy wire or cable and twisting wire ends together. To twist two wires together, hold them side by side with one hand, their stripped ends aligned, point the blunt end of the pliers in line with them, clamp down, and twist in a clockwise direction.

Neon voltage tester

This helpful little tool can tell you whether wires are hot (charged) or not. When using it, be sure to hold only the insulated probes—not the bare parts. Touch one probe to what you suspect is a hot wire and the other probe to a neutral wire or grounding wire (or grounded metal electrical box). If the small light glows, the circuit is live.

Circuit tester

Simple and inexpensive, a circuit tester plugs into a conventional outlet and will tell you whether the circuit is hot (charged) or whether it's properly grounded.

Continuity tester

A small, battery-operated continuity tester costs less than $10. It can be used to determine whether wiring is broken and whether electrical circuits are complete.

Multi-meter or volt-ohm meter

You'll want to have a multi-meter on hand for making a variety of continuity checks, voltage checks, and other similar tasks. Read the manufacturer's instructions for a thorough understanding of techniques. Multi-meters, which do the job of ohm meters, volt meters, and related tools, are sold at consumer electronics stores for under $20.

Screwdrivers

You'll want an assortment of screwdrivers with insulated rubber grips. Be sure to get both flat-bladed and Phillips-head drivers.

SYSTEM PROBLEMS

When the electricity in part or all of your home doesn't work, the outage may be caused by any of several problems. Your first step is to determine the extent of the outage. If you see sparks or evidence of electrical shorting, shut off the disconnect device that serves that portion of your home and call an electrician. Do not do your own electrical repair unless you are accomplished at and knowledgeable about electrical work.

Follow all safety precautions: never work on live electrical wires; always shut off the circuit first. Do not stand in water or on a damp floor, even when working on low-voltage wiring such as telephone wires.

No electricity

If all of your lights and receptacles go out, either your main breaker (page 101) has tripped or the electrical utility's delivery system is down. Look at your neighbors' houses. If they're dark, call your electrical utility company and report the outage.

If your neighbors appear to have power—or if you just want to be sure—check your main electrical panel. (Even if you see lights next door, the problem may originate with your utility.) If the main circuit breaker has tripped, the problem is likely to be an overload or short circuit within your house. Fuses blow or breakers trip when there is a short circuit or an overloaded circuit. See information on restoring electricity, below.

Partial electricity

If some lights or receptacles work but others don't, one or more of your circuits has overloaded or short-circuited. When the power failed, if someone was using a device that draws a lot of current—such as a hair dryer or electric heater—the circuit probably tripped or the fuse blew because of simple current overload. If the nonworking circuit has a GFCI receptacle or circuit breaker (see page 102), you can often solve the problem by simply pushing the "reset" button. If the circuit blows again, you must determine and eliminate the cause or call an electrician.

Restoring electricity

Follow this sequence to restore electricity:

Check the subpanel or main panel that powers that circuit (see page 104).
1. No circuit appears to be out.
   - Call your utility company.
   - Call an electrician—the outage may be caused by a loose wire.
2. Circuit tripped
   - Turn off or unplug everything from the problem circuit (see page 102).
   - Replace fuse or reset breaker.

   If it blows, call an electrician to check the circuit for a charred wire or defective device.

   If it works, turn lights back on and plug in electrical devices one at a time.

   If one device causes an overload or short circuit, the device is faulty—have it repaired.

   If one device seems to be overloading the circuit, turn off other devices when using it or have your electrical service upgraded.

CONVENTIONAL LIGHTING

Most problems with lights occur when power is interrupted to the light fixture or when the light bulb or its socket is defective. If you're not comfortable working with electrical wiring, voltage testers, and the like, try the first few simple procedures; if those don't solve the problem, call an electrician.

Light doesn't work

When a single light doesn't work, the problem is almost always either the bulb, the circuit breaker (or fuse), or the switch. The first and most obvious solution is to replace the bulb with a good one; if that doesn't work, track down the problem through a process of elimination.

1. Test the bulb and, if necessary, change it. Be sure the bulb is screwed into the socket all the way. If you put a new bulb in the socket and it still doesn't work, check the new bulb in a working socket to be sure it isn't defective.
2. Remove the bulb. Turn the light switch on and then check to see if the socket is receiving power by touching the two leads of a voltage tester so that one touches

the brass contact at the center of the socket and the other touches the threaded metal bulb housing. If you get a reading of current, try another bulb. If you don't, go on to the next step.

3. Be sure that the circuit breaker (or fuse) for the nonworking fixture has not tripped. If it has, reset the breaker or replace the fuse and try the light again.

4. If it still doesn't work, turn off the circuit breaker that serves the nonworking fixture, unscrew the cover plate from the light switch, and use a voltage tester to be sure none of the wires in the electrical box are still hot (charged). Then be sure the wires are securely fastened to the switch's terminals.

5. Put the cover plate back on, turn the circuit back on, and try the switch again. If it doesn't work, go on to the next step.

6. Turn the circuit back off, remove the cover plate, remove the switch, and, using a multi-meter or a continuity tester, check the switch (see below).

7. If the switch is defective, replace it with one that has the same amperage and voltage ratings. (Because switches are quite inexpensive, it isn't worth the effort to attempt repair.)

8. If the switch tests fine, remove the cover plate from the light fixture, use a voltage tester to be sure there are no hot (charged) wires in the electrical box, then repair or replace the light fixture.

9. If the light still doesn't work, call an electrician.

How to check a standard light switch

If a light doesn't work and you suspect the switch:

1. Turn off the power to the light circuit (page 103).

2. Remove the switch's cover plate and unscrew the two screws that mount the switch to the electrical box.

3. Use a voltage tester to check the screw terminals on the side of the switch to make sure they're not hot (charged); then gently pull the switch out from the box.

4. Unscrew the wires from the two terminals and straighten their ends with a pair of pliers.

5. Twist the two bare ends together and screw a wire nut onto the twisted pair.

6. Turn the circuit back on. If the light goes on, the switch is bad—just buy a new one and reinstall it. *Remember to turn the power back off first!* If the light still doesn't work, the problem is in the wiring or the light fixture, so turn off the

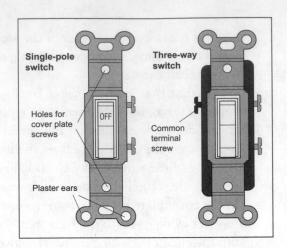

Single-pole switch

Holes for cover plate screws

Plaster ears

Three-way switch

Common terminal screw

OFF

FIGURE 5.5   Switches

power to the circuit, reconnect the original switch, put the cover plate back on, restore the power to the circuit, and call an electrician.

About three-way switches

When replacing a three-way switch (one that allows you to control one or more fixtures from two different places, such as from opposite ends of a hallway), be sure to return the wires to the proper screw terminals. On three-way switches, two terminals are the same color and the third terminal—called the common terminal—is a different metal or color. Put a piece of tape on the wire that goes to the common terminal screw. The other two wires can attach to either of the identical terminals.

Dimmer makes lights buzz

A dimmer switch can cause a light bulb's filament to vibrate, making a buzzing sound when its on a less-than-full setting. You can buy a new dimmer that's designed not to buzz and replace the old one as you would replace a switch (see page 108), but before you do, try replacing the bulb with a "long life" light bulb that has a sturdier filament and is rated at 130 volts instead of the far more common 120 volts.

Recessed lights go off and on

To minimize the risk of fire, recessed lights have a thermal protector that shuts them off when they get too hot. Be sure the bulb doesn't exceed the maximum wattage indicated inside the metal housing. And check whether a reflector-type bulb is required. If the bulb is the proper size and type, loosen the wing nuts or screws that adjust the bulb-holder's position inside the metal housing and slide the bulb unit down a little; then retighten. If possible, be sure insulation inside the ceiling is held back away from the fixture at least three inches. A flicker or spark indicates faulty wiring or a defective switch. If you're competent at handling electrical problems, shut off the power to the circuit and check wire connections at the switch and fixture. Otherwise, call an electrician.

Lights dim when appliances kick on

Too many electrical devices are drawing power from one circuit. If plugging some devices into receptacles on other circuits doesn't solve the problem, you may have to upgrade your home's electrical service panel. For today's electrical needs, a main electrical panel should deliver 100 amps of power or more; 150- or 200-amp services are even better for homes fitted with generous lighting and electrical amenities. A main panel sized smaller than 100 amps may be overloaded, which can cause lights to dim when appliances kick on or may allow frequent home power outages. If this is the case in your home, talk with an electrical contractor about installing a new, larger electrical service panel.

Replacing an electrical cord

When an appliance cord is defective, it should be replaced rather than repaired. If you can disassemble the appliance to see how the cord is connected, you may be able to handle this job yourself (be sure to unplug the appliance first). Otherwise, call an appliance repairperson.

Most cords are secured to the appliance with a strain-relief device, loops, or a clamp that you must loosen or remove. For screw-type, solderless connections, you unscrew the terminal screws that hold the cord and screw a new cord in its place. Cord wires that are twisted together and secured with wire nuts are easy to undo—just remove the wire nuts untwist the wires, and reverse the process with a new cord ($1/2$ inch of insulation must be stripped from the wire ends). If the cord's ends are soldered to terminals and you're familiar with soldering techniques, you can remove the old cord and solder a replacement to the terminals. Otherwise, leave this work to an appliance repairperson.

When you replace a cord, be sure to use an identical replacement; take the defective cord with you to the hardware store or electrical supply company to find a perfect match.

FLUORESCENT LIGHTS

Inside a fluorescent light, electricity is delivered to a ballast, which sends a spark through the mercury-vapor-filled tube (or bulb), creating light by activating phosphors that coat the inside of the tube. If any of the components are faulty, the light won't work right. Once you pinpoint the problem, most fixes are very easy. Remember to turn off the power first!

Old bulbs blink off and on just before they die; repairs are often simply a matter of replacing the tube or bulb. This problem may also be occurring because of poor contact between the pins at the ends of a tube and the tube holders. If the pins are bent, use needle-nose pliers to straighten them. Clean up the pins and socket contacts with fine sandpaper and brush away residue.

Though gray bands at the ends of tube are normal, black bands indicate that the tube needs to be replaced. If only one end is dark, turn the bulb end for end. If the tube is new and these fixes don't work, you may have to replace the starter or ballast as discussed below.

Some fixtures ("A-rated") are quieter than others, but most fluorescent lights have a slight hum. If the sound seems too loud—or if you can smell electrical burning—shut off the power. The ballast is probably either the wrong type, improperly installed, or defective. Replace it or call an electrician.

Brand new tubes tend to flicker, as do bulbs that are cold. If an old tube still flickers after it has had a chance to warm up (or after you've warmed up the room), rotate it a couple of times in the tube holders. Try cleaning the tube's end pins. If it still doesn't work, replace it.

If only the ends of the tube glow, either the starter or the ballast is defective. Replace the starter, then the ballast.

How to replace a fluorescent starter

Although newer fluorescent fixtures have built-in starters or no starters at all, most older lights have an easy-to-change, visible starter. It is a small, silvery cylinder that plugs into one of the tube holders.

1. Shut off the switch.
2. Remove the tube.
3. Give the starter a quarter-turn in a clockwise direction and pull it out.
4. Plug in the new starter, giving it a quarter-turn counterclockwise.
5. Replace tube.
6. Turn the switch on.

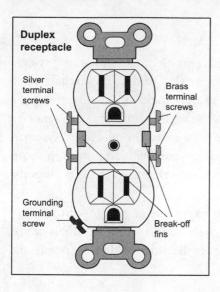

FIGURE 5.6   Receptacle

How to replace a tube holder or ballast

You can replace a ballast or tube holder if you're fairly familiar with wiring.

1. Turn off the power to the circuit.
2. Remove the tube and the cover plate that conceals the workings.
3. Disconnect or cut the wires to the tube holder or ballast and remove it.
4. Strip 1/2 inch of insulation from the ends of the wires.
5. Mount the component and connect the wires with wire nuts.
6. Replace the cover and tube.
7. Turn the circuit back on.
8. Turn the switch on.

RECEPTACLES

When you plug something into a conventional duplex receptacle (the type that receives two appliance plugs), and the device doesn't work, troubleshooting the problem is fairly simple. For large receptacles that run on 220 to 240 volts, such as ranges and dryers and air conditioners, call an electrician unless you're well versed in electrical repairs and safety issues.

Receptacle basics

Conventional duplex receptacles have two places to plug in electrical cords or devices. Each of those two places includes one narrow slot, one wide slot, and a semicircular hole. The narrow slot is the hot (charged) side, connected to the black wire of the electrical system. The wide slot is the neutral side, connected to the white wire. And the semicircular hole is the ground, connected to a bare or green wire or to the electrical system's ground. Many electrical plugs have one wide blade and one narrow blade (and, in some cases, a ground plug) that match the receptacle's slots to insure that the circuit is properly connected to the electrical device.

Wires may be attached to screws on each side of the receptacle or plugged into terminal holes in the back of the receptacle. Whether wires attached to screw terminals or are pushed into rear-mount terminals, the screw terminals on the sides of the receptacle are hot (charged), so don't touch them!

Receptacle doesn't work

For a nonworking duplex receptacle, first make sure the problem isn't with the appliance or lamp. Some appliances, such as hairdryers, have overload protectors that automatically shut them off if they begin to overheat. Try a second appliance or lamp in the receptacle.

If the receptacle still doesn't work, you'll usually find that the circuit breaker has tripped or the fuse has blown, the receptacle has become faulty, or there is a switch that operates that receptacle and it needs to be turned on. The problem is rarely the wiring.

1. Test the receptacle with a second lamp or appliance.
2. Be sure that one half of the duplex receptacle (or the entire receptacle) isn't controlled by a switch in the room.
3. Check the circuit breaker (or fuse) for that receptacle's circuit to be sure it has not tripped (or blown). If it has, reset the breaker or replace the fuse and try plugging a working lamp or appliance into the receptacle again.
4. If it still doesn't work, turn off the receptacle's circuit breaker, unscrew the cover plate from the receptacle, and use a voltage tester to be sure none of the wires in the electrical box are still hot (charged). Then check to be sure that the wires are securely fastened to the receptacle's terminals.
5. Look for signs of charring. Replace the receptacle if it looks damaged.

6. Put the cover plate back on, turn the circuit back on, and try the receptacle again. If it still doesn't work, turn the circuit back off, remove the receptacle cover, and replace the receptacle with one that has the same amp and voltage ratings.

7. If this doesn't solve the problem, call an electrician.

Receptacles wired backwards

"Reverse polarity" is the term used to describe the condition where electrical wires are connected to the wrong terminals of a receptacle; it's a common condition that can be hazardous if the hot (charged) side of your electrical system gets connected to certain types of lamps or equipment. It's common because it's an easy mistake to make when hooking up wires and because receptacles work fine even when the polarity is reversed. You generally don't know the condition exists unless you look for it. If you think your home's wiring is a bit haphazard or may contain some conditions of reverse polarity, it's a good idea to check for it.

You can buy a simple circuit tester (see above) for less than $20. Just plug it into all duplex receptacles; test both the top and bottom.

If the tester indicates reverse polarity:

1. Shut off the circuit breaker that serves that receptacle (the tester's lights will go out).
2. Unscrew the cover plate from the receptacle and use a voltage tester to be sure none of the wires in the electrical box are still hot (charged).
3. Unscrew or release the wires from the receptacle and refasten them to the proper terminals—white to the silver (neutral) terminal and black to the brass (hot) terminal. The bare or green wire should connect to the green screw.
4. Put the cover plate back on, turn the circuit back on, and test the receptacle again. *NOTE: If the tester indicates reverse polarity but the wires are hooked up to the proper terminals, call an electrician.*

GFCI receptacles

A special type of receptacle called a GFCI (or GFI), short for ground-fault circuit interrupter, protects kitchen, bathroom, and outdoor receptacles in a home from the serious shock that can occur where electricity and water meet. Identified by the reset and test buttons located on its face, a GFCI will sense even a tiny short and will shut down itself and, in some cases, other receptacles on the same circuit. Just push the reset button to reset the receptacles. Push the test button periodically to insure that the device is working.

DOORBELLS

Doorbells are simple electrical systems. Repairing one is normally easy and a good lesson in basic electricity—as long as you can find the key components. Because buttons, buzzers, and transformers are relatively inexpensive, replacing these faulty components usually makes more sense than trying to make involved repairs on them. Don't be intimidated by the steps involving a multi-meter (or volt-ohm meter)—see more about these important, inexpensive tools on page 105-106.

How a doorbell works

A doorbell, chime, or buzzer normally operates on low voltage—older systems may be six or eight volts, newer ones are twelve to fourteen volts for bells and buzzers, sixteen volts for chimes. To produce this power, a transformer converts standard household 120-volt current into the lower voltage. Two small-gauge wires run from the transformer to the bell or buzzer; a push-button switch interrupts one of these. When you push on the button, it completes the circuit, delivering low-voltage electricity to the bell unit.

At the bell unit, one or two spring-loaded pistons slide through the windings of an electromagnet. The electrical surge sent from the transformer charges the magnet, pulling the pistons against their springs; when the charge stops, the springs thrust the pistons against the bell or chimes: "ding dong!"

Many doorbell units make two sounds: one for the front door, the other for the back door. Terminals on the bell unit are marked "front," "back," and "trans" (for transformer). One wire from the transformer goes to the "trans" terminal; one wire from each button goes to either the "front" or "back" terminals. The button connected to the "front" terminal produces a "ding-dong" and the one secured to the "back" terminal just produces "ding."

FOR SAFETY: *The button and small-gauge wires that run from the button to the doorbell and transformer are normally safe to work on without shutting off the power. Nevertheless, be careful. Even the low-voltage side of an electrical system may carry dangerous current in certain conditions where the transformer has failed, though this is fairly rare. Avoid shock by testing the transformer first. You can also use an electrical tester (page 105-106) to check the two low-voltage terminal screws on the transformer—it should NOT light up if the transformer is working properly. See below for information on how to find the transformer.*

If you can't find the transformer, you can still check its voltage and see if it works. At the bell unit, remove one wire from the terminal marked "front." Have a helper push the button, if the button is known to be good, otherwise carefully remove the button and connect its two wires with a small wire nut (just to be safe, don't touch the bare wires at this point).

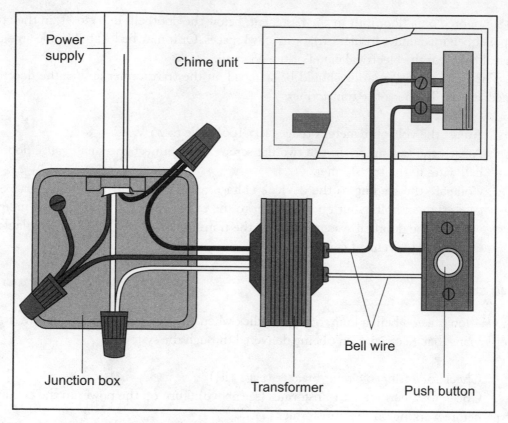

FIGURE 5.7 Doorbell Components and Wiring

Using a volt-ohm meter (set for voltage) at the bell unit, touch one test lead to the free wire from the "front" terminal and the other test lead to the terminal marked "trans." If there is no reading, start hunting for the transformer so you can replace it.

How to find and check the transformer

Sometimes finding the transformer is a challenge. It may be located inside the chimes or bell enclosure, but often it is located elsewhere. If you know where the doorbell wires run, trace along them to find the transformer's location. Newer homes often have doorbell transformers conveniently located in plain sight, high on a garage wall. Sometimes it's mounted on a floor joist in the basement, below the doorbell, in a closet, in the attic (possibly buried under insulation), or in crawl spaces. Or it may be located inside an electrical box near the electrical panel or the doorbell.

The proper voltage rating should be stamped on the transformer and/or the doorbell mechanism. To check the transformer:

1. Adjust the volt-ohm meter's (pages 105-106) scale to 25 VAC.
2. Attach the two probes to the two flat screws that connect the small gauge doorbell wires to the transformer.
3. Compare the reading to the device's voltage requirements. If it's too low or exceeds sixteen volts, shut off the power to the transformer before doing any more work on the doorbell system. Replace the transformer with a new one (available at home improvement centers).

No sounds

If you don't hear a bell, a hum, or even a click when you push the doorbell button, it often means that electricity isn't being delivered through the system.

1. Check for a tripped circuit breaker (page 104).
2. Check for a burned-out transformer (see above). Turn off the power to the circuit before working on the transformer.
3. Be sure all wires are connected securely at the transformer, the bell, and the button.
4. Remove and check the button.

Removing and checking the button.   Because the button is the primary moving part of the system, this tends to be the most likely component to fail.

1. Remove the button's attachment screws and gently pull the button out.
2. Be sure the two wires are connected securely to the screw terminals.
3. Touch a screwdriver's blade across both terminals (or remove the two wires and touch them together).

If the bell sounds, you're in luck—this is a very easy and inexpensive repair. Remove the wires and clean corrosion from the button's contacts and wire ends with fine sandpaper or electrical contact cleaner; then reconnect the wires. If the button still doesn't work, just remove and replace the button (available at hardware stores).

This button test will work if the power circuit is functional. If the button is faulty AND there is an additional problem, it won't. If the simple button test fails to ring the bell, you can make sure the button is faulty by doing a continuity test with a volt-ohm meter (set on ohms). Hold one of the meter's probes on each of the button's contacts; then push and release the button. The meter's needle should bounce up when the button is pushed and drop flat when it is released. If it doesn't, the button should be replaced.

Bell doesn't ring

If the bell doesn't ring but the transformer hums when the button is pushed:

1. Check the bell.
2. Check the piston.
3. Check the wiring.

To check the bell.   Be sure wires are connected to the terminals in the bell unit. If necessary, clean the contacts with fine sandpaper or electrical contact cleaner.

To check the piston.   It may be worn and jammed inside its sleeve or gummed up if someone has tried to oil it in the past (something you should not do). If this is the case, replace the electromagnetic/piston component or the entire bell unit.

To check the wiring.   Look for any breaks in the doorbell wiring. If you find one (or more), strip insulation from wire ends and splice with a short piece of matching wire, using properly sized wire nuts.

Doorbell hums

If your doorbell is relentlessly buzzing or humming, the button may be stuck in the contact position. If this continues for very long, the electromagnet will burn out and the bell unit won't work even if current is being delivered to it through the button. Immediately repair or replace the button (see above) or else you'll have to replace the bell unit.

TELEPHONES

If there is a problem with the phone lines that serve your house, nearly all phone companies will solve the problem without charge. Many phone companies offer a monthly plan for inside wire and phone jack problems—they charge a very small fee for this (normally less than $1.00 per month). If you have a fairly complex system, with old wires or several jacks, or if you don't want to hassle with trying to solve your own phone problems, such a plan is well worth the price. Call your telephone company's business office to inquire about this type of service.

Do not work on your own phone lines if you have a pacemaker.

Remove one of the handsets before working on any wiring to insure that the higher voltage needed to ring the phone will not shock you.

Loose connections or bad cords cause many problems. If tightening connections doesn't solve a problem, it's usually easiest to replace cords rather than to locate breaks and repair them.

Phones are dead

If one phone doesn't work, check all other phones on the same line to isolate the location of the problem. If none of them work, report the problem to your phone company from a neighbor's house or another phone.

One phone doesn't work

Be sure both the line cord and the handset cord are plugged in. If they are, plug a working phone into the dead phone's modular wall outlet. If it works, assume the problem is with the dead telephone.

Try plugging the dead phone into a working outlet. If it works there, its cord or modular plug may be making a poor connection with the first modular receptacle. Switch cords with the working phone and try again. If it works, replace the cord.

If it doesn't work with a good cord, plugged into a working outlet, the phone is probably defective. Further isolate the problem by substituting the handset from a working phone. If it works, repair or replace the dead phone's receiver. If it doesn't work, repair or replace the entire phone. Be sure the switch hook isn't stuck down or jammed.

The outlet is dead

If no telephone will work when plugged into a certain receptacle—but the phones work in other receptacles on the same line—assume that either the receptacle is bad or the wires that connect it to the rest of the system have become loose or severed.

Doesn't ring or rings too quietly

If the phone has a dial tone, adjust the ringer loudness (this adjustment is on the bottom of some phones). Also check to see if there is a switch for turning off the ringer—and turn it on.

In some cases, you can't connect more than five phones to a given line or they won't ring properly. If this is your situation, you may have to disconnect one or more phones, or at least turn their ringers off.

Rings but either can't hear the caller or can't be heard

This problem often results from a defective handset cord—check the handset cord by switching it with a good one. If that solves the problem, replace the cord. With a portable phone, substitute a transmitter from another telephone—replace if necessary.

Portable handset won't work

Some portable handsets have a static discharge protection circuit. When you walk across a carpet holding one, you may build up enough static electricity to cause the phone to turn off. If this happens, turn the handset off for a few seconds and then try it again.

Low batteries can also cause the handset to stop working, though this is usually not sudden. Recharge the handset. If that doesn't work, replace the batteries (see below).

Replace rechargeable phone's batteries

Rechargeable batteries are usually located behind a removable door on the handset. Disconnect the batteries and take them to a consumer electronics store and buy replacements.

Other problems

A number of other problems may occur if the telephone you're using is faulty. These problems include improper dialing, voice distortion, cutting in and out, and the like. Try another telephone in the receptacle to see if it works; if it does, the problem is with the telephone. In most cases, it's cheaper to buy a new phone than to have an old one repaired.

6

HEATING AND COMFORT PROBLEMS

Furnaces, air conditioners, air-delivery ductwork and equipment, air cleaners, and other components in a home that help provide warmth, cooling, and ventilation make up the "comfort systems." Most of the time these systems operate seamlessly and invisibly, providing a high degree of comfort regardless of outdoor weather conditions. But, when they break down, comfort goes out the window.

Though it's best to have a professional heating-and-air (HVAC) contractor or furnace repair technician handle major problems with your comfort systems, there are a number of tasks that you can handle yourself to keep things running smoothly. Here we will look at them. Keep this in mind: almost all comfort appliances utilize electricity to provide power and/or heat—*always disconnect the power from an appliance before working on it.*

Most work on heating and cooling equipment requires some of the same tools needed for electrical and plumbing jobs, as discussed on pages 73 and 104. You typically need screwdrivers, pliers, wrenches, a hammer, a flashlight, and so forth.

UNDERSTANDING HEATING SYSTEMS

Before you try to fix heating problems, you should have a basic understanding of how your system works. First identify whether your home has a central heating system—the predominant type—or heaters in each room that work independently of each other.

A central heating system has a primary heating appliance such as a furnace or boiler located in an out-of-the-way spot such as a basement or garage. It delivers heat throughout the house, either by pumping warmed air through a system of air ducts or by sending hot water or steam through pipes to room radiators or convectors. With both forced-air and gravity systems, one or more thermostats, operated either manually or automatically as room temperatures rise and fall, turn the heating (or cooling) plant off and on.

Homes without central heating normally utilize electric baseboard heaters or, in some cases, in-the-wall or in-floor gas heaters or radiant heat.

Central ducted air systems

In contemporary homes, ducted air systems are the most common type of central heating and cooling. If your home has an air conditioner, heat pump, or furnace, it is a ducted air system. There are two main types: forced-air and gravity.

A forced-air system.   In this system, a furnace warms air, an air conditioner cools air, or a heat pump either warms or cools air; then a blower forces the air through the system.

A gravity furnace.   In this system, convection currents (caused by the natural tendency of heated air to rise) carry heated air through the system from a furnace that is located on or below the main floor level. Gravity systems do not have blowers, tend to have very large air ducts, and can deliver only warmed air. If your system includes an air conditioner or heat pump, it is a forced-air system.

Radiant heating systems

Radiant heat is a comfortable, even type of heat that is radiated into living spaces by hot water, steam, or electric elements.

A hydronic radiant system.   This system uses a central boiler to heat water; the resulting hot water or steam then circulates through a system of pipes to room radiators or through circuitous routes of tubing that wind beneath a floor's surface to emit heat.

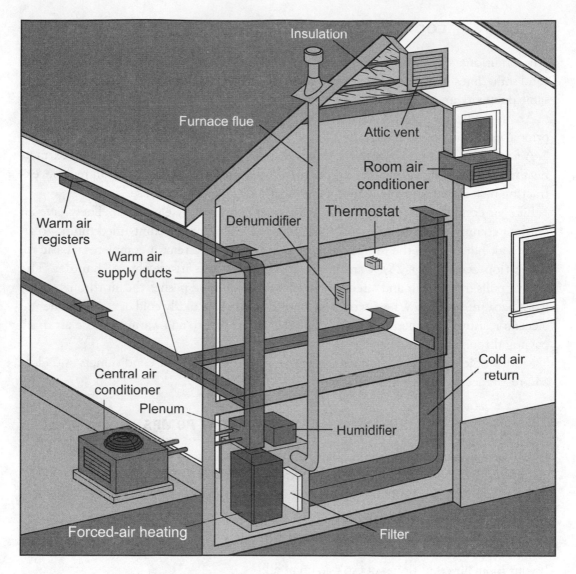

FIGURE 6.1 House Comfort Systems

Electric radiant systems.   These systems may have electric-resistance baseboard or wall registers or a system of electric cables or foils hidden beneath floors or above ceilings. When an electric current runs through an electric-resistance element, cable, or foil, it generates heat—and that heat is radiated into the room. Because radiant heating systems have very few moving parts, they rarely fail (most failures are caused by circuit overloads).

COOLING AND HEATING/COOLING SYSTEMS

Air conditioners and heat pumps are also forced-air systems. With these systems, cooled (and sometimes humidified or electronically cleaned) air is usually delivered through the same ductwork and registers used by heated air.

An *air conditioner* runs on electricity and removes heat from air with basic refrigeration principles, as discussed on page 25.

A *heat pump* can provide both heating and cooling. In the winter, a heat pump extracts heat from outside air and delivers it indoors. On hot summer days, it works in reverse, extracting heat from room air and pumping it outdoors to cool the house.

Like air conditioners, nearly all heat pumps are powered by electricity. They have an outdoor compressor/condenser unit that is connected with refrigerant-filled tubing to an indoor air handler. As the refrigerant moves through the system, it completes a basic refrigeration cycle (page 25), warming or cooling the coils inside the air handler. The blower pulls in room air and circulates it across the coils and pushes the air through ductwork back into rooms. When extra heat is needed on particularly cold days, supplemental electric-resistance elements kick on inside the air handler to add warmth to the air that's passing through.

Most problems with heat pumps are the same as those with air conditioners and electric-resistance forced-air heating systems.

AIR CONDITIONERS AND HEAT PUMPS

If you have an air conditioner or heat pump that doesn't turn on or cool properly, there are a few things you can try before you go to the hassle and expense of calling an air conditioning contractor or furnace repair technician.

Room air conditioner doesn't turn on

If your room air conditioner doesn't go on at all:

1. Check the power source first: be sure it's plugged in and turned on.
2. Then check the outlet by unplugging the air conditioner and plugging in a light that works (only for standard-voltage models—do not plug a light into a 220/240-volt receptacle!).
3. If the light doesn't go on, the circuit has probably overloaded—check the electric panel or fuse box and reset the breaker or replace the fuse (page 104).

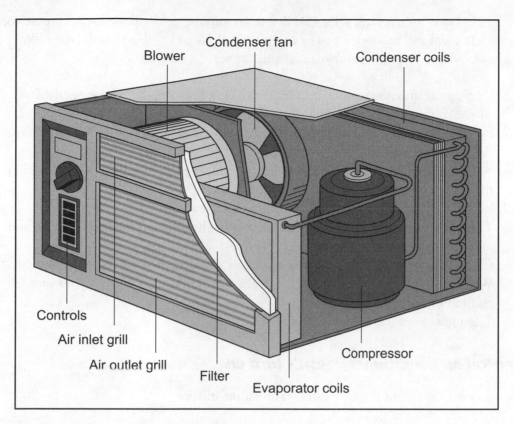

FIGURE 6.2   Room Air Conditioner

4. If the light works, it's likely that the air conditioner's switch is faulty or the thermostat needs adjustment or repair.
5. Be sure the thermostat is set to "cool" and below room temperature.
6. Refer to the manufacturer's instructions for thermostat repair. If adjusting or repairing the thermostat doesn't solve the problem, unplug the unit and call an air conditioning technician.

Room air conditioner doesn't cool

A room air conditioner that doesn't cool may need to be recharged with refrigerant, but the chances are good that it simply needs to be cleaned. You can do this work yourself, which involves disassembling the unit, or you can call a professional (see "Air Conditioning Service" in the Yellow Pages). Before attempting the work yourself, consult your owner's manual and make sure you have the right skills and tools to handle the task.

Here is what a typical owner's manual will advise:

1. Unplug the unit and remove it from the window (beware, these are heavy!). Put it where you can work on it outdoors.
2. Remove the grille and filter and unscrew the metal case. Be careful not to damage the coil's fins.
3. Wash out the filter or replace it with a new, inexpensive filter—cut-to-size foam filter fabric is available at most appliance stores.
4. Using a vacuum with a soft brush attachment, clean the inside coil's fins.
5. Then, from the fan side, spray water back through the fins (protect the wiring and motor with plastic).
6. Clean it up with a rag, making sure all drains are open. Allow it to dry thoroughly.
7. While you have the unit apart, lubricate the motor according to your owner's manual instructions.
8. Then reassemble and reinstall the unit.

Central air conditioner doesn't turn on

If your central air conditioner doesn't go on automatically:

1. Be sure the thermostat is set to "cool" and set below room temperature.
2. A central air conditioner should be on a dedicated 240-volt circuit; check the main electrical panel and any secondary circuit panels for a tripped breaker or blown fuse. If you find the problem here, reset the breaker or replace the fuse (page 104).
3. Make sure the furnace power switch is turned on and that the outdoor condenser's power switch, mounted on the outdoor unit, hasn't been shut off. Also be sure the 240-volt disconnect next to the compressor (in a metal box, usually mounted on the house wall) hasn't been shut off.
4. Turn off the power to the air conditioner and check the thermostat.
5. Remove the thermostat's cover and unscrew the wire from the Y terminal.
6. Turn the power back on.
7. Holding the wire by its insulation, touch the bare end to the R terminal; hold it there for about two minutes. If the compressor kicks on, the thermostat is faulty; replace it or call an air conditioning technician. If the compressor doesn't go on

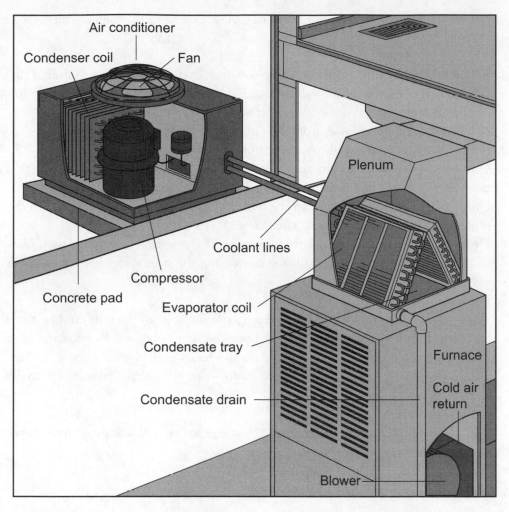

FIGURE 6.3   Central Air Conditioner

when you hold the two wires together, turn the power back off and call a service technician.

Central air conditioner doesn't cool

A central air conditioner that runs but doesn't cool may just need to be cleaned. Plan to do this on a relatively warm day. First look for your owner's manual and, if you can find

---

it, follow its instructions. If you can't find it, request one from the manufacturer (see resources, page 229).

1. Before you begin, turn off the power to the unit; there is normally a shutoff or disconnect panel on the house wall next to the outdoor compressor. Otherwise, shut off the air conditioner's 240-volt circuit at the main electrical panel.
2. Rake leaves and debris away from the outdoor condenser.
3. Remove any protective grille or cover from the condenser's fins.
4. Use a soft brush to clean dirt and debris from the fins; then vacuum them with a brush attachment (be careful not to bend or damage them).
5. Unscrew and lift the top grille off the unit, if possible. If the fan is attached to the grille, be careful not to pull any wires loose.
6. From inside the unit, hose out the fins (protect the wiring and motor with plastic). If your owner's manual calls for lubricating the motor, do that now—don't overlubricate.
7. Then reassemble the unit.
8. To test it, turn the power on and set the thermostat to turn the unit on. Let it run for a few minutes; then feel the two pipes that connect to the condenser unit (slide any insulation back). One pipe should feel warm, the other cool. Otherwise, call an air conditioning technician—the refrigerant may need to be recharged.

NOTE: *To avoid straining an air conditioner's compressor, wait at least five minutes between turning it off at the thermostat and turning it back on.*

Water pools next to air conditioner

Air conditioners and high-efficiency combustion furnaces create significant condensation, which exits through a plastic drain tube. This water should go into a floor drain or be carried away by a small "condensate pump." If water is pooling at the base of the appliance, something may be blocking the water's flow or leaking, or the pump may not be working.

1. Look to see if one of the tubes is leaking. If it is, replace it.
2. Test the condensate pump by pouring water into its pan. If the pump doesn't start, either it isn't receiving power, or it is broken. Be sure that it's plugged in and reset the circuit breaker (page 104). If it's broken, either get it repaired or replace it.
3. If the pump runs but doesn't empty the pan, the ball-like check valve just before the discharge tube is probably stuck. Unscrew the check valve and loosen the ball

inside it. Look for an obstruction. If it appears that a condensation drain tube is clogged with algae, remove it if possible (you may have to cut it and replace it later with a coupling). Run a wire through the tube to clear it. To kill algae, pour a diluted solution of bleach (one part bleach to sixteen parts water) through the tube.

With an air conditioner, ice may be blocking the tube. If this is the case, be sure the filter isn't dirty. If the filter appears to be fine, the air conditioner's refrigerant supply is probably low. This is when it's time to call an air conditioning technician.

Heat pump trips circuit breaker

Most heat pumps have auxiliary heating elements that provide heat when the weather gets really cold because the heat pump's efficiency drops too low. These elements automatically turn on at a fairly low temperature: around 20°F. When they come on, they may be drawing too much power, which trips the circuit breakers.

FANS AND VENTILATION

A fan is essentially an electric motor with propeller or drum-like blades. With bath and range-hood fans, the easiest fix for a motor that has burned out or stopped running is often to shut off the power, open up the fan, and replace the fan motor. A project like this usually doesn't involve doing any electrical wiring—most fan motors simply plug into a receptacle mounted inside the housing.

Fan doesn't work

When a fan doesn't work at all, be sure it is receiving electrical power—that it is plugged in and receiving power from the circuit breaker or fuse box (page 104). Look for a limit switch on the fan motor. If the limit switch has tripped, reset it.

Works but no (or poor) air flow

This is usually caused by a loose or broken belt that runs from the fan motor to the blower drum. Tighten or replace the belt. In some cases, it's easiest to call an appliance repair person for replacement.

Ceiling fan hums

If your ceiling fan makes a humming noise when it runs, you may be able to eliminate the noise by changing the control. This is a relatively easy fix, but it may not work if your fan has a cheaply made motor. Be sure to buy a control with an anti-hum feature and is compatible with your fan; the amperage rating must be equal or greater than the demands of your fan. Multiple fans or fans with lights may require special controls.

1. Turn off the power to the fan at the circuit breaker (page 103).
2. Check the fan at the switch to be sure it's off.
3. Remove the faceplate and the switch. Use a voltage tester to be sure the wires connected to the fan switch are not hot (charged).
4. Disconnect the wires from the switch.
5. Straighten the ends of the wires in the electrical box, if necessary, and twist them together with the wires on the new anti-hum fan control.
6. Twist on wire nuts. Screw the control to the electrical box, attach the faceplate, and restore the power.

Ceiling fan wobbles

Though a little wobble is typical for ceiling fans, significant wobble can be dangerous. Begin by checking for the source of the wobble. In many cases, wobble happens when a fan has been hung from a regular ceiling electrical box instead of an electrical box that's rated for fans. Because of its weight and constant movement, a fan exerts far more force on the electrical box than does a light.

If a fan works its way loose, it could fall.

1. Unscrew and lower the bracket housing at the ceiling. Check the electrical box for a label that designates it as a fan-rated box. Also check to see how it's fastened. U-bolts or lag screws should connect the metal box to a bracket or solid wood block in the attic.
2. If the fan hangs from the wrong type of box or is clearly undersupported, call a fan-installation specialist, an electrician, or a home handyperson to solve the problem.
3. If you can't determine the type of support from below, you may have to climb into the attic and check, but before you do, see if you can solve the problem.
4. Wiggle the support bracket. If it isn't firm, tighten it.

5. If your fan hangs from a drop rod, as most do, be sure the ball joint at the top of the drop rod is properly engaged with the fan support bracket.
6. Check and, if necessary, tighten all bolts and screws.
7. Measure to see if the blade tips hang an even distance from the ceiling. If they don't, one or more of the blades may be bent or warped. Report this problem to the manufacturer; most offer replacements.

FORCED-AIR HEATING

A majority of American homes are equipped with forced-air central heating systems. Inside the furnace of a typical forced-air system, fuel—either some type of combustion fuel or electricity—is converted to heat.

Combustion furnaces

In combustion furnaces, natural gas, propane, or oil is piped into a combustion chamber where it is mixed with air and ignited by a pilot light, spark, or similar device. The burner heats an air chamber, called a heat exchanger, and the exhaust gasses are carried outside through a flue. As discussed above, heated air is pushed through a forced-air system by a blower or moves naturally through a gravity system. In terms of repairs, gravity furnaces have the same combustion problems as forced-air systems, but they don't have blower breakdowns because they don't have blowers.

Electric-resistance furnaces

These furnaces work like a hair dryer: electric heating elements heat the air, and a blower pushes the warmed air through the system. Because combustion doesn't occur in an electric-resistance furnace, it doesn't need a flue. Most problems are caused by an interruption in the delivery of power, faulty heating elements, or blower breakdowns.

Regarding repairs

Normally, forced-air systems are very reliable. You can probably handle fixing minor problems yourself, but you're better off calling a heating contractor if a few basic repair steps don't work. Be aware that in many areas the utility company will send a technician to your home to check—and often repair—minor furnace problems for free. Call your utility to find out whether this is part of the service they offer before you go to the expense of hiring a furnace repair technician.

Gas leak

If you smell natural gas in your home or near the furnace, do not light any matches or turn off or on any switches. If the gas odor is strong, immediately evacuate your house, leaving the door open, and call your gas utility or the fire department from a neighbor's phone. Do not return to your home until you are sure it is safe.

If the smell of gas is faint, follow the steps for dryer problems under "Smells of natural gas" on page 40.

No heat

Most heating system failures are caused by thermostat malfunctions, a tripped circuit breaker or blown fuse, or—in the case of combustion furnaces—a pilot light that has gone out. If the heat doesn't come on even when you adjust the thermostat to a setting above room temperature:

1. Be sure the thermostat is set to "Heat" (if yours is a heating and cooling system). If it isn't, turn it to "Heat."
2. Be sure the furnace's circuit breaker is on or that its fuse has not blown (see page 104). Check both the main electrical panel and any secondary subpanels that supply power to the unit. If the circuit has blown or tripped, reset the circuit breaker or replace the fuse (page 104). If the circuit blows again, there is a probably a short in the electrical system providing power to the furnace. Either call an electrical contractor or see page 99 for electrical repairs.
3. Be sure the furnace's power switch is turned on; it is usually located next to or inside the furnace cabinet. If it isn't on, turn it on and wait a few minutes for the furnace to engage.
4. The motor may need to be reset because of an overload. Look for a reset button near the blower motor's housing and, if you find one, press it. If nothing happens, wait about thirty minutes for the motor to cool; then try the reset button again.
5. Turn off the power to the furnace at the main electrical panel or subpanel. Look for a fuse in the power switch. If there is one there, it may have blown. Replace the fuse (be sure to follow instructions in your owner's manual). If you don't have

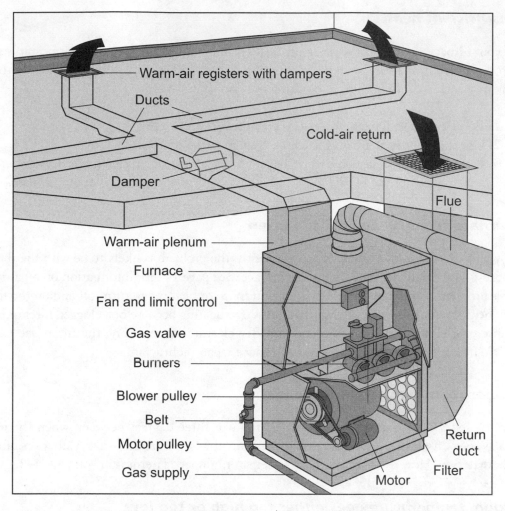

Warm-air registers with dampers

Ducts

Cold-air return

Damper

Flue

Warm-air plenum

Furnace

Fan and limit control

Gas valve

Burners

Blower pulley

Belt

Motor pulley

Gas supply

Return duct

Filter

Motor

FIGURE 6.4   Forced-Air Furnace

an owner's manual or are not clear about what it will take to do this, call a furnace repair technician.

6. With a gas furnace, the pilot light may have gone out or the gas valve may be shut off. Check the furnace's ignition, as discussed on page 139.

7. If it still doesn't work, be sure the thermostat isn't faulty (see page 142).

8. If none of this works, call a heating contractor or furnace repair technician.

Insufficient heat

If your furnace runs and provides some heat but not enough, be sure the thermostat is set properly. Try raising the set temperature five degrees and waiting a few minutes. If that doesn't work, be sure nothing is blocking the flow of warm air.

1. Be sure the room heating registers are open.
2. Check the furnace filter. If it's dirty, change it (see page 138).
3. If these simple steps don't work, have a furnace repair technician check out your system—either the blower isn't working properly or the system is out of balance.

Furnace turns on and off too often

If your furnace cycles off and on too frequently, the problem is likely to be with the thermostat—especially with a combustion furnace. See page 142 for information on repairing this problem. When an electric-resistance furnace or heat pump turns off and on too frequently, the problem may be that the unit is overheating because of a clogged filter or because of a blower that is malfunctioning. Try cleaning or replacing the filter (see page 138). If that doesn't do the trick, call a furnace repair technician.

Major room temperature swings

When room temperatures swing more than about three degrees between when the furnace goes off and on again, it generally means that the furnace isn't cycling on often enough. See "How to adjust the heat anticipator," under "Thermostat" on page 142.

Room temperature goes either too high or too low

When room temperature rises higher or drops lower than the set temperature on the thermostat, it usually means that the thermostat is improperly calibrated or installed where it doesn't sense a proper sampling of room air. See page 142.

Blower runs continuously

This may be caused by two things: the thermostat mounted on the wall or the limit switch located on the furnace just below the plenum (the box that distributes heated air to all of the ducts). The limit switch is designed to shut off the furnace if the air in the plenum gets too hot.

Check the thermostat to see if the "Fan" switch has been turned on. If it has, turn it to "Off" or to "Auto." If it is set to "Off" or "Auto" already, the furnace's limit switch must be adjusted.

Call a furnace repair technician to adjust the limit switch or, if you are handy with this type of repair, follow the instructions in your owner's manual to reset the pointers on the fan side of the limit control. The lower pointer should be set to about 90°F and the upper one should be at about 115°F.

Furnace squeals

Squealing sounds from a forced-air furnace generally occur when the belt that connects the motor to the fan slips. If the blower is making a grinding noise, shut off the unit and call a furnace repair technician—the motor's bearings are probably shot.

In most cases, the belt is improperly aligned or worn and needs replacement. Follow the instructions in your owner's manual (if you don't have one, contact the manufacturer and ask for one; see resources, page 229).

This job involves removing the access panel, loosening a couple of bolts that hold the blower motor at the proper tension, and realigning or adjusting the belt. In many cases, it's a good idea to remove the belt and buy a replacement at the hardware store. When reinstalling the belt, be careful not to overtighten it—this can ruin the motor bearings.

Furnace rattles

If the furnace makes rattling noises when it runs, be sure the cover panels are screwed on tight. If they aren't, tighten them. Other noises may be coming from squealing belts (see above), or rattling ductwork (see below).

Air ducts are noisy

Many heating ducts are metal, so they conduct noise quite readily from the air-handling unit to your rooms. To break the conduction of sound, you can have a heating contractor insert flexible insulation ductwork between the furnace or air conditioner and the duct-work runs.

If you hear a pinging or popping sound coming from the ductwork, this may be caused by thermal expansion or by air blowing past a loose flap of metal. Track along the duct runs, listening for the sound. If you find it, make a small dent in the sheet metal to provide a more rigid surface that's less likely to move as it heats and cools.

Basic forced-air maintenance

A little maintenance goes a long way toward keeping your forced-air equipment working properly. Start by cleaning or replacing the filter. With forced-air furnace systems, air returning to the furnace's blower first passes through an air filter designed to catch dust and debris and help clean the air before it's recycled to your home.

A good furnace filter can help reduce allergens but isn't designed to significantly improve air quality in your home. For that, you'll need a special air filter (talk to a heating specialist about this).

When typical filters become clogged with debris, they cut down on a furnace's efficiency and, over time, can cause parts to wear out faster. Change filters quarterly or sooner if they look dirty. Pleated fabric filters are a good, inexpensive choice for reducing dust and allergens.

Here's how to maintain your forced-air system:

1. Turn off the power to the unit.
2. Look for the door or panel that conceals the blower; sometimes this is marked "Filter." Lift this door or panel off of its holding hooks or unscrew its retaining screws to remove it.
3. Standard filters are mounted next to or under the blower motor. Slide the filter out along its tracks. Check to see whether it is a disposable filter or intended to be cleaned and replaced—this should be marked on the filter's edge, along with directions for cleaning if applicable. If it's a disposable filter, its size will probably be printed on the frame's edge also. Make a note of its size.
4. Buy a replacement and slide it back into place, noting that arrows stamped on the side indicate the proper direction of airflow; be sure you face these in the proper direction.
5. While you have the furnace open, it's a good idea to vacuum out the area around the blower. If possible, slide out the fan unit and clean each fan blade with a toothbrush; then vacuum with a brush attachment on a vacuum cleaner.
6. Look for oil ports on the motor, normally located near the motor shaft. If the motor has these, apply two or three drops of nondetergent motor oil into each port (you may have to remove a cover plate to do this). Note: Most contemporary motors don't require lubrication, but motors with oil ports should be lubricated once a year.
7. Look for worn belts between the motor and pulleys. If you see any, see "Furnace squeals" on page 137.

GAS BURNER FIXES

Gas burners serve as the primary source of heat in a variety of home appliances: water heaters, gas dryers, and gas cooktops and ovens, and—of course—furnaces and boilers. When the burner fails, most gas appliances are designed to stop working altogether to prevent a gas leak.

As a rule, it's best to have gas burner problems fixed by your gas utility service person or a qualified heating technician, but there are a few steps you can take to avoid paying for a service call.

How to check your furnace's ignition

Your gas- or oil-burning furnace must be receiving fuel to work. On a gas-fired furnace, be sure the valve on the gas pipe is turned on (the lug or handle should be in line with the gas pipe). On an oil furnace, check the fuel supply.

Unless your furnace has electronic ignition, be sure the pilot light is lit. Check your owner's manual or instructions posted inside the furnace cabinet for pilot light information, or see below. If necessary, relight the pilot.

Look for a reset switch (see your owner's manual) and push it. If the furnace ignites but fails again, call a furnace repair technician.

On an electronic-ignition furnace, turn down the thermostat or turn the power switch off and then on again to reset the ignition control module. Listen for the sound of the spark or watch for the hot surface ignitor to glow (see your owner's manual). If the furnace doesn't ignite, call a furnace repair technician.

Pilot goes out

If the pilot won't stay lit, the thermocouple may be loose or faulty, the pilot orifice may be clogged, or the pilot light's flame may be set too low and in need of adjustment.

You can clear a clogged orifice with a piece of thin wire, such as a bread tie with the paper stripped off of it. Be sure to turn off the gas to the furnace first! Also shut off the switch or circuit breaker that controls power to the furnace. Just poke the thin wire into the tiny orifice where the pilot flame normally burns to knock off any ash or debris.

Some pilots have a flame adjustment screw for adjusting the flame. To adjust this, refer to your owner's manual. Normally, this is simply a matter of turning the flame adjustment screw to achieve a full, steady $1^{1}/_{2}$-inch to 2-inch flame that doesn't have any yellow in it.

Gas burner doesn't work

Most appliances that utilize gas burners need electrical power in order to operate. If the burner doesn't work at all:

1. Be sure the circuit breaker serving the appliance is "On" or that its fuse has not blown (see page 104). Check both the main electrical panel and any secondary subpanels that supply power to the furnace or appliance. If necessary, reset the circuit breaker or replace the fuse (page 104). If the circuit blows again, there is probably a short in the electrical system. Call an electrician or furnace repair technician or see page 99 for electrical repairs.
2. Be sure that the appliance's switch is turned on and that the appliance is plugged in (when applicable). The switch may be on the appliance or, in the case of a gas furnace, next to or inside the furnace cabinet. If it isn't on, turn it on and wait a few minutes.
3. Be sure the thermostat or heat dial is set properly.
4. If the appliance has a pilot light, be sure it's working (see page 139).
5. If none of this works, call your gas utility or an appliance service technician.

Burner doesn't turn off

If the burner stays on and will not go off, the gas valve or furnace limit switch is defective. Immediately turn off the gas to the furnace by turning the inlet valve so that it is perpendicular to the gas pipe. Call your utility company or a furnace technician.

OIL BURNER FIXES

It's best to have a furnace repair technician solve most problems that occur with oil burners. One way to avoid problems is to have an oil-burning furnace or boiler serviced annually. Here are a few steps you can take to avoid an unnecessary service call:

Burner doesn't work

An oil burner won't work at all if it isn't receiving electrical power, if the thermostat is broken or turned off, or if a flame sensor in the burner or heat sensor in the stack have signaled the unit to shut off.

Burner doesn't light but works

This is usually caused by low oil level but may be caused by loose or defective parts. If filling the tank doesn't solve the problem, call a service technician.

Burner goes off and on

For this problem, clean or replace the filter. If that doesn't solve the problem, call a service technician.

HOT WATER HEAT

This type of heating employs a boiler and a network of pipes that delivers heated water (or steam) to convectors or radiators located in rooms. Types of systems vary, so if you are unsure of the proper maintenance for your system, it's a good idea to hire a service person to teach you. With periodic care, these systems should operate virtually problem free. When problems do occur, there are a few things you can handle yourself. For others, call a plumber or radiant heating professional.

No heat

If the convectors are cold:

1. Check the power at the master switch, circuit breaker, or fuse.
2. Be sure the boiler is receiving fuel—that the fuel inlet valve is open.
3. Check the thermostat (see page 142).
4. Bleed the air from convectors by opening each air valve with a wrench until water squirts out (catch the water in a bucket or bowl). Be ready for hot water.

Hammering noises

With a steam system, hammering noises may occur if the radiator isn't sloped slightly. Place small shims beneath one end to slope the radiator toward the outflow.

Inlet valve stem leaks

If the inlet valve leaks, the culprit is usually a worn valve stem packing. Repairing this involves draining water in the system until it drops below the valve, then dismantling the valve and replacing the packing (this is very similar to a faucet, discussed on page 81). If you don't know how to drain water from the system, call a plumber or radiant heating service person.

THERMOSTATS

Many heating and cooling problems first become evident when you adjust the thermostat—and the thermostat is often the cause of the malfunction. Fortunately, thermostat problems are easy to fix. At the very worst, you can replace a thermostat yourself for under $50.

Thermostat misreads temperature

When your thermostat says one temperature and you know the room is another, it may be dirty, tilted on the wall, or located where it can't get a proper reading.

1. Turn the power off to the heating system (see page 103).
2. Remove the thermostat's cover.
3. Use a soft brush or vacuum with brush attachment to gently and carefully remove dust and dirt. If the thermostat has two parallel metal strips, wipe them off with a soft cloth.
4. Look for corrosion. You can try to remove corrosion with electronic contact cleaner. If it's an outdated thermostat, consider replacing it with a newer model.
5. If you have a mechanical (not electronic/programmable) thermostat, be sure it is mounted level on the wall. Check it with a small bubble level.
6. A thermostat should be mounted about five feet from the floor and located where it can easily sense an air sample that is consistent with room temperatures. This means it should not be put in a corner, behind a door, in a closet, near a window or door, or near a heat source. If it is mounted in one of these spots, consider relocating it. This involves rerouting wires, so unless you're pretty handy with this sort of thing, it's probably better to hire an electrical contractor or heating technician to do the work.

How to adjust the heat anticipator

If your gas- or oil-burning furnace cycles on and off too frequently or there are major swings in room temperature before the furnace goes on, the thermostat may just need a simple adjustment.

To adjust the thermostat:

1. Remove the thermostat's cover. For a mechanical thermostat with a mercury switch (a small vial filled with mercury), first use a small level to make sure the thermostat is mounted level on the wall. If it isn't level, it won't measure temperatures properly.
2. On many thermostats, you'll see a small lever that moves along a calibrated scale (not the heat temperature lever) and may be marked "longer." This is the heat-anticipator adjustment.
3. Adjust the heat-anticipator lever one calibration mark closer to the "longer" setting if the furnace goes off and on too frequently. If the furnace allows room temperature to drop too low or rise too high before the furnace goes on or off, move the lever one mark away from the "longer" setting.
4. Wait several hours for the thermostat to stabilize at this new setting.
5. Repeat the adjustment if necessary.
6. If making these adjustments doesn't solve the problem, consider replacing your thermostat.

To check your thermostat

If your heating equipment isn't working properly, maybe the thermostat is defective. Here's how to see if it's any good:

1. With the power to the furnace off, remove the thermostat or thermostat cover to expose the wires.
2. Unscrew and remove the two wires from their terminals. Do not let them fall back in through the hole in the wall (you can wrap them around a pencil if necessary). If there are more than two wires, pick red and white—normally, these are standard colors for power and heat. For a problem with cooling, you would choose red and green.
3. Wrap the two wires together.
4. Turn the power on and watch the furnace. If the blower goes on and the furnace burner ignites, the thermostat is defective. Replace it. If the burner does not ignite, the wires from the thermostat to the furnace may be broken or disconnected. (If you're checking the air conditioning, only the blower will go on.) Check and tighten terminal screws at all wire connections. If it still doesn't work, call a service technician.

Heating and Comfort Problems

7

INTERIOR SURFACE PROBLEMS

Typical problems with your home's interior surfaces such as walls, ceilings, and floors are cosmetic: holes, scuffs, cracks, and the like. This means that the problems are rarely urgent and that, because the work is indoors and easily accessible, these are the kinds of repairs that most homeowners can tackle. On the other hand, because these repairs are cosmetic—and interior surfaces are highly visible—it's important to do them well.

For most interior surface repairs, you'll need an assortment of basic carpentry, painting, and, where applicable, wallpapering tools.

CABINETS

As a rule, few things go wrong with cabinets—they typically wear out from continual use, and when that happens, doors sag or drawers stick. Here is how to take care of the few kinds of problems that do occur.

Door swings poorly

Cabinet doors that get a lot of use can, over time, go out of adjustment for a variety of reasons. Most problems are easily corrected in the following order:

1. Tighten the hinge mounting screws. If this helps only for a while, or if the holes are so worn that the screws no longer hold, remove the screws one at a time and insert wood slivers or matchsticks into the holes, then replace the screws. A drop of glue on the slivers makes this repair even stronger.
2. Replace the hinge screws with longer or larger screws. This usually requires drilling deeper pilot holes, which may not be possible on some cabinets, and larger diameter screws may not fit the hinges as well as the originals, so consider this option carefully before you start.
3. Move the hinges. If the screw holes or mounting locations are badly worn, try shifting each hinge to a new spot where the wood is stronger. This works best if the hardware is hidden, because the old locations will be visible, especially where the hinge leaves mount to the face of the doors.

Door hinges need adjustment

Simple adjustments are easy to make, and many cabinets have hinges that allow you to make micro-adjustments in any direction.

For plain hinges, loosen the mounting screws just enough so that the hinges can move but not so much that the door droops. Prop the door so that it is square with the cabinet opening, using shims if necessary, then retighten the screws.

Most European-style hinges have built-in adjustment setups, and there are several types. One has a single screw connecting the two halves of the hinge. Loosen this screw slightly and you can reposition the door vertically or horizontally. Another type has a sliding bar with a setscrew for horizontal adjustments and a separate screw for vertical adjustments. The newest hinges have snap-on mounting plates that let you adjust height and depth and even remove the doors completely without affecting the adjustment.

Drawer stuck or jammed

A drawer that's off its track can be difficult to remove without damaging it even more. Try working the thin blade of a putty knife between the drawer and the runner and then gently tapping the drawer back in line. If you're successful, the drawer slide will pop into place; you can then remove the drawer and correct the problem that made it slip its track in the first place. Overloaded drawers—either too heavy or with contents piled too high—are often the cause of jams. Also check that the runners haven't worked loose or been forced out of alignment.

Drawer slide broken

Broken or damaged drawer slides have a way of reminding you over and over that they need to be repaired. In some cases, the problem is merely that one or more of the mounting screws on the slide has fallen out—you can repair this by replacing the screws. More commonly, the glides have become bent or broken. In this case, the easiest remedy is to replace the glides.

1. Remove the drawer by pulling it out and then lifting the front to disengage the drawer from its track.
2. Check the glides on the drawer and inside the cabinet. If they're just bent or misaligned, reshape them with a pair of pliers and slide the drawers back in.
3. If something is broken, unscrew the glides both from the drawer and from the cabinet.
4. Buy replacements at a hardware store or home improvement center. Be sure to take along one complete glide (both halves) as a sample of what you'll need.
5. Screw the new glides to the cabinet and drawer and replace the drawer.

Drawer box broken

Drawers are sturdy but simple in construction. When they break, more often than not it's caused by either a split in the wood or a glue joint that has come apart. Fix splits by re-aligning and gluing together the broken pieces (use wood glue); clamp them together for at least an hour. Do the same with separated joints; but first carefully clean away as much of the old glue as possible without damaging the joint or the wood itself.

Shelf paper won't come off

To lift old shelf paper, you'll want to warm and dissolve the adhesive backing. To start, peel up a corner. Continue to lift as you spray warm water on the backing. Stubborn residue can usually be removed with vegetable oil. Before painting, wash with sudsy water, rinse, and dry.

Cabinet wood is damaged

Repairs to the cabinet itself depend on whether the damage is structural—say, at a hinge location—or cosmetic, such as on a door face or visible part of the cabinet carcass. Structural repairs are easiest if the wood has cracked or even split away. If it's a clean break, a little wood glue can make the repair area stronger than the original piece. If a chunk has been gouged out, or if the wood is shattered beyond reassembly, you can often fix it in one of two ways:

1. Cut a new piece of the same size and the same wood species, if possible, and mechanically fasten it with dowels, screws, glue, or whatever means is most effective. Carpenters call this replacement piece a "dutchman." A piece that's slightly oversize can be sanded down to match the original, and if the cabinet is stained or painted you may be able to do some artistic retouching to blend it all together and make the repair nearly invisible.
2. Use an epoxy wood repair kit to fill the damaged area; then sand and stain or paint to match. This material works amazingly well, and the repair is often as strong as the wood. An added benefit is that the epoxy filler is also waterproof, so it can be used where the wood damage was caused by wet conditions.

If the damage is to an area that's prominently visible, it may be difficult to do a "seamless" repair. Small nicks and chips can be filled with plastic wood filler. This is sold in colors to match most wood stains, and it's available in putty consistency or in wax-like sticks. Experiment with blending and color-matching in an unseen area before attempting a repair on a cabinet face.

About painting cabinets

Touch-ups are most effective if you use the manufacturer's original paint or stain colors, although your cabinets may have faded over time. If you know the brand, contact a local distributor or cabinet retailer; these businesses usually stock touch-up paints, even for cabinets and colors that are no longer produced. Spot painting touch-ups are more difficult on parts of cabinets that have become discolored, such as around cooking areas affected by heat and airborne grease and soot. Often the best remedy is to repaint or stain the entire area. If you start and end at a cabinet edge, the slight color change from the original shade will be less noticeable.

About refacing cabinets

When your cabinet doors and fronts are worn beyond repair, or when you're just tired of looking at the same old thing, you have two choices: replace them entirely, or reface them. Refacing is such a popular option today that there are probably a number of trades people in your area (check the Yellow Pages) that specialize in this work alone. If you want to tackle it yourself, you can do a partial, intermediate, or complete refacing job.

At the least difficult level, you can add new hardware, moldings, or wood appliqués to plain cabinet doors and fronts. Depending on how elaborate you make it, this refacing can simply dress up your old cabinets or change their appearance entirely. Adding a new paint color or multicolor scheme makes this refacing even more effective.

The next step up is to buy new doors for your existing cabinets. Home centers and cabinet shops sell a wide variety of sizes and styles, and replacing an all-too-familiar panel door with a sleek new European style door—or a plain flush door with a raised panel style—can effect an amazing transformation. This option works best with overlay doors, which cover the stiles and rails and limit the amount of reworking necessary on those areas.

If you want to go the distance and completely reface your old cabinets, you can buy high-quality, self-sticking veneers in just about any wood species. Some of these veneers have a peel-off paper backing, and some are applied with heat. Professional cabinet refacers use special heat tools, but an ordinary clothes iron works just as well. After the veneer is on, you stain and finish it the same as any other new wood.

CARPETS

Carpets are durable floor coverings, but they can be stained, torn, or damaged. As you will see in what follows, some repairs are considerably easier to make than others.

Stained carpet

The most common problem with carpets is staining. Immediately following a spill, remove any semisolid material with a rounded spoon and place a clean, white absorbent material such as paper towel or a kitchen towel over the spot and press to draw the liquid away from the carpet fibers. The idea is to BLOT, not to scrub. As soon as the towels are wet, replace with dry ones and continue the process. Then place dry ones on the spot and weight them down with a heavy object. Again, replace them when they grow wet.

Use a carpet spot remover, following the manufacturer's instructions—but first pretest it in an inconspicuous place to avoid damaging the carpet.

Carpet snags

Fixing snags in looped carpets is a relatively easy job with the help of a nailset or small screwdriver and carpet seam sealer, available from home centers. Count the number of curls along the pulled-out strand and make a single cut to allow the right number of loops for each side of the run. Outline the run with masking tape. Apply the sealer/adhesive inside the run; then, with the nailset or small screwdriver, press the portions of yarn that have old adhesive stuck to them back down into the backing, creating properly sized loops.

Pet odors in carpet

If the odors are from a pet that still lives in the house, eliminating odors is probably a waste of time and money; most pets will revisit their favorite spots regardless. Ridding carpets of odors from pet urine is expensive, time consuming, and not always effective. Nevertheless, you can try this:

1. Call a carpet installer and have the carpet and pad removed; dispose of the pad and order a new one.
2. At a pet store, buy a liquid, enzyme-based odor remover and ask to rent a black light.
3. Go over the carpet and over the now exposed subfloor with the black light to locate every trace of urine, which should show up under the light. Circle the areas with chalk.
4. Saturate the marked areas on the carpet and subfloor with the enzyme, following label directions. Allow to dry completely; it usually takes several days.
5. Seal the subfloor with a stain blocker, such as KILZ; then have a new pad and the carpet reinstalled.
6. If necessary, have the carpet professionally cleaned.

Split seams and tears

For tears or problems with seams in wall-to-wall carpeting, it's a good idea to contact a professional carpet installer—for several reasons. To do the work properly, you must release the tension of the carpet, a job that requires a few special carpet installation tools and experience in working with carpeting. Most carpet installers are relatively affordable to hire for small jobs.

Carpet dents

Heavy furniture can leave indentations in carpet. To prevent this, put furniture glides or cups under the furniture legs, or occasionally move your furniture a couple of inches to give your carpet a break. When areas have become crushed, use a coin to work the carpet pile back upright; then hold a steam iron not more than four inches above the spot (don't touch the rug!) until the iron warms the fibers.

Carpet fading

Once carpet has faded, there is no way to revive the color, so protect it from damage by the sun's ultraviolet light with the help of shades or other window coverings. Or utilize window glazing or films that reduce ultraviolet rays.

Carpet rippling

If your wall-to-wall carpet suddenly appears to be rippled, it's probably because of high humidity. Normally, this problem disappears on its own when the climate becomes drier. If it doesn't, have a carpet installer restretch your carpet.

Sprouting tufts

If a tuft rises above the rest of the carpet pile, do not pull it out—just snip it off flush with the surface.

Squeaks beneath carpet

How you deal with squeaks beneath a carpet depends upon whether or not you have access to the underside of the floor.

Access below.   If you do have access from below, go under the floor and have someone walk around above to locate the squeak(s). If necessary, remove the insulation. Check for nails that have missed the floor joists and are rubbing up against the joists, causing the squeak. If you find these types of nails, cut them off with a good pair of diagonal cutters. Also check for areas where the subfloor may not be nailed down with enough nails. If you find spots that are loose because of insufficient nailing, slide small glued shims (small wooden wedges) in the gaps under the subfloor.

Nailing solid blocking between floor joists can also strengthen the support for subflooring, eliminating squeaks.

If finished flooring is obviously raised off of the subfloor, go below and drill a couple of 1/2-inch holes through the subfloor but not through the finish flooring. Press the nozzle of a carpenter's glue bottle into the holes and force glue up into the space between subfloor and finish flooring. Then have someone stand on the raised spot while you drive screws through the subfloor into the finish floor from below. Be sure screws all long enough to grip the finish floor without going all the way through.

Another method is to pre-drill pieces of two-by-two, eighteen inches long, at convenient angles for driving 2-inch or 2 1/2-inch screws into the subfloor and joists. Partially drive the screws into the pre-drilled holes. Coat with yellow carpenter's glue and power-drive the screws into place.

No access below.   If you can't get beneath the floor or if the underside is covered with a finished ceiling, drive trim screws (with very small heads). Walk on the floor to help determine the problem zones; then drive the small-headed screws through the carpet, padding, and subfloor into the joists. The most effective way to place these screws is to drive them into joists at an angle from both sides (in a V formation). Predrill screw holes through the subfloor and make a small incision in carpet so you don't wind its fibers onto the drill bit. If this doesn't work and the squeaks are too bothersome, you may have to pull back the carpet and screw down the subfloor. Call a carpet installer to handle reinstallation.

COUNTERTOPS

Countertops receive a great deal of wear and tear on a daily basis. Some hold up better than others; most materials—even stone and tile—can suffer from some types of damage. For information on repairing tile, see page 162. Here is a closer look at how to solve common problems with laminate and stone counters.

Laminate chipped or burned

Plastic laminate is popular for countertops because it offers a seamless, unbroken, and impervious surface. However, it can break if something hits it hard enough, and it will melt and scorch if you put something hot on it. You can fill small chip-outs with epoxy glue, but the odds of matching a laminate color or pattern are slim. Slight surface burns can sometimes be scrubbed away with a mild abrasive cleanser. Deeper burns usually can't be removed because they char the thin laminate all the way through. You can try cutting away the damage and filling the void with epoxy.

Laminate lifting

If a laminate surface starts to peel or lift at an edge, it means that either the glue or the substrate below it has failed. If the substrate is in poor condition (damp or rotted, for example) you won't be successful trying to glue the laminate back in place. If the substrate is sound, you can usually reglue the laminate using contact cement.

Paint both the underside of the laminate and the substrate with a thin coat of contact cement; then allow both to dry until tacky before mating the pieces (follow the manufacturer's directions for application and set-up time). It's critical to get the glue all the way to the joint where the two materials meet and to bond them so that no air voids are trapped between the joint and the edge of the laminate. Contact cement is a strong and aggressive glue—once the cemented pieces touch, you won't be able to pull them apart to realign them. After the pieces are joined, place a weight atop them until the glue dries.

Laminate countertop damaged

Laminate as a material is difficult to repair. If your countertops are the squared-off type and they're sound, it is possible to have new laminate applied over the top. If they are the rounded-over (post-formed) type, or if the laminate is not sound, you will need to have them replaced entirely. This is not as difficult as it sounds—most counters are only attached with a few screws from below, and sometimes they are not fastened at all. Once you remove the screws (and the sink, if there is one—it also helps to hold a counter in place), most laminate counters come off in one piece. Fabricators such as kitchen cabinet shops can make up any size, shape, and color counter to fit your dimensions, and they generally charge by the foot. Stock sizes can also be found in most home centers.

Stone counter is stained

Food spots, water stains, marks, and dull patches on stone can be prevented with an application of wax or a commercial sealer. If you have a stain that is difficult to remove with ordinary surface cleaners, start by polishing it with a nonabrasive cream sold for this purpose. All stone is porous, and some stains can become embedded in the surface. If polishing cream doesn't get out the stain, there are nonsolvent, nontoxic poultice powders sold for specific types of stains (rust, oil, ink, food and wine, etc.). Mixed with water, poultices reabsorb the stain out of the stone. Their effectiveness often depends on the surface texture and on the type of stone—marble, granite, limestone, slate, agglomerates, and terrazzo are the most common.

Stone counter is etched

Stone polishing cream can remove minor scratches in many types of stone, especially the softer marble, limestone, and terrazzo. Harder materials like granite, slate, and stone agglomerates may require a more aggressive abrasive compound like pumice, jeweler's rouge, or "honing powder" made especially for stone. Any stone surface that has been etched by food acids or crystallization must be repolished. Start with a more abrasive compound to smooth out the surface damage and finish with a polishing cream to remove fine scratches; then wax or seal the surface.

Stone counter is cracked or broken

If a small section of stone counter or table breaks off, you can use epoxy to glue it back permanently in place. Many kinds of stone are variegated in color, and this helps to hide the repair. There are also clear and colored epoxies that might closely approximate the color of your stone. If small chips are missing and you can't get the repair to mate precisely, you can try using colored wax to fill the cut line after you epoxy the break.

Large pieces, or sections that have to support their own or other weight, are more difficult to glue successfully. Professionals sometimes drill into the fractured edges and then insert metal pins to hold the pieces together and provide support. This takes skill and experience to prevent making the damage worse, so consider your chances carefully before you begin.

Cultured marble is scratched

"Cultured marble" is actually polyester resin; you can buff out light scratches using the same supplies and techniques a Corvette owner would use. At an auto parts dealer, buy a buffing pad that fits an electric drill, medium-cut rubbing compound, and paste wax made for fiberglass cars. Buff the surface with the compound and buffing pad, rinse, apply the wax, and buff until shiny.

For severe scratches, look up "Bathtub and Sink Refinishing" in the Yellow Pages; you can have the surface sanded and recoated with a special acrylic urethane.

HARDWOOD FLOORS

More than any other surface in a home, floors suffer the ills of daily wear and tear. Hardwood is a relatively easy material to care for and repair, unless large areas are damaged or need refinishing. In that case, you'll want to call a professional floor refinisher.

Dark and dirty wood

Filthy wood floors that don't come clean usually result from one of two things: the surface finish (Swedish oil, wax, varnish, polyurethane, etc.) has not been stripped in too long a period, or the surface finish is missing entirely. Test an inconspicuous area with a few drops of water—if it soaks into the wood, the finish is gone. If the water turns white, there is wax on the surface. If the droplets bead up, the floor has probably been oiled or coated with polyurethane or varnish. Use a commercial wood floor cleaner to strip away oil or wax finishes that have become discolored with ground-in grime. Dark stains in the wood may have to be sanded out with a professional floor sander.

Surface finishes like varnish and urethanes sometimes can be revived by buffing with steel wool or a special pad made for this purpose (rental stores have the machines and replacement pads). If that works, recoat the floor with the same type of finish. If the dirt doesn't come out, the floor may have to be sanded to remove the topcoat entirely, then refinished.

Squeaks

Squeaky floors are very common in older homes; squeaks are the sounds of friction—one piece of wood rubbing against another. You de-squeak the floor by either lubricating between surfaces that rub, to reduce the friction, or by stopping the movement altogether.

Lubricating is easy but not always effective. First, try working a little powdered or liquid graphite or talcum powder between floor boards. Then clean up the surface.

Stopping the movement is usually more permanent. First, determine exactly what is squeaking. Go under the floor, where possible, and listen while somebody walks above you. Where the floor squeaks, use a hammer to tap a wood shim (a narrow piece of tapered wood shingle) between the floor joist and the subfloor—just tight enough to kill the squeak. If that doesn't work, drive a screw through the subfloor into the underside of the surface flooring. Be sure the screw is short enough not to pop through the surface above; insert it through a large, flat fender washer before driving it. It's easiest to use

FIGURE 7.1 Fastening
Squeaky Floor Boards

square-drive or drywall screws and a power screwdriver or cordless drill with the appropriate driver tip.

If you can't get under the floor, try squirting wood glue into cracks between boards and working it in with a putty knife. Wipe up excess glue and weight down the surface. As a last resort, drive ring-shank nails at a slight angle into floor joists. Drill pilot holes and set and fill nail heads.

If none of these methods work, there is always one last answer: earplugs.

Damage and rot

Badly damaged or rotted sections of flooring must be removed and replaced with new pieces. This involves cutting out a section of the finish flooring, gluing or nailing replacements to the subflooring, filling cracks to match, sanding the surface, and refinishing. If you're not experienced with this type of work, you'll find that the most difficult part is getting the new to match the old. This job is usually best left to a professional.

Floor scratches and dents

Minor scratches often can be buffed away with steel wool or progressively finer sandpaper grits. Restrict your sanding to the scratched area, feathering only slightly into the surrounding surface. Sand or buff only in line with the wood grain.

Polyurethane finishes are difficult to sand—try using a scouring pad dipped in mineral spirits, or a sanding screen. Never wax a floor that has a polyurethane coating—this will negate your ability to recoat the floor in the future.

If paste wax will adhere to the finish, you can use it to hide scratches, and the wax is available in clear, honey tone, or brown to match most wood floors. Wood-repair wax sticks may help fill deeper scratches and dents.

You can sometimes raise small dents by placing a few drops of water on them, allowing the wood to swell back to its original shape. Applying mild heat with an iron or heat gun helps this process along.

Stains

Stains on wood floors are typically watermarks caused by spills or overwatering plants. To get to the root of the problem, the area must be sanded, sometimes bleached, and refinished to match the rest of the floor—that's the trickiest part. It's a good idea to hire a professional for this work, particularly if the stain is in a highly visible area.

Typically, the process is to:

1. Sand the area with a vibrating sander, first with 100-grit sandpaper, then with 150-grit sandpaper, and finally with 220-grit.
2. Vacuum the area.
3. Wipe the area with solvent: mineral spirits for oil-based stain or water for latex stain.
4. For a dark spot, apply bleach or an oxalic acid solution to lighten the spot, then lightly sand with 150-grit sandpaper.
5. Mix up one or more wood stains to match the existing floor color. This process usually requires testing possibilities on a piece of wood that's the same species as your floor.

When you must replace boards or sections of flooring and you can't find replacement pieces, cut replacements from a closet or another inconspicuous part of your existing floor, and then replace that cutout with newer flooring.

About recoating polyurethane finish

One of the nice things about a polyurethane finish is that when it becomes scratched and dull, you can usually have it recoated without sanding the entire floor first. Whether or not this is a possibility with your floor depends on a couple of factors: the existing finish must be polyurethane, and it cannot have a buildup of wax or other chemicals—these will cause the floor to reject the new finish. You can determine whether your floor qualifies by making a patch test on a small section of flooring (about four inches square).

Though you can do this in an inconspicuous place, such as in a closet, it's better to test along a wall near windows, where cleaners may have collected on the floor.

1. Thoroughly clean a small section of flooring, using a wood floor cleaner.
2. With fine (220-grit) sandpaper, lightly sand the area, working in line with the wood grain. Completely wipe away dust.
3. Apply polyurethane floor finish to the patch test area and wait twenty-four hours.
4. Check the finish. It should be smooth, not rippled or textured like an orange peel. Using a coin, scratch the surface with moderate pressure; it shouldn't flake or peel away. If the surface isn't smooth or if it flakes with this moderate scratching, you'll have to have the floor completely sanded and refinished.

RESILIENT FLOORS

Vinyl and other resilient floor materials are very durable. Even so, they need occasional care to keep them in top shape, and they can be torn or damaged with heavy wear. With resilient tile floors, it's usually easier to replace a damaged tile (if you can find a matching replacement) than to try and repair the floor. With sheet flooring, repair may be the only practical option. You can probably handle making minor repairs; for difficult jobs, contact a resilient floor installer.

Discoloration

Vinyl and most other types of resilient flooring don't need to be protected by waxing, but many floor products include wax to brighten the shine. Discoloration that results from wax buildup is easily remedied. Use a solution of white vinegar and water or a cleaner specifically formulated for your type of flooring.

Curled resilient tiles

When tiles begin to curl, they're telling you they need to be replaced. You might be able to get a few more years out of the flooring, but the repair may cost more than you bargain for.

Although heat from a propane torch or heat gun can soften the material enough so that it lays back down for regluing, many older resilient tiles were made of vinyl-asbestos—a material known to cause cancer when inhaled. Asbestos control experts often recommend encapsulation rather than removal of suspected materials. The best remedy, then, may be to not repair or remove the old flooring at all, but to cover it with new seamless sheet vinyl. Consult an expert if you're in doubt.

Scratches and blisters

Scratches that don't penetrate through resilient flooring often can be sanded out (sanding creates fine airborne dust, which may be hazardous if the flooring contains asbestos—use caution as noted on the facing). If you do sand, use a medium-grit sandpaper followed by finer grits until the scratch disappears. Apply floor wax to restore the shine on the buffed area.

Blisters in sheet vinyl can be reglued. Make a knife cut along the edge of the blister, just large enough to let you work glue into the void. Use an artist's brush to apply contact cement on both the subflooring and the blister flap. Let the glue dry until tacky; then lay the flap down and place a weight on the repaired area for several hours.

Seams separated

When the seams of vinyl sheet flooring separate and pucker, you can glue them back down with a vinyl flooring sealer kit. Generic types are available at home improvement stores; it's better, though, to order kits made specifically for your type of flooring (if you know the brand) from a flooring dealer.

1. Use a hair dryer to warm the edges of the raised seam so you can peel them back to work on them.
2. Brush and/or vacuum the dirt out from the subfloor beneath the seam area.
3. With masking tape, protect the flooring surfaces on both sides of the seam.
4. Use a brush to apply multipurpose sheet flooring adhesive to the back of the raised flooring.
5. Press the edges down and wipe off any excess adhesive. Then put a heavy, flat board along the seam and add weight with phone books or other heavy objects. Allow to dry overnight.
6. Use the seam-sealing kit as prescribed on the label to clean and permanently fuse the seam along the surface.

Old linoleum needs covering

Before pulling up old flooring, be sure neither the material nor the adhesive that holds it in place contains asbestos. You can remove a small sample of the materials, including backing and adhesive, and have it tested.

If any of the materials contain asbestos, leave the old floor in place and cover it with the new flooring, applied over lauan plywood underlayment.

Interior Surface Problems

About vinyl removal

Removing stubborn vinyl tile from a concrete slab can be hideous unless you use the right tool: a tile stripper, available through tool rental companies. This heavy contraption rolls on two wheels and chips up the old flooring, using a replaceable blade. The same tool will remove vinyl from wood floors, but you'll want to fit it with a flexible blade made for this task. Over solid finish or subflooring, work in line with the wood grain.

Replacing floor tiles

To replace tiles over a concrete slab—even one that has firm, residual adhesive from old linoleum or vinyl tile—first try to remove most of the old adhesive (a heat gun and a scraper help expedite this process); then use a latex-modified thinset over the mastic. If you're tiling over a new concrete slab or where two subfloor materials meet, first cover the floor with a self-adhesive, antifracture membrane, which comes in fifty-foot rolls. This will help prevent any new cracks in the concrete from being transmitted up through the tile.

STAIRS

Staircases are generally built for the life of a home, but they can be damaged, repaired, and even replaced like any other part of the house. Because many of the accidents that occur in homes typically include falls on stairs, you want to be sure your stairs are in sound condition. Loose treads and handrails are an invitation to a fall. Lesser, but still significant, problems include wear, settling, and wood deterioration.

Stair handrails are even more difficult to design, build, and repair than the stair carriage itself. If you even attempt to take one apart by yourself, be advised that you may never be able to restore it to its original strength or condition. Some basic repairs are manageable, though.

Stairs squeak

Most steps in older homes creak and squeak underfoot because the wood has dried and shrunk over time. Stairs are made up of many individual parts, and as these parts begin to separate slightly and wear on each other, they make noise when you put your weight on them. This is usually not a problem unless the parts become very loose, or the creaking indicates that a section of the stairs is nearing the breaking point.

If you're worried about the noises, start by investigating the source of the sound. Stairs with open undersides (such as those that go down to a basement or that have closets beneath them) make this job easier. Where the underside is not accessible, you may have to pull down a finished ceiling underneath the stairs to get a good look. Check that the wood wedges used to lock the treads into their mortised slots haven't worked loose or fallen out. If they have, glue them back in place and tap them tightly home. Glue blocks under the treads where they meet each riser also can fall away. If they have, nail and reglue them as well. Look for longitudinal splitting or cracks across the width of the stringers that carry the treads. Also check the vertical plumb and horizontal level of the major parts to determine if the stairs are leaning in any particular direction—all the noise you hear could indicate that the structure is moving or in danger of collapsing.

Broken treads

Individual treads can be replaced when absolutely necessary. Depending on how the staircase is built, this can be simple or far too complicated for an amateur to tackle. If you can, try to repair the tread without removing it. If this proves impossible, consider your options carefully.

If the treads are "open" on both sides and resting atop the stringers, and if the handrail balusters aren't attached to the steps, removing a damaged tread might require only pulling it up and removing the nails that hold it to the risers above and below it. New, unfinished hardwood treads can be purchased and easily cut to fit.

However, if the treads are glued into mortises cut into the stringers on both sides (a "closed" run), or if they are held in place by balusters mortised into each step, then removing a single tread could entail disassembling (and possibly destroying) much of the staircase in the process. Before you begin this work, get an estimate from a professional with proven experience in stair building and repair.

Loose baluster

Use a syringe-type glue bottle to squeeze wood glue into the baluster sockets at top and bottom. Drill pilot holes sized for small (2d to 4d) finishing nails through the baluster ends and into the wood holding them in position. Use a nailset to bury the nails into the wood; then fill the nail holes with wood putty.

Broken baluster

If you can't reglue a split baluster, carefully saw through it and remove both parts by "working" them out of their sockets. Buy or make a replacement baluster and cut it so that it is $3/8$ inch longer than the original. Bore the existing top hole in the handrail

---

$^1/_2$ inch deeper, but take care not to bore through the top of the rail. You should be able to insert the baluster into the top hole far enough to allow the bottom end to drop into its socket. Glue and nail the replacement into the sockets.

Loose newel post

Because they anchor the handrail and must be able to take the weight and stress routinely imposed on them, stair newels must be well secured to the staircase or floor framing. When one becomes loose, and when you can't see its anchoring point under the stairs, it may be necessary to work through a ceiling to get at the underside, or to remove a piece of flooring on a stair landing, in order to make the repair. On older stairs, the base of a newel is often doweled or mortised and glued in place. Modern stairs may use bolts, lag screws, or other conventional hardware to hold the newel. Once you've located the problem, reinforce the newel with new hardware. Use hefty connectors that can hold their own against everyday use, and be sure the newel is vertically plumb when you fasten it permanently in place.

TILE AND GROUT

Ceramic tile is impervious to water and a very durable material—that's why it's such a popular surface for countertops, floors, bathroom walls, and more. But tile can be cracked or broken and the grout that fills the gaps between tiles is vulnerable to several problems.

Tile is dirty

Clean the tile on walls and countertops with a damp sponge or cloth. For floors, use a damp mop. To scrub out stains, utilize a nylon scrubbing pad or a stiff scrub brush.

Stubborn stains on tiles can often be scrubbed out with a white cleansing powder; don't use cleaners that contain bleach, because these can bleach the grout. For cleaning grout, scrub with a toothbrush and household cleanser (chlorine free). Test the cleanser first in an inconspicuous place.

Soap film and lime deposits can be taken off with household ammonia or a mixture of equal parts vinegar and water. Rinse and dry.

For stubborn dirt stains, you can buy commercial tile cleaners; be sure to follow the label directions. Never mix a tile cleaner that contains ammonia or acid with chlorine bleach—this mixture releases the chlorine as a poisonous gas.

Tile grout is stained

The grout used to fill the voids between individual tiles often becomes dingy and stained, especially on countertops where food is prepared regularly. At a tile store, you can purchase a pH-neutral tile-cleaning solution. Unless your grout is white-white, do not use a cleanser that contains bleach because it could lighten your grout's color. Mix the cleanser according to label directions (wear rubber gloves). Permanently stained grout will have to be removed and replaced as discussed below (see "Tile grout cracked or crumbling").

1. Pour the cleaner onto the counter and scrub it in to the grout lines with a soft-bristle brush.
2. Using a sponge and clear water, rinse the surface completely. With a rag, sop up the water so the grout will dry quickly—damp, dark grout will hide stains.
3. If necessary, repeat the process. To remove stains that won't come out when you use these methods, consult your tile dealer about a stronger cleaner.

Removing Stains from Grout

Coffee, wine, mustard, fruit juice	Scrub with a nonbleaching cleaner. Allow to sit for several minutes. Then rinse.
Hard water, rust	Scrub with a nonbleaching scouring powder; then rinse thoroughly.
Fresh paint	Remove stain with commercial paint remover, per label directions.
Oil	Scrub with detergent or with a mixture of 10 percent sodium carbonate in water.
Old paint	Carefully loosen paint with a razor blade. If necessary, follow up with paint remover.

Tile grout cracked or crumbling

Though most cracks start small, they grow over time. Eventually, water seeps in and damages the base beneath the tile, and eventually the tile crumbles. To repair the grout, you'll need a few inexpensive specialty tools, including a toothed tool called a grout saw (available at tile dealers), a sponge, and a rubber grout float. You'll also need to buy replacement grout that is the same color.

1. Use a grout saw or the pointed end of a lever-style can opener to remove cracked and loose grout and to score stable grout. Brush away dust and vacuum the surface.
2. Mix replacement grout according to label directions.
3. Holding the rubber grout float's leading edge up at a slight angle, spread grout across the surface. Be sure to work it into all joints completely.
4. Use your finger to smooth the grout at the joints.
5. Allow the grout to set up for about a half hour; then use a damp sponge to wipe excess off of the surface.
6. Let the grout dry for several days; then apply penetrating silicone sealer for protection.

NOTE: If you have a newly tiled interior floor and the grout is cracking, consider removing the grout between tiles (as discussed above) and replacing it with a sanded caulk. This works only if grout joints are narrower than 1/4 inch because the caulk is not designed for wider gaps. Because the cracking is probably caused by floor deflection from foot traffic, consider trying to reinforce the floor from below to strengthen it.

Small crack in tile

If you have a small, narrow crack in a tile, you may be able to fill the crack with paintable caulk and, if necessary, touch up the caulk with an artist's paintbrush and acrylic paint. But in most cases, you're better off removing and replacing the tile (see below).

Tile is cracked or broken

Replacing a cracked or broken tile isn't as difficult as you might think. Of course, you can only replace the tile if you have—or can find—an appropriate match. If you can't find a match on your tile dealer's shelf, ask whether they have a "bone pile" of rejects and extras you can check.

Here's how to replace a tile:

1. Use an inexpensive grout saw or the sharp point of lever-style can opener to scrape most of the grout out of the joints around the damaged tile.

FIGURE 7.2   Grouting New Tile

2. Wearing eye protection, use a hammer and a nailset to punch a hole in the center of the damaged tile. Avoid driving the nailset into the wall or surface material behind the tile.
3. Score an X across the face of the tile, from corner to corner, using a glass cutter.
4. Rapping a cold chisel lightly with a hammer, break away the damaged tile, starting at the center (wear eye protection).
5. Using an old chisel, finish removing grout and adhesive from the area.
6. Paint the surface with latex primer (fill with vinyl spackle if necessary). Allow the primer to dry.
7. Spread tile adhesive onto the back of the replacement tile, using a notched trowel made for this purpose. Hold the adhesive back from the tile edges by about $1/2$ inch.
8. Position the tile, and with a rubber mallet or a hammer and block of wood tap it gently to level it with the surrounding tiles. Remove excess adhesive from the grout joints, using a stick or old screwdriver. If necessary, tape the tile in place until the adhesive dries.
9. Wearing rubber gloves, mix grout to match existing grout and apply it to the joints, using your finger or, for large areas, a grout float. Clean excess grout from the tile surface, using a damp sponge.

WALLBOARD AND PLASTER

Most homes built in the past fifty years have interiors made with drywall—large, thin sheets of paper-covered gypsum nailed directly to wall studs and ceiling joists. Drywall is inexpensive to buy and install and easy to repair. Although durable, it is also easy to damage. The areas between wood framing members are unsupported and particularly vulnerable. Before drywall, most homes had plaster interiors. Plaster work is still done in new construction, but it requires more skill and is usually found in higher-priced homes today. Working with plaster requires practice—when mixed, it has a very brief "open" time when the material is liquid and pliable; it sets quickly and becomes rock-hard in an instant. Premixed drywall joint compound can be used to make minor repairs in both drywall and plaster.

Dirty walls

When ordinary cleaners don't work, stubborn stains on plaster often can be scrubbed away with a strong solution of trisodium phosphate (TSP) and water or with a nonphosphate substitute. Unpainted plaster is porous but generally nonsoluble, and unless you really drown the wall, it can take a good bath and rinse. Drywall, on the other hand, has a paper coating and its gypsum base is water soluble. Since water can penetrate a thin coat of paint, be careful not to treat drywall the same as plaster. Scrub drywall gently with a soft sponge and a mild TSP solution, and try not to use too much water. Let the drywall dry thoroughly and consider repainting it with a higher-gloss paint that resists stains and is easier to clean.

Holes in wallboard

Use vinyl spackling compound to fill holes in gypsum wallboard, but first slightly dent the surface with a hammer to produce a void for the filler. Apply the spackling compound with a putty knife, drawing it smoothly over the dent, flush with the wall's surface. For a deep hole, allow the patch to dry, sand lightly with 120-grit sandpaper, and reapply spackling compound. Sand very lightly; then touch up with paint to match.

Holes are easy to make in drywall, and they're just as easy to fix. Repair kits are sold for this purpose—they usually have some sort of backer board that inserts into the hole and suspends itself in place while you cover the now plugged opening with joint compound. The dried compound and the backer board become part of the wall, and the rest of the job is just smoothing over the damaged area and repainting it to match the rest of the wall surface. You can also make your own backer from a piece of scrap plywood or drywall. Thoroughly smear it with joint compound (this "glues" it to the inside wall face), and use a string to hold it in place while the compound dries. Then cut the string off and use more compound to smooth out the repair, as above.

If the hole is very large, it's often better to cut the drywall back to a stud on each side of the break. Use a screw gun to fasten a two-by-four nailer to the open face of each stud; then cut a new piece of drywall to fit the opening. Tape and compound all of the joints as you would a new drywall installation.

Holes in plaster

Small holes in plaster are also easy to repair, providing that the lath backing that held the original plaster is still intact. If it is, simply mix joint compound with plaster of paris and use it to fill the hole (the compound retards the plaster setting time and makes it easier to work with). Clean away any loose plaster and dust and fill from the edges in, working the plaster mix into and through the lath for a good bond. Do one rough, or "scratch," coat and allow it to dry; then apply a finish coat.

If the lath has broken away, enlarge the plaster hole just enough to reveal some remaining well-anchored lath. Cut a piece of wire mesh to fill the opening and attach it to this lath with screws or wire. Apply the plaster/compound mix in layers, allowing each to set hard before adding another. If the hole is large and your plastering skills are weak, use joint compound only for the finish coat; then sand it smooth.

Stress cracks in wallboard

Hairline cracks in gypsum wallboard (drywall), particularly at the top corners of windows and doors, are signs that the wall framing has settled or moved a little—a common condition and one that's easy to repair. If the crack isn't repaired properly, it's likely to reappear later.

1. Using a utility knife with a sharp blade, widen the crack so that it has a V-shaped profile.
2. Use a broad-bladed putty knife to spread drywall over the groove so that it fills the area and covers an inch or two on each side of it; smooth it out evenly; then allow it to dry.
3. Apply self-adhesive fiberglass joint tape over the groove.
4. Using a six-inch drywall knife, completely cover the tape with a second coat of joint compound, "feathering out" the compound smoothly and evenly a couple of inches beyond the earlier coat. Allow it to dry.
5. Sand the repair smooth with fine sandpaper. Be careful not to sand down to the tape or to scuff the paper surface of the surrounding wallboard.

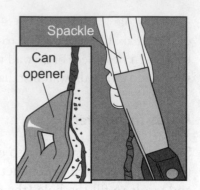

FIGURE 7.3   Repairing
Plaster cracks

6. Touch up with paint to match (it may be necessary to repaint the entire wall for a perfect match).

Cracks in plaster

Small cracks in plaster are relatively easy to repair, with one condition: the plaster must be firmly anchored to the lath behind it. If, when you push on the wall, it flexes as though it has broken away from its support base, call a plaster specialist—the repair will involve removing the loose plaster and replacing it.

Here's how to repair a simple crack in a firmly anchored plaster wall (Figure 7.3):

1. Wearing safety glasses, turn the crack into a groove that is about ³/16 inch wide and ¹/4 inch deep—you can use a can opener, a screwdriver or a utility knife (throw away the knife blade afterward) to do this.
2. Using a medium-bristle brush, scrub the area with a solution of water and TSP or with a nonphosphate detergent.
3. Cut short pieces of self-adhesive fiberglass mesh joint tape and cover the groove with them.
4. Dip a sponge in clean water and dampen the area.
5. Mix setting-type joint compound and apply it over the tape and groove, using a three-inch-wide putty knife. Smooth it out evenly and allow it to dry.
6. Apply another coat of joint compound with a drywall knife or wide-blade putty knife. Apply it smoothly and "feather" the edges so that they taper into the

undamaged area. Allow to dry; then sand lightly to blend the patch into the wall at the edges.

7. Prime with a high-quality latex primer; then paint.

Dinged drywall corners

Drywall corners are vulnerable to getting banged and bruised by traffic through a house. Beneath the joint compound that covers and finishes the corner is a length of light-weight metal "corner bead" with either a right-angle or curved profile. The object is to straighten out this dented piece of metal and re-cover it with drywall compound. Here's how to do it:

1. Use a utility knife to cut away loose drywall compound from the damaged area.
2. Reshape the dented corner bead. To sculpt flattened or bent areas, gently pound a bolt or an upside-down nailset with a hammer.
3. Tack down one edge of the loose metal with drywall nails.
4. Using a putty knife, remove all loose existing joint compound.
5. Tack down the other edge of the metal corner bead.
6. Using a six-inch-wide drywall knife, fill one side of the corner and draw it out so that it's smooth. Allow the compound to dry.
7. Fill the other side of the corner and allow it to dry.
8. Gently sand with fine sandpaper wrapped around a block. Fill with a second coat if necessary and sand again.

Popped nails

When wood wall studs and ceiling joists bend and twist—which often happens in new homes built with wood that dries after it is installed—the framing members can push and pull away from the drywall, causing the drywall nails to literally pop up out of the wood. This usually happens near the center of the boards, where the most pronounced bending is likely to occur. If it's too late to call the builder back to take care of this annoyance (it's rarely structurally threatening), you can do the repairs yourself (Figure 7.4). Here's how:

1. Use drywall screws, not nails, to replace each nail "pop" that you find.
2. Don't pull out the old nails. Drive a new drywall nail or a drywall screw in so that it overlaps each popped nail to re-anchor the drywall at that spot. If you're lucky, you may need to do only a surface touch-up over the fasteners, using drywall patching compound.

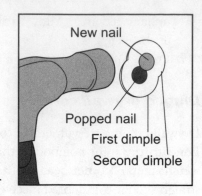

New nail

Popped nail

First dimple

Second dimple

FIGURE 7.4   Popped Nail Repair

3. If the nails protrude far enough, they can tear or push the drywall tape off the wall. Where this happens, you'll have to cut away and replace the tape (see "Peeling drywall tape" below). Cut back only as far as necessary—the ends of the tape still firmly embedded in joint compound should not have to be removed.

Unwanted wall anchors

When you remove certain types of hollow-wall fasteners, the expanding, umbrella-like sleeve may be left behind permanently. To hide the sleeve, use a hammer and a short bolt to set the sleeve further into the wall. Then just fill the surface hole as you would any other hole (see "Holes in wallboard" on page 166).

Peeling drywall tape

Drywall tape can peel for a variety of reasons—poor application, high room humidity, nail pops (see above), even destructive kids and pets. You can make repairs easily enough, but it may keep happening unless you find and eliminate the cause, such as by placing a dehumidifier in a room where dampness persists. If the problem is confined to a small area, you don't need professional drywall skills to do an adequate job, but if the tape is peeling off the walls in several places, or in areas of prominent visibility, consider calling in a pro who can give you quality results. Here's how to do it yourself:

1. Use a sharp razor knife to cut away each end of the tape a foot or so beyond the damaged area. Sand down the remaining ridges of dried drywall compound with a

moderately coarse drywall sanding pad. Sand almost to the drywall surface (you don't want to go too far and cut into the drywall paper) and vacuum away the dust.

2. Use a five-inch taping knife to lay a thin bed of joint compound over the drywall joint. This compound bed should be uniform in thickness and width, with no gaps or large air pockets, and it should extend at least two inches on each side of the joint.

3. Cut a piece of drywall tape slightly shorter than the missing tape section. Place it atop the joint and use your taping knife to smooth the new tape into the compound. Be sure there is no air trapped under the tape or wrinkles anywhere along its length.

4. Smooth a second thin coat of joint compound over the tape. Keep the knife blade flat and take care not to disturb the tape's position. Allow it to dry overnight.

5. Carefully sand and scrape away any high spots where the compound has dried; then use a wide-bladed taping knife to lay another bed of joint compound over the entire area of repair. Allow it to dry thoroughly. Sand again, using progressively finer sanding sheets to blend or "feather" the compound into the rest of the wall surface.

Sagging plaster

Flaking and cracking plaster are relatively minor maintenance items, but when the plaster starts to sag or "belly" out from a wall or ceiling, it indicates deeper problems that require your full attention. Plaster is heavy, and it needs a solid, well-anchored base to support its weight. This base is usually made of strips of wood or metal wire mesh (both referred to as lath) that are nailed to the wall and ceiling framing. When the plaster is applied, it squeezes through the lath, creating "keys" that harden to form a strong mechanical bond with the wall. Over the years, plaster can dry out and lose its holding strength, or it can weaken from vibration, and the keys begin to break away. The lath can also pull away from the framing. Gravity and the weight of the plaster exert themselves, and the first sign is often sagging—followed eventually by the collapse of the plaster surface.

At this point, you may want to call in a professional. Repairing a large wall area is difficult enough, but if the ceiling is beginning to sag, working over your head with heavy, hard to handle materials is not an easy job. If you still want to attempt your own repairs, here are a couple of ways to proceed:

1. First, protect the flooring under your work area, because once you begin, the entire affected area could give way. To prevent plaster dust from spreading into the rest of the house, hang damp sheets or tape plastic sheeting over the doorways and put an exhaust fan in a window. If you're worried that much of the ceiling

could come down at once, build T-shaped supports from two-by-fours and use them to hold a piece of plywood flat against the ceiling while you work.

2. Use a hammer and cold chisel or wrecking bar to chip out a small area at the edge of the bulge (wear safety glasses). Once you can see behind the surface, you should be able to tell if the plaster has pulled away from the lath, or if the lath itself has come loose from the framing. If the lath has pulled away and the plaster is still well-adhered to it, you may be able to refasten the lath to the framing without removing the plaster.

3. Use long drywall screws that will penetrate at least half their length into the wood framing. Start near the edge of the bulge and press the ceiling upward as you drive the screws (you may have to shift your plywood support, and the tees holding it, ahead of you as you work). Because the plaster and lath form an integral sheet, like a piece of drywall, it may go back up without a problem. However, if the lath has warped, or if the old nails in the framing prevent the lath from returning to its original position, this may prove impossible. You might have to first remove much or all of the plaster just to get the lath back up.

4. If the lath is still anchored to the ceiling joists, and the plaster has pulled away, your only option is to remove the old plaster. It's a dirty job, but if there's nothing holding the plaster to the framing, it will come down quickly.

NOTE: There is another trick that professionals use to repair plaster walls and ceilings that have failed—leave the old plaster in place and reface the entire area with new drywall. Long screws with washer heads are used to pull the drywall and old ceiling back up to the framing, or as close to level as possible. You end up with a drywall surface, but it eliminates the problems of sagging, cracking, and flaking plaster once and for all.

Water damaged ceiling

If roof or plumbing leaks have caused yellow or brown water stains on your ceiling, don't try to paint right over the stains; the stains are likely to show through. Of course, fix the source of the leak first. If the ceiling is not textured or if the texture isn't loosened by the water damage, simply seal the stain with a stain sealer and repaint.

Large ceiling hole

If you have a fairly large hole in the ceiling—the type of hole that might be left behind when moving a ceiling fixture—you'll need to give it some backing before filling the hole with patching material.

Here's how to do it:

1. Cut a piece of pegboard (hardboard with holes in it) sized to overlap but slip through the hole.
2. Loop a six-inch-long piece of stiff wire through two of the holes in the pegboard. Twist the ends of the wire so that it forms a complete loop.
3. Coat the pegboard with drywall compound, using a putty knife.
4. Slip the coated pegboard piece into the hole, coated side facing down.
5. Pull down on the wire loop, insert a pencil, and wind up the wire by twisting the pencil to pull the pegboard snugly down against the backside of the ceiling.
6. Let the compound dry; then take out the pencil and snip off the wires, flush with the ceiling.
7. Fill the hole with two coats of drywall compound, allowing the first to dry before applying the second.
8. Let the second coat dry; then apply a third coat, flush with the ceiling. Let that dry for twenty-four hours.
9. Lightly sand with fine sandpaper to "feather" (blend) the patch with the surface. Paint to match the ceiling.

Ceiling texture needs repair

After repairing a stain or hole in the ceiling, it may be necessary to repair the texture. Here's how you do it:

1. Use a putty knife to scrape off any loose or damaged ceiling texture around the stain or repair.
2. With drywall sanding paper wrapped around a small block, gently sand the edges of the damaged area.
3. Using a broad-bladed putty knife, fill the void with a smooth coat of drywall compound and allow to dry.
4. Sand smooth again; then spray stain sealer over the patched area to prevent the patch from bleeding through later. Allow to dry.
5. If you have a cottage-cheese type of texture, buy canned ceiling texture and spray it onto the repaired area. If the ceiling has a splotchy-style texture, you may be able to recreate the look with drywall compound and a special texturing brush, also available at home improvement centers. Texturing takes a little practice— just use your artistic talents; keep scraping the damp compound off until you achieve the look you want.

6. Touch up with paint to match (if necessary, repaint the entire ceiling for a perfect match).

Dust streaks on ceiling

Below poorly insulated attic spaces, dust sometimes leaves streak marks along the ceiling; these marks are caused by temperature differences between insulated spaces and joist locations. Short of repainting, the only solutions to this problem are to add insulation or to spread existing insulation more evenly in the attic.

WALLPAPER

Unless the wallpaper is damaged, a simple tear can be reglued so as to be almost unnoticeable. Seams that have lifted also can be reglued. Wall-covering and hardware stores sell mending kits that include contact cement, wood rollers to press the repair back down, and small pieces of various color papers to match (more or less) most walls. If you were smart when you installed the wallpaper and saved some pieces for repairs, use that instead.

Removing wallpaper

You can steam wallpaper off of walls, but be careful not to damage the wall beneath it. If the wall is old, damaged, or particularly porous plaster, a steamer could damage it, so test the steamer in an out-of-the-way place.

Misting wallpaper with a hand-pump garden sprayer filled with a mixture of hot water and wallpaper remover is another option. Of course, the wetter the wall becomes, the messier this method gets.

One of the easiest methods for removing wallpaper is to use a special enzyme-based gel made for the purpose and sold at paint stores. All you do is score the surface of the wallpaper with a special scoring tool, apply the gel with a brush or roller, allow the enzyme time to dissolve the wallpaper adhesive, then peel away the paper.

Removing wallpaper adhesive

Use the same enzyme-based gel wallpaper remover discussed above to remove wallpaper adhesive from a wall. Just paint it on with a roller or brush; then use a wide-blade putty knife or scraper to scrape and scoop off the dissolved adhesive.

Wallpaper bubbles and loose seams

To remove air bubbles from wallpaper, use a syringe-like glue injector, available at hardware stores and home centers, to inject wallpaper adhesive into the bubble's center. Use a wallpaper seam roller to work the adhesive throughout the bubble and to squeeze the excess back out through the hole. Wipe away excess with a damp sponge.

Patching damaged wallpaper

Cut and remove the damaged paper (see facing page) as far back as a seam, a corner, or the least visible part of the design, such as a line in the pattern. Be careful not to pull away the drywall's paper covering when you remove the wallpaper. Clean away any residual glue and apply a thin coat of wallpaper sizing. Allow it to dry; then repaper.

How to cover over wallpaper

Sometimes it is easiest to cover over old wallpaper instead of repairing it. Smooth any visible seams with a thin layer of drywall compound and sand lightly. Next, apply a coat of "paper-to-paper primer." Allow to dry; then hang new wallpaper, offsetting the new seams with the old ones.

WOODWORK

Repairing scratches, cracks, dings, and similar problems with wood trim, paneling, and other woodwork is easy in most cases. One of the reasons wood is the most popular building material is the fact that it's easy to machine and work with standard tools. If you'd like to get help with woodwork repairs, you can call a finish carpenter or cabinetmaker.

Scratched paneling

Real wood paneling is usually made of individual boards jointed together; often, however, "wood" panels are actually thin photo-lamination sheets designed to look like solid wood. This is an important distinction, because real boards can be repaired using conventional woodworking methods, whereas the faux wood requires more cosmetic treatment. A slight scratch in a board, for example, simply reveals more of the same wood below, whereas a deep scratch in paneling can expose a paper backing or plywood core.

Interior Surface Problems

Paneling sheets also have a clear surface film that is hard to match with any type of protective finish.

Minor scratches in solid wood can be sanded out and refinished. Sometimes you can do a bit of sanding on a paneling sheet; then apply paste wax in a shade close to the original finish. If the damage goes deeper, you may need to replace a section or the entire sheet.

Surface repairs

A deep gouge in woodwork can be repaired in one of two ways: fill the hole with wood putty or wax filler, or glue in a new piece of the same type of wood. If wood filler is used, it may be difficult to match the wood's original color or stain. Experiment with different stains mixed into the filler, and allow these "test patches" to dry in an inconspicuous location before you choose one to repair the problem area. If you glue in a new section of wood, clean away any dried glue around the edges of the repair and sand the entire section around it before you restain.

Dirty woodwork

Interior natural woodwork is usually protected with some kind of clear finish. To clean any wood effectively without ruining this topcoat, you need to know what it was finished with in the first place. Here's a quick primer on finishes and how to clean them:

- Natural "drying" oils like linseed and tung oil soak into the wood surface and then dry hard to form a protective film that is all but invisible. Manufacturers recommend lemon oil polish, which partially dissolves the old topcoat. As you wipe it on, you also wipe away surface grime that has become embedded in the finish.
- Wax imparts a surface coating that can be felt and seen. It doesn't dry as hard as oils and builds up in the wood pores after repeated applications. To clean waxed wood, you can use a commercial wax stripper, a mild solution of white vinegar and water, or lemon oil polish, but you'll have to reapply a new wax topcoat afterward.
- Polyurethane and varnish are basically the same, although one is made with plastic resins and the other with natural resins. Both create a hard, waterproof coating that is impervious to most dirt and stain. Woodwork wearing these protective finishes may not look "natural," but it can be cleaned by simply wiping with a damp cloth.

Trim needs to be paint-stripped

See information on stripping paint and finishes on page 214. Before applying a stripper to your trim, be sure it's made of wood, not plaster. Strippers can damage plaster trim.

Damaged trim

If moldings and trim are badly damaged, it's best to replace them. This work isn't particularly heavy or difficult, but it does take a little experience at making accurate cuts using a miter box. If this isn't something you've done before, you're probably better off calling a finish carpenter or cabinetmaker to do the work. You may be able to save a few dollars by removing the old trim yourself.

Here's how:

1. Use a utility knife to cut through any paint seal between the trim and the wall.
2. Slip a putty knife or scraper in behind the trim and pry it gently away from the wall—don't bend the tool. Next, fit the hooked end of a flat prybar into the separation behind the putty knife and pry against a flat wood block that has been placed against the wall (so you don't damage the wall).
3. Door and window trim is often nailed with a small nail at the mitered corners. If you pry at these points, the wood may split. First, use a mini-hacksaw to cut off the nails at the joint. If you do split trim when removing it, just glue it and rubber band or tape it together with masking tape until the wood dries.
4. When you remove the trim, don't knock out the nails from the backside—they'll break away the face of the moldings. Instead, use slip-joint pliers to pull them all the way through from behind.
5. Replace with new trim, using a fine-toothed saw, backsaw, or miter box to make the necessary cuts.

Gaps along moldings

To fill gaps between moldings and the ceiling or walls, apply a bead of siliconized-latex caulk. This is flexible enough to ride out any movement caused by moisture changes. Apply a 1/8-inch bead with a caulking gun; then dampen your finger with water and smooth the caulk.

Molding corners coming apart

If mitered corners of base moldings are separating, squeeze a little wood glue in the joint and renail with finishing nails. Set the heads and putty to match. If nails don't hold, ask your hardware dealer for trim screws—very narrow screws with a tiny head that can be driven with a drive bit in an electric screwdriver or drill.

8

DOOR AND WINDOW PROBLEMS

Doors and windows play an extremely active role in a house. We use them to control access, views, light, privacy, heat, and more. In fact, doors and most types of windows are some of a home's most frequently used—and largest—moving parts. This frequent handling, coupled with exposure to the elements, calls for a high degree of durability. Some measure up; some can't handle the pressure. Here we look at how to solve common problems with various types of exterior and interior doors; locks and latches; and windows and screens.

GENERAL DOOR PROBLEMS

The most common problem with a door is that it doesn't open or close quite right—either it binds against the doorjambs, or it doesn't close tightly. Most problems of the latter type have more to do with the latch and knob than the door itself (see page 186 for more about this). Of course, because doors are moving parts, they also can suffer from a variety of other maladies.

Door binds, sags, or drags

Many doors bind against the upper corner of the jamb or drag across the carpet. Close the door and check how it fits in the jamb. Look for tight spots and make sure the top edge of the door is level. If it appears to be more than 1/4 inch out of level, the cause is probably settling or sagging. You can usually solve this by replacing the center screw of the upper hinge with a longer, 2 1/2-inch screw, angled slightly toward the jamb's center. Drive it in tightly and tighten the other screws that secure the hinge.

Humidity can cause a door to swell and stick in the frame. To solve this, you have to mark the areas where the door is binding (use a pencil), remove the door, and plane or sand the high spots slightly. Don't take off too much! Remember that the door will shrink back up when the air is drier.

Hinges squeak

Squeaky hinges are easy to fix. First try spraying them with a light coat of penetrating oil (such as WD-40). If that doesn't work, pull out the hinge pin from the squeaky hinge, clean it with steel wool, spray both the pin and the leaves with penetrating oil, then replace the pin.

Door rattles

When an interior door rattles, it means the door stop and/or the strike plate are not tight enough. If the strike plate has a flange in the center that can be bent slightly to tighten the fit, remove the plate and use a pair of pliers to bend the flange. Otherwise, you may have to adjust the position of the door stop on the latch-side jamb. To do this, first use a utility knife to cut the paint seal between the molding and the jamb. Then place a wooden block against the door stop and hammer the block gently toward the door to provide a tighter fit.

The best way to stop an exterior door from rattling in the wind is to install resilient weather stripping around its perimeter. Look for the vinyl bulb type and follow package instructions.

Wood door damaged

There are many methods for repairing or restoring woodwork (see page 175), and they work just as well for all-wood doors. You can sand out minor scratches, fill gouges with wood putty, replace rotted or broken sections with epoxy filler or a new piece, and so on.

If a panel in a colonial-style door has cracked or split, you may be able to reglue it without removing it from the rest of the door. If you have to remove a panel, try prying off the moldings that surround it and hold it in place. On some panel doors, the moldings are routed in and can't be removed. In this case, one option is to carefully cut away these integral moldings. After you've fixed the panel, buy new moldings to match the rest of the door's trim.

EXTERIOR DOORS

In addition to the problems discussed above, exterior doors are vulnerable to damage because of constant use and exposure to the elements.

Steel door is dented

To repair a dent in a steel door or garage door, buy auto body filler at an auto parts store and follow the label directions. With most types, you sand down the dented area until you reach bare metal, then apply the filler in thin layers to build up the patch. When it's flush with the surface of the door, sand it smooth. Prime the patch with 100 percent acrylic latex primer; then paint the entire door with 100 percent acrylic latex paint.

Fiberglass composite door is damaged

To repair a dent or ding in a fiberglass door, buy a Corvette body repair kit at an auto parts store; follow the label directions. Once you've finished the repair, prime the patch with 100 percent acrylic latex primer; then paint the entire door with 100 percent acrylic latex paint.

Air leaks around a door

If air is leaking around the perimeter of a door, simply replace the weather stripping (if there is any). Compression weather stripping is the most common type; steel doors may utilize a magnetic weather strip along the top and down the knob side. It's easiest to remove the door before replacing weather stripping, so plan to do this on a warm day. Also, buy your replacement material before you remove the door.

1. Use a hammer and a small pin punch or a nail to tap out the hinge pins.
2. Grip the knob, slightly open the door, and lift it off the hinges.

3. Pull off the old weather stripping. If it's the type that fits into a groove in the jamb, don't attempt to pull the brads that hold it in place. Instead, shear them off or drive them into the groove with an old chisel.
4. Cut the replacement weather stripping to length, push it into the groove in the jamb, and refasten with new one-inch brads. Then replace the door.

Door sweep damaged

If a vinyl door sweep on the bottom edge of your exterior door is broken and providing an inadequate seal, remove the door as discussed above. Pry off (or, on a steel door, slide out) the old sweep and take it to your home improvement center to buy a replacement. If an exact replacement isn't available, buy the type with a U-shaped profile that screws onto the door bottom. Run a bead of caulk along the bottom edge of the door, tap the sweep into place with a hammer and small wood block (or a mallet), and fasten the new replacement sweep in place with $1/2$ inch staples or fasteners provided with the sweep. Last, replace the door.

Threshold gasket worn

If you have an exterior door with a threshold that's capped by a rubber gasket that is broken or badly worn, you can replace the gasket. Remove the door as discussed above. Use an old chisel or screwdriver to pry out the splines that hold the gasket in place (if there are splines); then pry up the gasket and pull it out of its groove. Take the old gasket to your home improvement center or hardware store and buy an exact replacement. Most new gaskets just press in place (you can force them, if necessary, by pushing against a short wood block). Finally, replace the door.

Storm door closer is broken

When a storm door is wrenched open by a gust of wind, the door-closer's plunger may become bent, or the closer may be torn completely away from the jamb. Once it's badly bent, the only thing to do is replace it. If it has just pulled loose from the jamb, reattach it with longer screws.

Here's how to replace a pneumatic door closer:

1. Open the storm door and lock the plunger in the open position.
2. Remove the pins that attach both ends of the closer to the brackets and disconnect the closer.
3. Unscrew the old bracket from the jamb.

THE HOME PROBLEM SOLVER

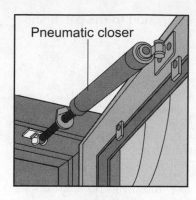

Pneumatic closer

FIGURE 8.1
Storm Door Closer

4. Buy a replacement closer; it's a good idea to take along the old one so you can choose a close match.
5. Screw the new bracket into position (if necessary, first fill the old screw holes with glued dowel plugs and cut them off flush with the surface).
6. Attach the closer to the bracket. If possible, connect it to the old door bracket; otherwise, remove the old bracket and replace it with the new one.

INTERIOR DOORS

Minor problems with interior doors are relatively easy to fix. You'll see some general fixes on page 179 under "General door problems." The issues discussed here are specific to interior doors.

Hole in hollow-core door

If you have a hollow-core door with a serious hole in it, consider replacing the entire door; hollow-core doors are modestly priced. You can repair a hole if you're willing to paint the door to hide the patch. For this repair, you'll need a can of spray foam insulation, vinyl spackling compound, and touch-up paint.

1. Fill the hole with the foam insulation.
2. Let it dry and expand overnight.
3. Use a razor blade to slice off the excess, cutting the mound just slightly lower than the door's surface.

4. With a three-inch putty knife, apply vinyl spackling compound to the patch and draw it smooth to the door's surface. Allow to dry.
5. Sand lightly with fine sandpaper; then touch up with paint.

Pocket door is off track

To repair a pocket door, you first have to remove it. To do this:

1. Use a utility knife to break the paint seal along the stop moldings on each door jamb; then carefully pry off the moldings with an old chisel or a five-in-one tool and flat bar.
2. Position the door so that it's centered in the doorway; then tilt it toward the room and lift the roller out of the overhead track.
3. Inspect the rollers to see if they're broken, worn, or otherwise fouled. If one or both are, repair or replace both of them (take one to the hardware store to find replacements that match).

Damaged pocket door track

Repairing the track can be tricky because it's located inside the pocket. If possible, slide your arm into the pocket and make sure the track is screwed soundly in place. If it isn't, do your best to tighten screws.

A hopeless track will have to be removed and replaced. This task involves removing enough of wall covering up near the track to let you access the old track. Unless you're accomplished at home carpentry, call a professional.

Sliding door rolls poorly

When a sliding door doesn't work right, the problem is often that the rollers have come off the track. Check to be sure they're fitted into the track properly. If you see that a roller is broken or has come loose from the door, you'll need to repair or replace it. To repair a sliding door, you have to first remove it.

To do this:

1. Tilt the door toward the room and lift the roller mechanism out of the overhead track.

2. Inspect the rollers to see if they're broken or have come loose. If the problem is just a loose roller, tighten or replace the loose screws. You'll have to replace a broken roller (take it to the hardware store to find a matching replacement).

Bifold door out of alignment

When a bifold door opens or closes poorly, adjusting it is usually easy. On the "hinge" side of the door, a pin at the door's bottom corner typically rests in a floor bracket, and a spring-mounted pin at the top corner engages a sliding bracket that locks into the track. When the door drags or pops out of its track, it usually means that one of these two pivots has moved.

1. Open the door, making sure its upper guide roller is in the track.
2. Check the bottom corner pivot pin. Be sure it's properly engaged in the floor bracket and that it is adjusted to allow about $1/16$-inch clearance from the jamb at the bottom corner of the door when the door is closed. To adjust its position, lift the door upward (the top pin is spring loaded to allow this).
3. Check the top pivot pin. A very common occurrence is that the sliding bracket has loosened and slid out of position. Align it so the "hinge" side of the door is plumb, with about $1/16$-inch clearance from the jamb when closed, and tighten the sliding bracket into the track.
4. If necessary, you can usually adjust the "hinge" side of the door up or down by turning the bottom pin, which is threaded like a bolt. With some types, you must first lift the pin out of the floor bracket.

Bifold door wobbles

If your bifold door is loose and wobbly, one of the pivot pins has probably worn away at its seat in the door—a hole—and become loose. The fix is to remove the pin, fill the hole with a dowel plug, then redrill a round hole.

Here's how:

1. Lift the door up and out at the bottom to remove it.
2. Pull the loose pivot pin out of its hole.
3. Enlarge the hole with a drill or hole saw so that it's perfectly round and will receive a wooden dowel plug.
4. Spread glue onto the dowel plug and tap it into the hole. Wipe away excess glue.

Door and Window Problems   185

5. Cut off the dowel, flush with the door.
6. Redrill a new hole to receive the pivot pin. If the pin is damaged, replace it.

Shower door is mildewed

Mildew is a growing fungus that thrives in damp, cool places. Warm, well-ventilated areas—even frequently wet areas like shower stalls—seldom have this problem. When you find mildew, clean it away with any of the commercial cleaners available; then take steps to remedy the cause.

Shower door is water-spotted

Household water with a high mineral content leaves behind deposits of these minerals when it evaporates. Water softeners help to eliminate this problem at the source, but you can find ways to reduce water-spotting without buying equipment. Wipe up drips and drops when they occur, before they have a chance to form stains. Keep a squeegee near the shampoo, and give the walls and door a quick wipe after each shower. To clean up those pesky spots that escape, try one of the new citrus-based cleaning solvents, which are especially effective against organic stains.

LOCKS AND LATCHES

The chances are good that if you're having trouble with a door lock, it's only going to get worse unless you remedy the problem. Most lock troubles are caused by parts that have become worn or that have shifted out of alignment over time. Some problems are easy to fix. For others, you're better off disassembling the lock and taking the faulty part to a locksmith. Fortunately, unless a house call is needed, locksmiths are relatively affordable tradespeople.

Key is hard to turn

The first and most obvious step is to be sure you're using the right key. Then open the door and try the key again. If it works easily, the dead bolt isn't engaging the strike plate properly (see page 189). If it doesn't work any easier, lubricate and/or clean the lock. Spray a little graphite into the cylinder and try the key several times. If this doesn't help, consider calling a locksmith.

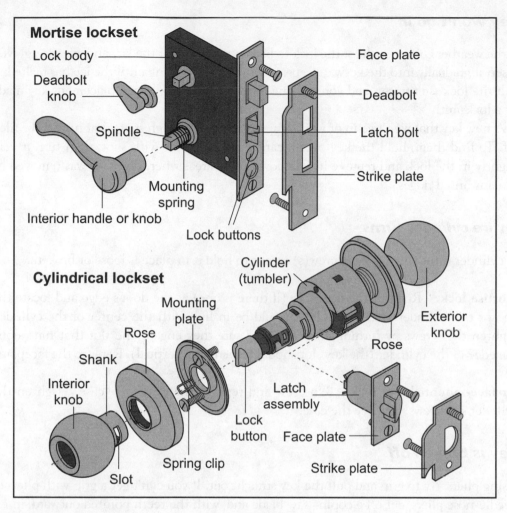

FIGURE 8.2 Mortise and Cylindrical Locksets

Key turns but doesn't work

Disassemble the lock so that you can be sure the cam or tang in properly engaged with the bolt. Re-engage it if necessary. Replace any broken parts and reassemble the lock.

Key won't go in

Is the weather cold enough for the lock to be frozen? If so, heat the key and, wearing gloves, insert it gradually into the keyway. Repeat heating and inserting until the ice has melted.

If the lock isn't frozen and you're using an old key, have a new replacement key made by a locksmith.

A new key that won't go in or work properly may have rough spots that need to be filed off. To find them, hold the key over a candle to blacken it with soot, then turn it very slightly in the lock and remove it. File down shiny areas where the soot was removed by the unwanted ridges.

Entire cylinder turns

A cylinder turns when the setscrew(s) meant to hold it in place is loose or broken.

Mortise lock. Remove the faceplate (if there is one) at the door's edge and locate the one or two cylinder setscrews. They should be in line with the center of the cylinder. Tighten the screws by turning clockwise—be sure they engage the slot that runs along the edge of the cylinder (the key slot should be perfectly vertical). Replace the faceplate.

Surface-mounted rim lock. Unscrew and remove the cover or "case." Tighten the cylinder set screws. Replace the case.

Key is broken off

Using pliers, try to grip and pull the key straight out. If you can't get a grip with pliers or needle-nose pliers, cut off a coping saw blade and, with the teeth pointed outward, insert the blade into the keyway and try to hook and drag the key out. As a last resort, remove the cylinder. Insert a stiff wire into the cam slot at the back of the cylinder and push the key out, or take the cylinder to a locksmith.

Doesn't latch shut

When a door latch doesn't click into position, it usually means the latch and the strike plate are out of alignment. When possible, it's easiest to file the slot in the strike plate a little bit so that it will receive the latch—shifting the strike plate's position usually involves mortising the jamb, filling part of the old mortise, and so forth. You can also solve misalignment by replacing the strike plate with an adjustable one.

Latch sticks

A latch can stick for many reasons, most of which are easily fixed. Check that the hinge screws are tight. If the door is out of alignment, the latch will bind. Also check the knob and lock assembly for loose screws or misalignment. Finally, look closely at the strike on the door jamb—if it's blocked or out of adjustment, the latch won't run freely in and out.

Lock works slowly

Exterior locks can freeze; interior locks get dirty; and small internal parts eventually wear out or break. Before you buy a replacement, try some quick remedies: put some graphite into the keyhole, either by squeezing it from a tube or by dusting a key; then operate the lock a few times to work the graphite into the mechanism. Lock deicers contain alcohol and other lubricants that help to dissolve gummy, dirty deposits. The last resort is to disassemble the lock to see if something has jammed or broken—you may be able to set it straight or replace the part without buying a whole new lock.

Dead bolt hard to bolt

The chances are good that the bolt is having a hard time finding the throat in the strike plate. Be sure the strike plate is secure and is in reasonable alignment with the bolt. You can file the edges of the strike plate a little and even slightly round the edges of the dead bolt's end. If this doesn't work, you'll probably have to remove the strike plate, fill the screw holes with glue and wood matchsticks, reposition it properly, and rescrew it.

Doorknob is loose

If your door has a loose knob, look for two screws that hold the decorative escutcheon plate and tighten them. On an older doorknob, position the knob on the spindle and tighten the setscrew that locks it in place.

Brass hardware is tarnished

Either remove or mask-off the hardware. Restore the shine with a good brass cleaner; apply it with a soft cloth (protect your skin with rubber gloves). A soft buffing wheel fitted into an electric drill speeds polishing. Protect the finish by spraying on a light coat of clear lacquer or brass sealer.

Remove badly tarnished hardware and place it in undiluted ammonia for about an hour before polishing.

WINDOWS AND SCREENS

Most windows operate reliably for years, but with time, certain types of windows can become balky in the way they operate. Double-hung windows—the type that has a bottom section you can raise and a top section you can lower—are the biggest offenders, and when they go bad, they're almost impossible to open. Here are helpful tips for handling the most common window problems:

Glass pane is broken

A small broken windowpane can be relatively easy to replace—but it may not be worth the hassle. Roughly measure the broken pane and call a couple of glass dealers for replacement prices, both with and without installation. If you decide to do the work yourself, wear eye protection and leather gloves when working.

1. Use an old chisel to remove the broken glass and old glazing compound. Compound doesn't always come willingly. You can soften it with a heat gun, if necessary. Also pull out the little metal triangles (glazier's points), using a pair of pliers.
2. Measure the exact size of the opening and deduct 1/8 inch in both directions when ordering a replacement.
3. Roll glazing compound between both hands to form a long, skinny snake. Run this around the perimeter of the opening.
4. Press the replacement glass into the compound and seat it firmly. Use a putty knife to press glazier's points into the sash every four to six inches to hold the glass.
5. Use your fingers to apply compound around the perimeter; then smooth it at an angle with the putty knife to match other panes (wet the blade if necessary). Allow to cure about one week; then paint.

Scratched glass

For an unsightly scratch, try applying a coat of clear nail polish. Remove the excess with nail polish remover on a clean cloth.

Another option is to buy a very gentle metal polishing compound, such as Brasso, and polish out the scratch with a soft cotton cloth. This takes a lot of elbow grease, and you do run the risk of creating tiny abrasive scratches.

FIGURE 8.3   Removing Putty
from a Broken Window

FIGURE 8.4   Installing a New Pane
with Glazier's Points and Putty

Crumbling glazing compound

Old glazing compound may become brittle and fall out. When this happens, air can leak in around the glass panes or—worse—the glass can fall out.

1. Remove the old glazing compound with an old chisel and hammer (wear safety glasses and be careful not to drive the chisel into the edge of the glass). If necessary, soften the compound with a heat gun, but be careful not to train the heat on the glass—it may break.
2. Use your fingers to apply glazing compound around the perimeter; then smooth it at an angle with the putty knife to match other panes (wet the blade if necessary).
3. Allow compound to cure about one week; then paint.

Window sash is painted shut

Use a utility knife—or better, a special little tool called a window saw (available for about $10)—to cut through the paint all around the moveable sash. Be careful not to leave any areas uncut (inside or out). Then unlock the window and try to force it open with abrupt force, using the heel of your hands. If that doesn't work, try to free it with a wood block and a hammer or mallet.

Door and Window Problems

Window sash is stuck

Sometimes a double-hung window won't slide freely simply because it fits too tightly within its tracks. Tightness may be caused by swelling of the wood due to moisture, by a build-up of paint, or by long-term settling of the house. When a double-hung window sticks, use a hammer and chisel to pry off the interior stops that form the track, as discussed on the facing page in "Double-hung window falls shut." Sand off any bumps or irregular areas and nail them back in place, allowing a slight bit of play by placing a spacer such as a very thin piece of cardboard between the stop and sash as you nail.

Window sash is loose

The opposite problem to the one above is a sash that is too loose. All wood shrinks to some degree over time, and wood wears down from repeated use. Replacing the parting track with a new one often solves this problem. An easier fix is to add an insulation strip to the face of the old parting strip—the strip may take up just enough "slack" in your window, and it adds a measure of protection against the elements.

Woodwork is rotted

Where wood sills or sash have rotted because of serious abuse from weather, you can use epoxy wood filler, available at home centers, to repair the area. (If large areas are affected, talk with a carpenter or cabinetmaker about replacing sections of the wood or the entire sash.)

Here's how to make the repairs with epoxy:

1. Use a chisel to dislodge most of the loose, rotted wood. Drill a few 1/4-inch holes into the damaged wood.
2. Soak the entire rotted area with liquid epoxy "consolidant" to transform the area into a sturdy base for filler. Let the wood absorb the consolidant for about five minutes; then reapply, wait, reapply, and continue until the wood ceases to accept consolidant.
3. Knead a batch of epoxy filler, according to label directions, and mold the repair. As the material cures, dip a putty knife in solvent and use it to sculpt and shape the repair.
4. Sand, file, or rasp as needed; paint the area within three days.

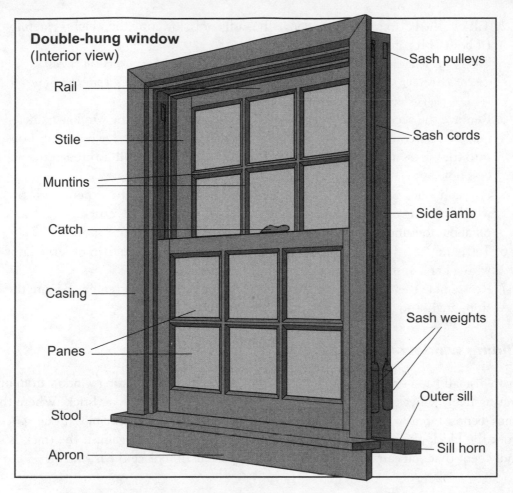

Double-hung window
(Interior view)

Rail

Stile

Muntins

Catch

Casing

Panes

Stool

Apron

Sash pulleys

Sash cords

Side jamb

Sash weights

Outer sill

Sill horn

FIGURE 8.5   Anatomy of a Double-hung Window

Double-hung window falls shut

Do you have a double-hung window that won't stay open unless you prop it up? Most of the time, this is caused by a broken sash cord. This is an inexpensive and relatively easy thing to fix, but it does take time—you're likely to spend the better part of your weekend messing with it.

1. Remove the interior stops. To do this, you'll probably have to slice the paint seal with a utility knife and then, using an old chisel, pry off the moldings. If necessary, remove weather stripping.

2. Tilt out the bottom sash and remove the sash cords, lowering the weights carefully (if both sash cords aren't broken).

   NOTE: If you want to repair sash cords in the upper sash, you'll have to pry out at least one of the parting strips to remove that sash. When you pry these out, they'll probably be ruined, so plan to buy new ones at a lumberyard.

3. Remove the access panel covers located on the inner face of the window frame.

4. Pass new #7 cotton sash cord over each top pulley and feed it down until it drops into the access area. If necessary, use a bent coat hanger to pull it through the access hole.

5. At each side, tie that end of the cords onto the sash weights; then, with the weights sitting on the bottom of their channels, pull the cords taut and cut them off about four inches from the top pulleys.

6. Tie a knot and push it into the top slot at each side of the sash; then tack the knot with a brad. Test the action of the window up and down.

7. Reassemble the rest of the window, reversing the order of disassembly. Be sure the stops are not so tight that they cause the window to bind.

Sliding window track is bent

Even a small bend or dent in an aluminum track will prevent a sliding window from operating freely. Check the track with a straightedge such as a metal yardstick. Where the track bends, tap a wood block gently with a hammer. But don't just tap in one spot— work the block along the track until the entire track is straight again. If the track is so badly bent that you can't straighten it, you may be able to replace the track.

Sun fades floors or furnishings

When floors and furnishings are becoming faded due to sunlight, you can control the fading by blocking the sun with shades or curtains, but then, of course, you'll lose the natural light. Fading is caused by ultraviolet light, heat, and visible light from the sun. Overhangs, awnings, and shade trees can help, but the best solution is to apply window film tints that are designed to block UV rays, reflect heat, and slightly reduce visible light.

Sold in rolls at home improvement centers, window film tint is a thin, plastic-like material that is easy to apply to the inside surfaces of windows with a soapy solution of water (directions come with the film). Choose reflective low-e films to cut back on UV rays and heat; beware of the darker films—with these, you'll sacrifice visible light.

Screen is torn

The easiest way to fix a torn window screen is to remove it and take it to a glass shop for repair—this usually costs less than $25. But if you'd like to do the work yourself—and save most of that money—the job of replacing screen fabric in an aluminum frame is relatively simple.

1. Use a narrow, flat-bladed screwdriver or an awl to pry up the vinyl spline that circles the perimeter of the screen fabric and seals it into the groove in the aluminum frame.
2. At a home center, buy replacement fiberglass screen fabric and vinyl spline; an inexpensive spline roller; and a utility knife with blades.
3. Place the aluminum frame on a flat surface, with the spline slot facing up. Tack a couple of thin wood slats against the inner faces of the long sides to keep the frame from bowing inward when you stretch the new fabric in place.
4. Spread the new fabric on the frame, overlapping all sides by about one inch.
5. Snip off the corners just beyond the slot at a 45° angle, to eliminate excess material. Lay the spline in place; then, starting at one corner, push the spline and screen fabric in place, using the rolling tool. If the fabric bunches or wrinkles, pull up the spline, straighten the fabric, and continue.
6. When you've completed the perimeter, use a sharp utility knife to trim off the excess fabric.

Condensation between thermal panes

Unfortunately, when a thermal window fails, there is no cost-effective way to remove condensation from between glass; the glazing must be replaced. Your best bet is to buy quality thermal windows that are backed by a strong warrantee (at least ten years). One mark of quality is "IGCC approved," a certification by the Insulation Glass Certification Council.

Condensation on interior glass

Because windows are usually the coolest surfaces in a house, they may collect condensation in winter, when outdoor temperatures are low and indoor air is warm and humid. These conditions encourage mold and mildew and can cause wooden window frames and sills to rot.

To reduce condensation, increase ventilation—just using bathroom and kitchen fans can make a big difference.

Running the air conditioner also reduces humidity. Also keep showers short and run only full loads in washers and dishwashers.

If doing these things doesn't help, contact an insulation contractor.

9

EXTERIOR PROBLEMS

Nothing makes you feel less secure in a house than the "drip, drip, drip" of a leaky roof. In this section, we'll look at how to handle repairs on your home's exterior—how to repair various types of roofs and how to fix other problems that occur on top of your house—notably chimney, flashing, and gutter problems. We'll also look at a variety of fixes for your home's siding, decks, basement, and driveway.

If you have a particularly steep, high, or slippery roof—or if you are not comfortable working at heights—call a professional roofer or repair person to handle roof repairs. *Always follow safe practices when on top of the roof or working on walls from a ladder or scaffolding* (see page 7).

BASEMENTS AND DRIVEWAYS

Basements and driveways have one key commonality—both are lined with masonry (typically concrete) that is in direct contact with the earth. As a result, basements are often damp, and both basements and driveways frequently suffer from cracked surfaces. You can handle minor basement and driveway problems yourself, but for major repairs, it's well worth the expense to hire a foundation, waterproofing, or concrete contractor.

Wet crawl space

Dampness in a dirt floor crawl space calls for improving ventilation and blocking the rise of moisture from the earth.

1. Begin by making sure the crawl space area is fully ventilated—that no foundation vents are blocked.
2. Then spread a vapor barrier made of 6-mil polyethylene (plastic sheeting) across the dirt area, reaching up to the top of each foundation wall.
3. Staple the barrier to the mud sills. Be sure to cut the barrier away around foundation vents and openings so it doesn't block airflow.

Mold or mildew on floor framing

If mold or mildew are growing beneath the floor, the conditions are far too damp. The first step is to eliminate sources of moisture. Then mix about 3/4 of a cup of bleach with one gallon of water in a clean garden-style sprayer. Wearing old clothing and goggles or safety glasses (and a respirator if the conditions make one necessary), spray the framing with this bleach/water mixture. If you don't wear a respirator, avoid breathing the spray. Following application, wipe off the mildew with a rag (or scrub with a brush, if necessary).

Driveway cracks

For cracks in a concrete driveway, see "Concrete cracks" on page 227. For small cracks in asphalt, buy a tube of asphalt crack repair compound, sold in a tube that's meant to fit into a caulking gun. Sweep loose dirt and debris out of the crack. Then apply the asphalt repair compound according to the label directions.

For large cracks in asphalt:

1. Use a broom or stiff brush to sweep out the cracks. If you have a shop vacuum, use it to vacuum up loose dirt and debris.
2. Use a cold-process asphalt repair compound to patch holes and large cracks. Follow the directions on the label. *Note: You can also ask your home improvement dealer whether they carry a self-adhesive polypropylene rubberized fabric, sold in rolled strips, that you just cut, peel, and stick over a crack or small hole.*

Oil stains on asphalt

Though oil stains on asphalt are difficult to remove, you can try to scrub them out with a detergent and bleach or, as an alternative, with a commercial driveway cleaner, sold at home improvement centers. If you buy a driveway cleaner, be sure to get one that is made for asphalt; a concrete cleaner can damage asphalt. Follow label directions explicitly. But first, try the household cleaner route:

1. Using a stiff, long-handled brush and a solution of trisodium phosphate (TSP) or a phosphate-free substitute, scrub the stain.
2. Following label precautions and directions, scrub remaining spots with full-strength household bleach. Wear old clothes, rubber gloves, and safety glasses.
3. Rinse thoroughly with a hose.

Asphalt driveway coating and sealing

One way to extend an asphalt driveway's life span is to seal coat it (apply an asphalt-based sealant). As moisture penetrates cracks, then freezes and thaws, cracks grow and allow more water in. The problem grows. At the same time, sunlight fades and dries the asphalt, making it brittle. Seal coating a driveway is like painting or staining siding—it helps block damaging sunlight and seals out moisture. It also helps a driveway to repel gasoline and oil, which disintegrate the asphalt. One gallon of seal coat covers about eighty square feet, but be sure to check the actual coverage listed on the can.

1. Pull any weeds and sweep the surface.
2. Use a cold-mix asphalt patch to fill holes or wide cracks, and remove stains, as discussed above.
3. Sweep again; then hose off the surface.
4. On a fairly warm day, apply the sealer according to label directions. Normally, you do this while the driveway is still wet. Allow the sealer to cure; avoid using the driveway for twenty-four hours.

DEALING WITH ROOF AND SIDING LEAKS

Most roof and siding leaks are hard to find because they originate away from where they show up. In order to find the source of a leak, follow a roofer's advice and "think like water." Water typically comes in through worn, broken, or missing shingles; where nails have worked loose; or through corroded or poorly sealed flashings around vents, skylights, chimneys, and along the intersections of roof planes. Once water passes the roofing, it flows along the sheathing, the roof rafters, or the topside of ceilings until it finds a place to drip down—inevitably onto your favorite piece of furniture.

Look for a roof leak during the day. Go into the attic with a bright, portable light; step only on secure framing members—never on the insulation or the topside of the ceiling below; it won't support you! Start above the place where drips occurred and work your way back, up-roof. Look for wetness along the framing members. Or, if the weather has been dry for a while, look for water marks—stains or discolorations on the wood made by dampness. Then switch off the light and try to find a hole where daylight shows through the roof. (On a wood shingle roof, you'll see too many such places because the overlapped shingles shed water but let light show through.) If it's still raining, put a bucket under the leak (again, properly supported).

Water testing for roof leaks

If you can't find the cause of a leak, wait for dry weather and ask a friend to help you do a water test. To do this, one person goes onto the roof with a garden hose; the other person goes inside the attic with a bucket and a strong light. The person in the attic watches carefully while the one on the roof floods the roof with a hose, starting at the eaves and slowly working up-roof until the leak appears in the attic. Once the leak is found, push a nail up through the hole to mark its location for rooftop repair.

Temporary roof repairs

For information on temporarily repairing a roof leak, see "Roof leak" in chapter 1 on emergencies, page 6.

Handling ice dams

Heavy snowfall can create ice dams that cause a roof to leak along the eaves. An ice dam forms when snow melts over a house's heated spaces and runs down the roof, only to freeze again over the cold eaves. This ice builds up along the eaves, trapping snowmelt water that eventually flows under the shingles into the attic. When putting on a new roof in a cold climate, it's smart to install a special membrane called an "ice shield" beneath the shingles along eaves to prevent ice-dam water penetration (talk to a roofer about the difficulty of installing one of these on an existing roof).

Quick Tip: In the event of leaks caused by an ice dam, photograph the damage and check with your insurance company regarding coverage. Immediately remove as much snow from the eaves as possible, or call a roofer to handle this job.

Here's how to solve ice dam problems:

1. Check and, if necessary, improve the attic ventilation to minimize the thaw/freeze cycle. Cold air should be able to circulate from eaves vents to ridge vents or gable vents, minimizing temperature variations on the roof. Be sure the soffit vents are not blocked by insulation. If the underside of the roof is insulated, be sure the insulation is held back from the surface by at least one inch for air circulation.
2. Improve the ceiling insulation to help keep heat from leaving the rooms below during winter months.
3. As a last resort, you can install electric heating cables made for this purpose along the section of roof above the overhangs. These melt enough of the ice to provide an escape route for runoff.

FLASHING

If your roof leaks, the chances are pretty good that deteriorating metal roof flashing may be the culprit. Flashing protects the intersections between roof planes; the joints where roofs meet dormers, skylights, and chimneys; and roofs' edges. Given enough time, these formed sheet metal (or sometimes plastic) angles and troughs can rust or deteriorate or simply work loose from the surfaces they protect, opening up places for water to penetrate. Because flashing tends to be used where there is heavy water flow, leaking flashing can funnel streams of water into your house.

Chimney flashing leak

Along the joint where the flashing meets the chimney, remove old caulking and chip out the mortar that seals the cap flashing. Scrub out the area with a stiff brush. Use special masonry caulk to seal the joints between the flashing and the chimney. Seal the seam between the cap and step flashings with urethane roofing cement or silicone caulking compound.

Leaking skylight flashing

Next to the skylight, lift the shingles, one at a time, and brush out dirt and debris. Force roofing cement into the area where they meet the skylight flange and/or the roofing felt. Seal any obvious seams or joints with silicone caulking compound or urethane roofing cement.

Leaking dormer flashing

Scrape out old caulking compound, if any. Wire brush the flashing and apply urethane roofing cement between the siding or shingles and the flashing. Be sure to seal any obvious seams.

Leaking vent pipe flashing

Remove shingles covering the flange at the back and sides of the vent pipe flashing. Pry and lift off the flashing. Pull or cut off any nails. Position a new vent pipe flashing over the vent, push it down into place, and nail where shingles will cover. Replace shingles, and cover nails with roofing cement.

GUTTERS AND DOWNSPOUTS

Most gutters become corroded, out of alignment, or broken, given enough time. Nearly all gutter-related problems are caused by the fact that they become clogged with leaves and debris. When this happens, water fills up gutters, causing them to sag or pull away from the eaves, to corrode, and to drain poorly, permanently. When water overflows the gutters, it can damage siding, windows, and roofing. The secret is to keep gutters free of debris so they don't clog in the first place.

Clogged gutters and downspouts

On most roofs, it's easiest to clean out gutters from a ladder; as you move around the house, be careful to position the ladder on sound footing and lean it where it won't bend or scratch gutters. To strengthen a lightweight aluminum gutter, you can set a short two-by-four inside it, flat side down. Consider installing a gutter guard, available at hardware stores, to minimize leaves and debris from entering gutters.

Clean your gutters at least twice a year to keep them from getting clogged. It's easiest to do this when the leaves and gunk in the gutters has had a chance to dry out. A leaf blower works pretty well for blowing out loose debris; wear eye protection. Otherwise, starting at the gutter's high point, just scoop out the debris with your hands; wear protective gloves to protect your hands from screws and sharp edges. When most of the debris is out, use a stiff brush to loosen caked-on dirt. Mount a high-pressure nozzle with a shut-off valve on the end of a garden hose, so you can control the flow from your ladder, then flush out the gutters.

Gutters sag

Check for signs of standing water or water marks along the inner sides of gutters. With a level, check the slope—gutters should drop about 1/4 inch for each ten feet of run toward the downspouts. Adjust, reseat, or add gutter hangers as needed.

Gutters leak

Standing water in gutters eventually will rust galvanized steel or seep through seams of aluminum gutters. Check for signs of standing water and sagging (see above). Adjust or add gutter hangers as needed. Allow insides of gutters to dry out, brush leaking seams clean, and then caulk the seams with silicone.

Gutters overflow

If your gutters overflow, either the gutters or downspouts are clogged (see above), or they are too small to handle the volume of runoff. If they're not stopped up, install new, larger downspouts first. If that doesn't solve the problem, have larger gutters installed by a professional gutter installer.

Downspouts are broken loose

Downspouts may break loose or disconnect from the gutter outlet or between sections. To refasten them, push them together, drill pilot holes, and fasten them with two 3/8-inch by #8 galvanized sheet-metal screws. (Don't use longer screws because debris will hang up on them.) Be sure the anchor straps that hold downspouts to the wall are secure.

   Note: By fastening the top downspout to the S-curve outlet with only one screw at each joint, the downspout is much easier to take down for regular cleaning.

Water pools at house

Divert downspout runoff away from the house, using downspout extenders. Though you can make an extender from a section of downspout material, flexible plastic pipe extenders will carry runoff several feet away, are easy to adjust, and move out of the way when they're not needed.

ROOFING: ASPHALT SHINGLE

Repairing or replacing the most common type of roofing—asphalt or asphalt-fiberglass shingles (sometimes called "composition roofing")—is relatively easy, but be sure you can work safely and comfortably on your roof before you decide to make your own repairs. Whether or not you do your own work, don't delay fixing roof problems: they only get worse. Small tears, cracks, and holes can be repaired, but missing or severely damaged shingles must be replaced. *Be sure to follow safe practices when on the roof* (see page 7).

When your roof has multiple leaks or many damaged shingles, it usually means it's time to replace the roofing. To test an asphalt-shingle roof's condition, bend over a corner of one or two shingles on the sunniest side of the roof; if they break rather than flex, the material is nearing the end of its serviceable life. Wear is another factor; a collection of mineral granules in gutters or at the base of downspouts indicates that the protective mineral surface of asphalt shingles is wearing away.

When you put on a new roof, it's helpful to store a few extra shingles so you'll have matching replacements for repairs. It's best to work on a warm day, when both roofing and asphalt- or plastic roofing cement will be more pliable.

Torn or curled asphalt shingle

It's important to fix or replace torn asphalt shingles before the problems get severe enough to permit leaks, or before the pieces break apart and blow off the roof.

1. Carefully lift the torn piece or damaged corner and, using a putty knife, spread a layer of roofing cement under it.
2. Tack down a curled corner with one roofing nail or the two torn halves with two roofing nails on each side of the tear. Spread roofing cement over the crack and on top of the nail heads to seal up any potential leaks.

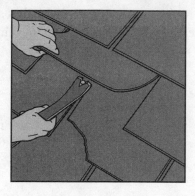

FIGURE 9.1   Removing a
Damaged Asphalt Shingle

FIGURE 9.2   Nailing a
Replacement Asphalt Shingle

Badly damaged asphalt shingles

When an asphalt shingle is beyond simple repair, it's best to replace it. Asphalt shingles are relatively easy to replace, but the repair may stick out like a sore thumb if you don't have an exact replacement for your type of roofing. When you visit a roofing dealer or home improvement center, take along a small, broken piece of your existing shingles to help you find a good match. (It pays to store a few shingles for repairs when you roof your home.)

If a ridge or hip shingle is damaged, don't remove it. Instead, nail down each corner with roofing nails and apply a second shingle over the top, first coating the bottom of that shingle with roofing cement. Nail down the corners and cover roofing nail heads with plastic roofing cement.

To remove and replace a damaged shingle:

1. Use a flat pry bar to gently lift the two shingles directly up-roof from the damaged one. Break the black, self-sealing strip that holds the shingles in place by sliding the pry bar along the length of each shingle.
2. Raise the shingle tabs and carefully pry up the nails holding the damaged shingle and the shingle directly above it (this means you'll have to go two shingles up-roof).
3. Slide out the damaged shingle.
4. With a utility knife, cut off a small piece from the top corners of the replacement shingle, then slide the shingle into position.

Nail the new shingle in place with galvanized roofing nails. Cover the nail heads with plastic roofing cement, and to help glue them back down spread a little extra cement beneath the tabs that you folded back.

ROOFING: BUILT-UP AND ROLL

Roofs covered with built-up or roll roofing are most likely to leak along deteriorating flashing (see page 201) or where the surface has puckered, blistered, or cracked. The difficulty of making repairs depends on the size of the problem; for large problems, call a roofer.

Flat roof blisters

Blisters on an almost flat roof may be caused by heat and sun but often signify moisture under the surface. The chances are good that water has penetrated the roof membrane through a nearby hole or flashing. If there are several blisters or if the blisters are quite large, consider calling a roofing contractor to handle the work.

1. Sweep gravel and dirt away from the blister.
2. Use a utility knife to slice through the top layer, releasing the pressure from the bubble.
3. Feel inside the hole for moisture. If it feels wet, look for possible sources of leaks along flashings or in the same general area as the blister—and fix those leaks (see below).
4. With a putty knife or caulking gun, work plastic roofing cement into the pocket and around the surface of the cut. Carry the cement beyond the damaged area at least two inches in all directions.
5. From an asphalt shingle or piece of roll roofing, cut a patch to fit the cemented area. Press it into place and nail it with roofing nails. Cover the patch and nail heads with more cement.
6. When the cement begins to set up, sweep the gravel back over the top of the patch.

Flat roof damage

You can fix a small damaged area on an almost-flat roof by cutting out a small section and replacing it with a new piece. Because this type of roof is designed to hold standing water, making a watertight repair can be tricky. If it sounds like more than you want to attempt or risk, call a roofing contractor.

1. Sweep gravel and dirt away from the hole.
2. Cut out the damaged area, making a rectangular cut with the aid of a straightedge and utility knife. Slice through the top layer and, if necessary, cut through other damaged layers.
3. From roll roofing or an asphalt shingle, cut a replacement piece sized the same as the cutout. Spread plastic roofing cement inside the cutout area and up over the edges. Fit the patch in place and nail it around the perimeter with galvanized roofing nails spaced about two inches apart.
4. Cut a second patch four inches larger than the first one, large enough to overlap by two inches on all sides.
5. Cover the first patch with roofing cement, carrying the cement about three inches beyond the patch's perimeter.
6. Press the second patch into place and nail and cement it as you did the first one.
7. When the cement begins to set up, sweep the gravel back over the top of the patch.

ROOFING: MASONRY TILE

The most common problem with tile, concrete tile, fiber cement, and other types of masonry roofing is cracking. For anything but an occasional cracked or broken tile, hire a roofer.

Small holes or cracks

1. Scrub the area with a wire brush.
2. Fill area with plastic roofing cement and use plastic roofing cement to seal or join the crack.

Long crack or broken tile

Replace a tile that is severely cracked or broken.

1. Carefully pry up the tile (or tiles) just above the cracked or broken one.
2. Break the faulty tile and remove the pieces. Also pry out or force out any nails.
3. Spread a small amount of roofing cement along the underside of the replacement and slide it into place. Adhesive, rather than nails, will hold this one.
4. Press all tiles snugly down.

ROOFING: METAL

Metal roofs are very durable but occasionally dent. Though you can replace a section, it's generally best to call an installer who is trained in working with your particular type of roof. If you have any paperwork on the original purchase of your roof, check it to see if the warranty will cover repairs. Seal small holes or cracks with roofing cement after cleaning the area with a wire brush.

Metal roof repair

1. Look for loose nails, pull them, and renail.
2. Look for holes, rust patches, or other signs of deterioration.
3. Seal up leaks with urethane roof cement, which has better protection against ultraviolet breakdown than common asphalt- or plastic roof cement. (Even so, the cement will deteriorate over time and the flashing will need replacement.) For a finger-size hole, make a small patch from the same material as the flashing and cement it over the hole.
4. Recaulk all seams and edges along the flashing, using a urethane roofing cement.
5. Replace severely damaged flashing; for this repair, call a roofer.

ROOFING: WOOD SHINGLE

Wood shingles and shakes last a long time, but like any other roofing material, they eventually fall prey to the elements. Fortunately, replacing wood shingles is relatively easy.

Split, warped, or damaged wood shingles

Cracked, warped, missing, or broken wood shingles are not something to repair. Instead, they should be replaced.

Here's how:

1. With a hammer and chisel, split up the defective shingle and pull out the pieces.
2. Slide a flat bar up under the shingles and force out the nails with a few hammer blows. (Or, for a neater job, you can cut off the nails, using a hacksaw blade or a special shingle ripper, available at hardware stores or roofing supply companies).

FIGURE 9.3 Using a Shingle Ripper

FIGURE 9.4 Replacing a Wooden Shingle

3. Cut a replacement shingle to fit the space, making it $1/2$ inch narrower than the space ($1/4$ inch clearance for each side).

4. Tap the replacement into place with a hammer, stopping about $1/4$ inch before the shingle is flush with its neighbors. Drive two roofing nails, angled slightly upward, just below the butt of the shingle above it. Then place a wood block against the replacement and tap it upward the final $1/4$ inch.

Moss on shingles

In particularly moist climates, moss can grow on shingles, particularly beneath trees that provide heavy shade. Cutting back tree limbs to encourage sunlight helps eliminate the cause, as does hosing down the roof twice a year. Once it becomes established, moss can be removed by a pressure washing specialist, using a power washer with hot water and fungicides. See more about pressure washing on page 210.

SIDING: COMMON PROBLEMS

What begins as a small crack in your home's siding can become a major headache. As wind-driven rain works its way into cracks and fissures in deteriorating siding, the water can get inside walls, causing paint to peel and fostering damaging dry rot in the structure. It pays to take care of siding problems when they occur. Some repairs are relatively easy to handle yourself—some should be handled by contractors. The line between doing it yourself or having it done professionally is often drawn both by the material and by your skills.

Dirty, stained siding

Perhaps the most common problem with all types of siding is that they get dirty. Even when siding looks like it desperately needs a new coat of paint, it may really only need a good washing. The most time consuming—and thorough—way to wash siding is the old fashioned way: with a bucket of sudsy water, a hose, and a stiff-bristle nylon scrub brush screwed onto the end of a pole. Considering the hassle of washing your car or bathing your dog, you might think that cleaning the whole house could take you forever—but it doesn't necessarily have to. Depending upon the type of siding your home has, you may have an easier method: pressure washing (see below). But beware: if your home's paint is not sound, pressure washing may cause it to peel.

Mildew on siding

Scrubbing or pressure washing a house will remove dirt and grime but will not necessarily remove mildew. To determine whether blackish areas are mildew or just dirt, take a little bleach and apply it to the area with a sponge. If the black spots disappear, they are probably mildew. If they don't go away, the discoloration is probably just dirt and should come off with a good scrubbing, using TSP or a nonphosphate detergent substitute.

To get rid of mildew, mix one part bleach to four parts water and scrub the area with this solution. Be sure to wear safety glasses and avoid getting the bleach solution on your body or your clothes. After scrubbing, rinse with clear water.

How to pressure wash siding

Pressure washing—also called power washing—is a good way to clean a house exterior or prep it for a new paint job. Spraying water and, in some cases, detergent at high velocity, a pressure washer cleans dirt, grime, and the chalk-like residue that comes from deteriorating paint from the surfaces of siding and trim. This is an excellent first step to ensure that a new coat of paint will last.

A pressure washer is not meant to be used for removing paint from wood siding or brick—holding a strong spray in one place long enough to remove paint can erode soft wood grain or dislodge mortar from between bricks. Though it can be used on most siding materials, including wood, vinyl, metal, and some types of masonry, a pressure washer should not be used on hardboard siding because moisture is hardboard's worst enemy, and it shouldn't be used on stucco because it can ruin the material. Also, do not pressure wash your house if you suspect that it may have been painted with lead paint prior to 1978 (contact your public health department or the EPA at 800-424-LEAD). If your home is two stories or very large, it's safer to let a professional do this job for you.

You can rent a pressure washer from most rental equipment dealers for about $50 to $75 a day. They come in various sizes for different types of jobs, from about 1,200 to 3,000 psi (pounds per square inch, the power of the spray). A 1,200 to 1,500 psi model is safer to use with vulnerable materials such as wood, aluminum, or steel; you can use a stronger 2,500–3,000 psi model for a material that doesn't have a painted surface, such as vinyl. The stronger types work faster. Choose one that will allow mixing detergent into the spray. Plan to mix about one pound of TSP (or a nonphosphate substitute) into every four gallons of water for the washing (but rinse with water only).

Scrub any mildew from the surface before power washing (see facing page).

Use both hands when operating the equipment, and never use it while standing on a ladder. For high areas, also rent a six- to twelve-foot adjustable extension shaft, but be aware that this can be a bit tricky to handle. Start with the nozzle about three feet from the wall and work your way closer until you feel the spray is strong enough—but not too strong. Never get closer than twelve inches from the siding or you may damage it; do not point it at windows and avoid aiming it upward, where it might drive water under siding. Remember: this is extremely high pressure, so never point the nozzle at anyone and be sure to wear safety glasses. Also keep the wand, the water, and your self away from any electrical wires or devices.

Here are the steps to follow:

1. Protect any plants, light fixtures, and any breakable materials around the house with plastic bags, duct tape, and drop cloths. Move obstacles and outdoor furniture away from the house.
2. Connect the pressure washer to a garden hose. If the machine has a detergent dispenser, fill it with a cleaning solution (a mixture of water and TSP [or a nonphosphate detergent substitute]).
3. Working from the top down, hold the wand at about a 45° angle and spray soffits, overhangs, gutters, and downspouts. Then move it across the siding from side to side at a steady pace. Hold the nozzle a couple of feet from the wall and adjust its distance back and forth for the best cleaning action. As well as you can, direct the water slightly downward so it isn't blasted up under horizontal lap joints of the siding. When working near windows, direct the nozzle away from the window, holding the wand at an angle so you don't drive water into the window or frame.
4. Rinse off the siding with clear water, using a garden hose—work from the top down. If you plan to paint, allow the siding to dry for at least two days.

SIDING: PAINT PROBLEMS

Painting a house is expensive and laborious, so you don't want to have to do the job more than once every five years. In order to get maximum life from a paint job, you will need to buy high quality, appropriate paint and to prepare the surface properly. If you fudge on either one of these tasks, you'll find yourself back on a ladder ahead of schedule. See the table on page 216 for information about how to choose appropriate paint for your situation; regardless of the type of siding your home has, buy only top-quality paint.

Preparation is the key to giving a house a paint job that will last. Be sure to follow preparation instructions fully.

If your home was built before 1978, the old exterior paint may contain lead—a health hazard. Call your public health department for information on testing for lead, and for information on reducing lead hazards, contact the EPA at 800-424-LEAD.

Paint problems

If your house needs a new coat of paint, figure out why the old coat failed first. Then tackle the cause so that the same thing doesn't happen with your new paint job. Pay special attention to preparation when you paint: this is the most common culprit behind paint failure.

Lead content

Houses painted before 1978 may have paint that contains lead, which can be hazardous, especially to children, both through physical contact and through breathing dust from sanding or scraping. If you suspect that your home may have lead paint, request information on proper handling from your public health department or from the EPA at 800-424-LEAD.

Peeling

Peeling paint usually indicates that the paint did not adhere to the surface during painting. This happens when paint is applied to damp wood, loose or flaking paint, or a dirty or greasy surface. To avoid peeling paint in the future, thoroughly wash (see page 210) the surface and scrape any loose paint. Only paint in dry weather.

Peeling paint can also occur when moist interior air compromises the paint from behind. If this is the case, solve the humidity problem in your home by improving ventilation or through dehumidification.

Peeling paint usually calls for repainting. Be sure to completely scrape loose paint from the surface, sand and fill if necessary, and prime before repainting.

Blisters

Cut open a blister and break away the paint. If you discover bare wood, you know the blister is caused by moisture in damp wood, trapped behind the paint seal and fighting to get out. If the surface beneath the blister is painted, paint solvent was probably trapped under a surface layer that dried too quickly. To avoid both of these problems, be sure the surface is completely dry and do not paint in direct sunlight.

Blisters are often localized, so complete repainting may not be necessary. Scrape the blistered area, sand it smooth, then prime and paint.

Wrinkles and sagging

Lumps, wrinkles, sagging, and similar imperfections in the surface texture indicate that someone was in a hurry when they painted. These problems are usually caused by careless paint brushing or rolling and by applying a too-heavy top coat. Be sure to apply the paint according to the paint label directions.

Alligatoring

When the surface is cracked like alligator skin, it usually means one of two things. One possibility is that the paint is so old that it no longer has any resilience to changes in weather. Another is that a newer top coat didn't adhere properly because it was not compatible with the primer or bottom coat, or because the paint was applied before a previous coat was dry. Avoid the latter problems by always using compatible paints and following the label directions.

A badly cracked paint surface should be repainted, but before you do this, you often need to remove the old paint. Obviously, this is a big job—one that you should discuss with a painter.

Chalking

The fact that siding paint produces a slight, chalky-like substance is fine: this allows a good rain to rinse dirt off of the siding. Excessive chalking, on the other hand, dulls the paint's sheen and color. Pressure washing (see page 210) may solve the problem; if not, you'll probably have to repaint. Use only high-quality paint.

Stripping interior and exterior finishes

Before stripping paint from a home built before 1978, test the paint for lead. See more about this on page 212.

There are several ways to strip finishes: heat gun stripping, chemical strippers, scraping, and sanding, to name the primary ones. Stripping paint can be a real hassle and often lends marginal results—it can be very tedious to get paint out of all the nooks and crannies, and when the finish has been entirely stripped, the wood may not look the way you hoped it would.

Chemical strippers are normally the least damaging to the surface and work best at removing paint from fine woodwork or irregular surfaces. It's also the safest way to remove paint that contains lead, when done properly.

If you plan to repaint, however, keep in mind that you can fill nicks and gouges before painting. In this case, stripping with a combination of heat gun and scraper is usually faster. It's often most effective to use a heat gun on flat expanses and a chemical stripper on details.

Tip: When using a heat gun, have a fire extinguisher (or a bucket of water) on hand in case wood begins to burn.

When using chemical strippers, wear rubber or neoprene gloves to protect your hands; eye protection; and—for some chemicals (see the table below)—an organic vapor respirator with new cartridges. Good ventilation is imperative.

Apply the stripper in one or more thick coats and let it work—don't scrape too soon. All layers of paint should be easy to lift with a scraper or—better—a plastic household spatula. On vertical surfaces, choose a stripper that has plenty of body and be sure to protect the floor with plastic masking taped around the perimeter and with newspapers on top to absorb the sludge. If you're stripping woodwork, also protect the walls by taping newspapers to them. Be sure to follow label directions.

You can hire a professional to strip furniture and loose parts: see "Furniture Refinishing" in your Yellow Pages.

Chemical Strippers

Methylene chloride strippers

Pros	Cons	Notes
Lift multiple layers quickly.	Considered hazardous; require good ventilation; require reapplication because they evaporate quickly.	Wear an organic vapor respirator with new cartridges.

THE HOME PROBLEM SOLVER

Pros	Cons	Notes
Considered safer to use than than methylene chloride.	Slower-acting; require good ventilation; and may require wearing an organic vapor respirator with new cartridges.	None.

Caustic strippers

Pros	Cons	Notes
Work on multiple layers of paint; nontoxic fumes.	Require vinegar rinse.	Not recommended for hardwoods or veneers.

Painting aluminum siding

When it's time to paint aluminum siding, be sure to start by thoroughly cleaning it. Scrub it with water and TSP or a nonphosphate detergent and rinse; or better, pressure-wash it (see page 210). Allow the siding to dry completely; then sand any previously painted areas that have chipped or peeled so that they're smooth. Remove any chalk from the surface, using a buffing pad. Prime any exposed metal with a high-quality acrylic latex metal primer. Finish with one or two coats of a high-quality, 100 percent acrylic latex paint that is specifically made for metal siding (satin or eggshell finishes offer the best longevity). Do the painting on an overcast day (avoid painting in direct sunlight).

Painting stucco

When stucco is applied, pigment is mixed right into the concrete-like material to give it its color—typically, this color will hold up for many years. But when stucco grows dingy looking—or when home owners just want a change—stucco can be painted. Keep in mind, however, that once you paint it, it will need to be repainted every few years.

For good adhesion, the surface must be clean and sound. If the stucco is in good shape, scrubbing the surface with a stiff nylon-bristle brush and a detergent may be all it takes. If any of the old paint is peeling or flaking, you'll have to use a wire brush or, for smooth-finish stucco, a scraper.

If the stucco was painted before with a glossy paint, the new surface coat will have problems adhering. Either scuff the surface with a wire brush to give the new paint some "tooth" or talk to a painter about having it professionally sandblasted. Don't pressure-wash the surface; this can damage it.

If the surface has a white, crusty powder on it in certain areas, see page 228 for information on removing efflorescence.

Exterior Paint Recommendations

Bare wood   Prime bare wood with oil/alkyd or acrylic latex primer, applied according to label directions. Use alkyd or stain-blocking acrylic latex for knots or for redwood or cedar, because of oils in these woods that can leach through the paint. Be sure the primer you use is compatible with the paint (buy your paint first).

Chalky or poor wood   Oil may be better where adhesion is a serious problem—chalky surfaces, for example. And when you need to paint in extremely cold weather, oil can be applied without freezing.

Smooth wood siding   Choose 100 percent acrylic latex paint for top performance. Eggshell finishes are relatively flat, so they hide imperfections well, but they're easier to clean than truly flat finishes.

Rough wood siding   For rough siding, such as resawn plywood, choose semi-transparent oil stains (or water-based stains that contain alkyd resins) that soak into the wood fibers, because they are much less likely to peel than other finishes.

Hardboard siding   For hardboard siding, which is given a factory finish, follow the manufacturer's recommendations. For most types, prime with acrylic latex primer and apply two coats of 100 percent acrylic latex paint. Be sure to prime and paint all cut edges.

Vinyl siding   No primer needed. Apply two coats of 100 percent acrylic latex paint.

Steel or aluminum siding   No primer is needed for aluminum. For steel, use a metal primer (galvanized metal primer if the metal is galvanized). Then apply two coats of alkyd paint.

Stucco and concrete   No primer is necessary. Apply two coats of flat 100 percent acrylic latex paint.

Trim   Choose 100 percent acrylic latex enamels in gloss or semigloss finishes. Remember, the higher the gloss, the more it will show imperfections. If painting over an existing oil-based paint, sand the surface first so the new coat will adhere well.

SIDING: SYNTHETIC

Like wood siding, small repairs are within the scope of many experienced home do-it-yourselfers. However, because both vinyl and metal siding require special tools and techniques that most homeowners don't have, serious repair jobs are usually handled by the pros. Check the Yellow Pages under "Siding Contractors."

Cracking or checking plywood siding

When plywood's surface veneers become weatherworn, they may crack and begin to peel. Repair is easy. Just sand down the area and apply a flexible, all-purpose filler, using a putty knife. Allow to dry, lightly sand the area again, and finish the area to match your siding.

Plywood siding coming apart

When the sandwich-like plies of plywood separate, it usually means that water has penetrated the material and compromised the glue. Force waterproof carpenter's glue into the area between plies, then nail the areas with galvanized common nails. Be sure the edges are properly flashed with sheet metal or caulked to prevent moisture from getting back in. And be sure the plywood has a durable finish.

For plywood that has numerous delaminations or serious damage, have the entire sheet replaced by a carpenter or handyperson.

Hardboard siding has small holes

Hardboard's worst enemy is moisture. Immediately fill holes with a flexible, all-purpose filler such as premixed bridging and patching compound, according to label directions. Sand the area smooth; then paint to match. For deep holes, build up the patch with several successive layers, allowing each to dry before applying the next.

Hardboard buckled or moisture damaged

Buckling is usually a sign of moisture, which destroys hardboard. Have any buckled or moisture-damaged hardboard siding replaced. Check your manufacturer's warranty or ask a lumberyard about consumer information on your type of siding.

Hardboard siding stained

To remove stains from hardboard, wash with a mild detergent. Oil-based stains may require scrubbing with a solvent.

Aluminum siding dented

Repairing a dent in aluminum siding is a little bit like doing body work on a car. In most cases, you can pull the dent out.

Here's how:

1. Drill a 1/8-inch hole into the center of the dent.
2. Put a washer onto a one-inch self-tapping screw and drive the screw into the hole.
3. Grasp the washer and gently pull until the dent pops back out into position. If necessary, pull with pliers.
4. Remove the screw, then use a tube of plastic aluminum filler to patch the hole (follow label directions).
5. Lightly sand the hole patch, if necessary, and touch up with paint that matches the siding.

Aluminum siding scratched or corroded

If aluminum siding has corroded or been scratched down to bare metal, lightly sand the problem area, apply a metal primer, and allow to dry. Finally, apply 100 percent acrylic latex paint.

Aluminum siding badly damaged

Serious damage calls for replacing a section of the siding. This can be problematic if your siding manufacturer is no longer in business—often the case with sidings installed thirty or forty years ago. If you can't find a perfect match, consider sequestering a piece from an inconspicuous place, such as the backside of the garage, and replacing that piece with a compatible but inexact match.

1. Using tin snips, make a vertical cut at each end of the damaged section. Then cut horizontally along the center of the damaged piece.
2. Leave the nailed, upper section in place and remove the lower half.
3. Cut the nailing tab off of the top of the replacement piece.
4. Spread butyl gutter seal generously along the upper nailed section.
5. Fit the lower replacement piece into place and press it firmly into the gutter seal.
6. Caulk the joints with silicone caulking compound or butyl gutter seal.

Metal siding faded

The factory coating on most metal siding is very durable, but the surface can fade or scratch. Sometimes power-washing the siding is enough (see "How to pressure wash siding" on page 210); other times the siding may need a new coat of paint.

For painting, don't use oil/alkyd-based paints or dark colors that can cause the metal to expand excessively. Instead, choose light tones of high-quality, 100-percent acrylic latex paint. Most houses look best with the slight luster of an eggshell finish.

Vinyl siding cracked or damaged

Small cracks in vinyl siding can be patched with silicone caulking compound, but larger cracks and damaged areas call for replacing a section. Begin by buying a replacement piece and a "zip tool" for unlocking vinyl siding at your home improvement center. Plan to work on a warm day, when the vinyl will be reasonably pliable.

1. Use the zip tool to unfasten the panel directly above the damaged section. Lift that panel to access the nails that fasten the damaged one.
2. Pry out the nails holding the damaged section.
3. Use a square to mark straight, square cutting lines at each end of the damaged section.
4. Using tin snips or a sharp utility knife, cut the panel along the lines and remove the damaged piece.
5. Make the replacement piece two inches longer than the damaged one, allowing an inch for overlap at each end.
6. Clip the top edge into place; then nail with galvanized box nails (these should be long enough to penetrate the sheathing by one inch).

---

7. Use the zip tool to hook the upper panel onto the replacement piece's locking edge.

SIDING: WOOD

Wood siding comes in many forms, including several types of boards, shingles, and sheets. If you have woodworking skills, you can tackle small repairs by duplicating the way the siding is installed in undamaged areas. Special tools like shingle-nail pullers are needed for certain jobs. Large repairs generally require more equipment and more hands, and the work becomes more difficult the higher up the wall you go. If the work extends beyond replacing a board or a shingle or two, you might want to find someone equipped for the job. Most general carpenters can handle repairs on all types of wood and hardboard siding.

Caulking joints

Siding is most vulnerable to water infiltration at vertical joints such as where doors and windows intersect, or where siding boards butt against one another. Tube caulking is easy to apply, and it's available in colors to match natural or painted finishes. Choose a quality caulk that will maintain its elasticity over a range of temperatures. Cut the tube's tip at a slight angle, and push it forward into the joint as you apply the caulk.

Hole in board siding

For repairs that will match natural wood siding, you'll want to use stainable wood putty. If you intend to paint the patched area to match siding, use premixed bridging and patching compound, sold at paint stores and home improvement centers. Follow the label directions; most advise you to:

1. Remove any loose material from the hole and brush it clean.
2. Apply the filler with a putty knife. Small holes require only one application; build-up the patch with several layers (allowing each to dry) for large holes.
3. Sand the surface and finish to match the siding.

Cracked board siding

Wood cracks and splits are quite easy to glue and refasten. Here's how:

1. Pry apart the split and force waterproof wood glue into the cracked area; be sure to coat both meeting surfaces.

THE HOME PROBLEM SOLVER

2. Force the crack back together and nail with galvanized finishing nails. Set the nail heads below the surface.

3. Wipe off any excess glue from the crack and allow the glue to dry. Fill the edges of the crack and the nail holes with a flexible wood filler, such as vinyl spackling compound, according to label directions. (For natural wood siding, use an appropriate shade of wood putty.)

Warped board siding

If board siding is butted together too tightly during installation, it may warp when it tries to expand with moisture changes. You can try pulling the board in flat and tight by driving a couple of long, galvanized screws through the siding into studs (drill pilot holes to avoid splitting the siding). But chances are good that you'll need to slightly shorten the board that is warping.

Here's how:

1. If the boards seem to be jammed together at the ends, pry out the nails from the warped area and then continue pulling nails (or you can cut them with a hacksaw blade), working your way toward the nearest end of the siding board.

2. Pry the end of the board away from the house and put a block behind it. Be careful not to damage any building paper beneath the siding.

3. Shorten the board. Sometimes it's easiest to do this with a saw; other times a rasp, plane, or perforated rasp works better. Allow about 1/6-inch of clearance to the next board.

4. Replace and renail.

How to replace a damaged board

A section of damaged or decayed board may require complete replacement. Before you tackle this project, be sure you can find a replacement piece that matches. If you can't find a perfect match, you may want to "steal" a piece from a less conspicuous part of the house and then replace that piece with a less-than-exact match. If you're not used to handling a power circular saw or similar carpentry tools, you may want to hire a handyperson or carpenter for this job.

The object is to cut the damaged piece, remove the nails that hold it in place, pry it out, repair any damage to the building paper, and replace the section. Here's how to do this:

1. Using a prybar or nail puller, pry out the nails holding the damaged piece. Depending upon the type of siding, it may be helpful to drive a couple of small wooden shingles or wedges beneath the board to pull it outward.
2. Use a square to mark a straight, square line across the board on each side of the damaged area.
3. Set the blade depth on your circular saw so that it will cut almost—but not quite—all the way through the siding. Carefully hold back the blade guard and make a "plunge cut" just to the waste side of each cutting line. Be careful not to cut into surrounding or lapped boards; if necessary, pry adjacent boards away from the wall and finish your saw cuts with a sharp chisel and hammer.
4. On tongue-and-groove siding (or other interlocked types) make another cut lengthwise across the damaged area so you can easily split the piece in half.
5. Repair any cuts or tears in the building paper beneath the siding by spreading roofing cement over them with a putty knife.
6. Cut a replacement piece to exact fit. When replacing a piece of tongue-and-groove siding, cut the back side of the groove edge off. Fit the replacement piece into place and nail it to wall studs with 8d galvanized finishing nails.
7. Set the nail heads and fill the nail holes.

Siding shingles damaged or missing

You can usually nail down warped or loose shingles, but if a shingle is broken or missing, you'll need to replace it.

1. Pull out the broken pieces.
2. Pry out the nails that held the missing shingle (located under the next course up the wall). Usually the easiest tool to do this with is a flat bar, but sometimes it's easier to cut the nails off with a hacksaw blade.
3. Cut a replacement shingle to the proper width; allow about $1/4$ inch of clearance between this shingle and its two neighbors.
4. Install the shingle in position, but leave its butt about $3/8$ of an inch below the butt line of adjacent shingles; nail it with two shingle nails, spaced about one inch in from the sides and located immediately beneath the butts of the shingles above. Once nailed, drive the replacement upward the last $3/8$ of an inch; doing this hides the nails above the upper shingles.

To blend the shingle with the grayed tones of aged shingles, brush on a mixture of baking soda and water.

STUCCO, BRICK, AND MASONRY

Unless you have masonry skills, the extent of the actual repairs you will be able to do in this area are limited. But you can look for signs that repairs are needed. Crumbling mortar joints; cracks that extend from one wall to another or "stair-step" up a block wall; and walls that lean, sink, or bulge under a structure are all warning indicators that require action.

Repointing brick takes a bit of practice, but it can be a do-it-yourself project. Use a chisel or other convenient tool to rake out loose grout between the bricks, then trowel new mortar into the joints. You can also replace individual bricks this way, but if the damage extends beyond a brick or two and threatens the structure, it's usually a job for a professional.

Holes in stucco siding

Though you're better off leaving major stucco repairs to a mason or stucco specialist, you should be able to handle fixing minor holes or cracks. Repairing a hole in stucco calls for cleaning out the area and applying a new patch of stucco mixture.

Here's how:

1. Use a cold chisel and ball peen hammer to clear loose stucco from the damaged area; then blow out the dust.
2. To provide a backing for the stucco patch to grip, staple new wire mesh over any damaged mesh.
3. Spray the damaged area with water.
4. Mix up some stucco patch and apply it according to the label directions.

Large hole in stucco

Patching large holes in stucco is a job that homeowners adept at basic home repair skills can handle—but it may be difficult to create a patch that blends perfectly with the existing wall (unless you repaint). If you think this may be the situation in your case, hire a professional. Otherwise:

1. Remove loose stucco from the hole with a cold chisel and ball peen hammer; blow out the dust. Staple new wire mesh over any damaged mesh. Spray with water.
2. Apply the first coat of stucco to within $1/4$ inch of the surface, using a mason's trowel or putty knife (stucco should ooze behind mesh). When firm, scratch with a nail. Cure for two days.

3. Apply the second coat over the dampened first coat to within $1/8$ inch.

8. Po inch of the surface, using a mason's trowel or putty knife. Smooth the stucco and let it cure for two days.

4. Apply the final coat over the dampened second coat with a metal float or mason's trowel. Smooth it flush with the existing surface. Texture as desired; cure for four days.

Stucco cracks

Cracks in stucco are a common problem. You can caulk narrow cracks with a high-quality caulking compound. For wider cracks, use an all-purpose filler such as premixed bridging and patching compound, according to label directions. For deep holes, build up the patch with several successive layers, allowing each to dry before applying the next. Do your best to match the texture by touching it up with a float or a small brush.

Stucco stained or weathered

Though stucco is a very tough surface, it can look weathered and dirty with time. But unlike other siding materials, you shouldn't use ordinary house paint to paint stucco because walls need to "breathe"; they need to let interior moisture escape the house. Trapped moisture can get behind the paint and cause it to blister or peel. Instead of painting your wall, have it "redashed" by a stucco contractor. If your stucco is white, a simpler (though more temporary) solution is to have it whitewashed with a mixture of water and white Portland cement. It's best to have this done by a professional painter or stucco contractor.

Brick or stone veneer mortar problems

If the mortar joints in your home's brick or stone veneer have cracked or crumbled, the problem probably occurred because of settling, of shrinking as the material dried, or of freeze-thaw cycles during the winter. The fix for these cracks and crumbles is to "repoint" the brick, which means to remove some of the mortar and apply new mortar to the joints.

1. Buy weather-resistant Type N ready-mixed mortar at your home improvement center and mix it according to the label directions.
2. Using a cold chisel and hammer, chip out crumbling mortar to a depth of $1/2$ inch; then brush vigorously with a wire brush.
3. Dampen the mortar joints with water; then, using a small metal trowel, pack mortar into them. Tamp it down with a short wooden block.

4. Allow the mortar to set up until it's somewhat firm; then finish the joint by drawing a jointer (or similar tool) along it. Most often, the object is to give the joint a slightly concave profile.
5. Remove excess mortar from the surface of the brick, using the clean trowel.
6. Allow the mortar to set up. Then sweep it with a stiff brush.
7. Use a damp rag or sponge to keep the mortar joints moist for about four days. This ensures that the mortar will cure properly so that it doesn't crack again.

Paint drips on brick

Spray the brick with a hose. Mix two pounds of trisodium phosphate (TSP) or a strong detergent in with water, apply, allow it to soak in, then scrub with a stiff nylon-bristle brush (don't use a wire brush). For resistant spots, repeat several times. If scrubbing with this solution doesn't work, try applying a water-base paint stripper (first test it where it won't show).

Hard water stains on brick

If a sprinkler or garden watering has splashed hard water spots on your home's brick exterior, buy an acid-based brick cleaner from a masonry dealer. Follow the label directions. Generally, these directions instruct you to cover plantings with plastic sheeting and, wearing rubber gloves and plastic glasses, to wet down the brick, apply a mixture of the cleaner and water with a stiff-bristled nylon brush on an extension handle, and rinse. To protect the brick, seal it with a silane- or siloxane-based sealer (also purchased from a masonry dealer).

YARD: DECKS AND CONCRETE

Decks, patios, and walkways set the stage for outdoor living—and because they are exposed to the elements constantly, they occasionally need a little care and repair.

Debris between decking

Debris between deck boards looks bad and soaks up water, promoting rot. To remove it, blast it out with a high-pressure nozzle attached to your garden hose. Push out any remaining debris with a putty knife or an old saw that you can slide between the deck boards.

Deck boards look dingy

The sun's ultraviolet radiation breaks down surface fibers and lignin, causing graying and surface erosion. In addition, moisture encourages surface mildew and causes stains, particularly in damp or humid climates. In some cases, a good washing as discussed below will solve the problem, but for a complete solution, you'll want to acid-wash and refinish the surface (see below).

How to wash a deck

You can wash a deck by hand or, for a large deck, using a pressure washer.

Using a stiff fiber bristle brush on a broom-type handle, thoroughly scrub the surface with a sudsy solution of water and laundry detergent. Rinse with clear water and allow to dry.

If you decide to use a pressure washer, get one that delivers 1,200 psi (pounds per square inch) of pressure or less and that has a spray nozzle that fans an arc of about 25° to 40°. See more about properly using a pressure washer on page 210. Be careful: the powerful spray can erode soft wood grain. Allow the deck to dry for several days before applying any type of finish.

How to acid-wash a deck

Purchase a premixed oxalic acid deck cleaner or oxalic acid crystals from a hardware store or home improvement center and mix a solution of four ounces crystals to one quart water in a nonmetallic container.

1. Wearing protective glasses, rubber gloves, and old clothes, apply the acid solution to one board at a time and scrub with a soft nylon brush attached to a broomstick-length handle.
2. Let a section dry; then rinse with clear water.
3. Allow the deck to dry for several days before applying any type of protective finish.

Choosing a deck finish

The preferred deck finish—one that takes advantage of the wood's natural beauty—is a clear finish or light stain. Once painted or stained with a heavy opaque stain, a deck will require repainting or restaining every couple of years. If you decide to paint, apply a stain-blocking oil or alkyd primer first.

With clear finishes or light stains, choose the type that is "water repellent" or "water proof," not just "water resistant." Be sure it offers UV (ultraviolet) protection and contains a mildewcide (a "wood preservative" does). "Toner" products offer good UV protection and may last up to four years. Read the label for application directions and to be sure the finish is appropriate for your deck.

Concrete cracks

Concrete is tough, but it can crack because of settling, moisture, or extreme temperatures. For narrow cracks, less than about 1/8 inch wide, simply buy a concrete patch sold in a caulking tube and apply it according to the label directions. Wider cracks require a little more work to prevent them from reoccurring.

1. Wearing safety glasses, use a hammer and a cold chisel to deepen the crack to at least one inch. Undercut the sides of the crack so the patching material will grip.
2. Brush away loose debris with a wire brush; then sweep or vacuum the crack to remove dust.
3. Mix a patching compound specifically made for concrete, following the label instructions.
4. Trowel the patching compound generously into the crack, overfilling the crack slightly. Skim off excess with the trowel.
5. Once the patch has set, smooth it out with your trowel so it's flush with the surface.
6. Sprinkle the patch lightly with water several times a day for about a week, to help it cure properly.
7. Apply a concrete sealer for lasting protection.

Step edges broken

To repair the broken leading edge of a concrete step, first brush away loose concrete and dirt. Fasten a length of scrap lumber along the front, flush with the top of the step. To attach it, use a 1/4-inch masonry bit to drill a hole through each end and into the concrete riser. To hold the board, drive two 16d nails into each hole, forming a wedge. Fill the broken area with patching concrete, allow it to set up slightly, then remove the board, fill the nail holes, and trowel smooth.

Concrete spalling

In regions where freeze-thaw cycles are severe, concrete surfaces may show damage of flaking and chipping, known as spalling. For all but the most experienced home improvers, the best strategy for repairing this problem is to hire a concrete contractor or mason to break away and patch the damaged area.

Efflorescence

Concrete, stucco, brick, and other masonry surfaces may have a white, powdery substance on them known as efflorescence. You can brush away this powder with a wire brush, but unless you eliminate the cause, it will return—and it's existence indicates that more serious moisture damage may occur. Efflorescence is caused by moisture from poor drainage, roof leaks, sprinklers, and the like that penetrates walls and other masonry surfaces. If you can't determine and repair the source of the moisture, call a masonry or concrete contractor for help.

Resource Guide to Manufacturers

The following is a listing of telephone numbers and Web site addresses of major manufacturers and information sources. (Phone numbers are less likely to remain current than Web addresses—if the number is out of service, check the Web site for an up-to-date number.)

APPLIANCES

Admiral	800-688-9920	www.amana.com
Airtempt	908-722-4500	
Amana	800-843-0304	www.amana.com
Arcoaire	615-359-3511	www.arcoaire.com
Asko	800-367-2444	www.askousa.com
Bosch	800-944-2904	www.boschappliances.com
Brown	800-251-7224	
Bryant	800-468-7253	www.bryant.com
Caloric	800-843-0304	www.amana.com
Carrier	800-422-7743	www.carrier.com
Comfortmaker	615-359-3511	www.comfortmaker.com
Dacor	800-772-7778	www.dacor.com
Day & Night	800-468-7253	www.bryant.com
Fedders	217-342-3901	www.fedders.com
Frigidaire	800-374-4432	www.frigidaire.com

Gaggenau	617-255-1766	
General Electric	800-626-2000	www.GE.com
Heil	615-359-3511	www.arcoaire.com
Imperial, Kelvinator	800-272-4723	www.frigidaire.com
Insinkerator	800-558-5712	www.insinkerator.com
Jacuzzi	800-288-4002	www.jacuzzi.com
Jenn-Air	800-688-1100	www.jennair.com
Kenmore	(local Sears Store)	www.sears.com
Kitchenaid	800-422-1230	]www.kitchenaid.com
Lennox	800-953-6669	www.lennox.com
Magic Chef	800-688-1120	www.maytag.com
Maytag	800-688-9900	www.maytag.com
Miele	800-843-7231	www.mieleusa.com
Modern Maid	800-843-0304	www.amana.com
NuTone	800-543-8687	www.faucet.com/faucet/ nutone/nutone.html
O'Keefe & Merrit	706-860-4110	www.frigidaire.com
Payne	800-468-7253	www.bryant.com
Peerless Premier	800-858-5844	
Rheem, Ruud	501-646-4311	www.rheem.com
Roper, Estate	800-477-6737	www.roperappliances.com
Scotsman	708-215-4524	
Speed Queen	800-843-0304	www.speedqueen.com
Sub Zero	800-222-7820	www.subzero.com
Tappan	800-537-5530	www.frigidaire.com
Tempstar	615-359-3511	www.tempstar.com
Thermador	800-735-4328	www.thermador.com
Trane Company	903-581-3568	www.trane.com
Uline	800-779-2547	
Viking	800-467-2643	www.vikingrange.com

Whirlpool	800-253-1301	www.whirlpool.com
White Westinghouse	800-456-4407	www.frigidaire.com
York	717-771-6225	www.york.com

OTHER

Alcoa Bldg. Prods.	800 962-6973	www.alcoahomes.com
American Olean	888-AOT-TILE	www.aotile.com
American Standard	800-752-6292	www.us.amstd.com
Andersen Windows	800-426-4261	www.andersenwindows.com
Armstrong World Industries	800-233-3823	www.armstrong.com
Artistic Brass, a Masco Co.	317-574-5550	www.masco.com
Broan Mfg. Co.	800-356-5862	www.broan.com
Bruce Floors	800-722-4647	www.brucehardwoodfloors.com
Carpet and Rug Institute	800-882-8846	www.carpet-rug.com
Casablanca Fan Co.	888-227-2178	
CertainTeed	800-233-8990	www.certainteed.com
Chicago Faucets	847-803-5000	www.chicagofaucets.com
Congoleum Corp.	609-584-3000	www.congoleum.com
Delta Faucet Co.	800-345-DELTA	www.deltafaucet.com
Dornbracht USA	800-774-1181	www.dornbracht.com
Eljer Plumbingware	800-435-5372	www.eljer.com
Elkay Mfg. Co.	630-574-8484	www.elkay.com
Formica Corp.	800-FORMICA	www.formica.com
Franke Inc.	800-626-5771	www.franke.com
Grohe America	630-582-7711	www.groheamerica.com
Hansgrohe	800-334-0455	
Harden Industries	800-877-7850	
Honeywell Inc.	800-345-6770	www.honeywell.com

Jado Bathroom & Hardware Corp.	800-227-2734	www.jado.com
Kohler Co.	800-4KOHLER	www.kohlerco.com
Kolson, Inc.	800-783-1335	www.kolson.com
KWC	770-248-1600	www.kwcfaucets.com
Mannington Wood Floors	800-814-7355	
Marvin Windows & Doors	888-537-8628	www.marvin.com
Master Lock Co.	414-444-2800	www.masterlock.com
Merillat Industries	800-575-8763	www.merillat.com
Moen Incorporated	800-289-6636	www.moen.com
Peerless Faucet	317-848-1812	www.masco.com
Pella Corporation	800-84-PELLA	www.pella.com
Price Pfister, Inc.	818-896-1141	www.pricepfister.com
Schlage Lock Co.	800-847-1864	www.schlagelock.com
Sterling Plumbing	800-STERLING	www.sterlingplumbing.com
Wheather Shield Windows & Doors	800-477-6808	www.weathershield.com
Wood-Mode	717-374-2711	www.wood-mode.com
Yale Residential Security Products	800-438-1951	www.yaleresidential.com

Index